D1563081

Taking the Air

Paul Kopas

Taking the Air: Ideas and Change
in Canada's National Parks

UBCPress · Vancouver · Toronto

BRESCIA UNIVERSITY
COLLEGE LIBRARY

© UBC Press 2007

All rights reserved. No part of this publication may be reproduced, stored in a retrieval system, or transmitted, in any form or by any means, without prior written permission of the publisher, or, in Canada, in the case of photocopying or other reprographic copying, a licence from Access Copyright (Canadian Copyright Licensing Agency), www.accesscopyright.ca.

15 14 13 12 11 10 09 08 07   5 4 3 2 1

Printed in Canada on ancient-forest-free paper (100% post-consumer recycled) that is processed chlorine- and acid-free, with vegetable-based inks.

Library and Archives Canada Cataloguing in Publication

Kopas, Paul Sheldon, 1949-
  Taking the air : ideas and change in Canada's national parks / Paul Kopas.

Includes bibliographical references and index.
ISBN: 978-0-7748-1329-7

  1. National parks and reserves – Government policy – Canada – History.
2. National parks and reserves – Canada – History. I. Title.

FC215.K66 2007   333.78'30971   C2007-904414-X

Canada

UBC Press gratefully acknowledges the financial support for our publishing program of the Government of Canada through the Book Publishing Industry Development Program (BPIDP), and of the Canada Council for the Arts, and the British Columbia Arts Council.

This book has been published with the help of a grant from the Canadian Federation for the Humanities and Social Sciences, through the Aid to Scholarly Publications Programme, using funds provided by the Social Sciences and Humanities Research Council of Canada, and with the help of the K.D. Srivastava Fund.

UBC Press
The University of British Columbia
2029 West Mall
Vancouver, BC V6T 1Z2
604-822-5959 / Fax: 604-822-6083
www.ubcpress.ca

Contents

Contents

Preface

National parks are icons of Canada. Canadians and foreign visitors alike regard national parks as national symbols on par with the maple leaf and the Royal Canadian Mounted Police. As expressions of Canada, national parks are immensely complex, perhaps also reflecting this country's breadth and diversity. Parks are about history, healthy and wholesome living, opportunities for learning, national memory, recreation, relations between different groups of Canadians (especially between Aboriginal people and the Canadian state), and they are about environmental protection. This complexity presents a challenge for anyone wanting to reach a singular understanding about them.

When I began this analysis, I approached parks as instruments of environmental protection, but I knew that there was also a strong emphasis on their use for tourism and recreation. As a policy analyst, I wanted to understand the relationship between these two elements – protection and use – and sought to explain the growing importance of environmental protection in parks policy from the late 1950s to the present. While the growth of environmental protection continues to be the central theme of this book, the pursuit of ideas about parks has led me through many other subjects, no one of which could capture the diverse character of these special places.

Despite devoting some attention to diverse concepts about parks, this book is primarily a policy analysis. It seeks to understand and explain the development of the environmental components of national parks policy in the latter half of the twentieth century. In order to analyze policy, one must first define it. As outlined in the first chapter, definition is particularly difficult for national parks. As a government program over a century old, it has grown, changed, and adapted without necessarily shedding its nineteenth- and early-twentieth-century characteristics. Therefore, policy must address everything from managing municipalities to protecting caribou migration. Interestingly, tracing that history helps to define the policy change that needs to be explained. It soon became apparent that in the contest between protection and use, environmental protection gained priority, so in 1988 ecological integrity became the legislated first priority for managing parks. Explaining and understanding this development is the purpose of this book.

As I approached the analytical question, I reasoned that it can be answered best by concentrating on one category of protected area. Therefore, this book addresses terrestrial national parks. While it would be desirable to examine protected areas in their entirety, each category of them inhabits a distinct policy universe occupied by its own participants, institutions, and political forces. Efforts to combine categories for analysis may seem orderly and comprehensive at one level, but these efforts introduce additional variables that impair the ability to reach definitive conclusions. An added complication for parks is that there is little existing policy analysis with which to engage. The necessity to begin at (or near) the beginning has been one of the challenges of this research. Ambitions to analyze policy issues about protected areas more broadly speaking must be part of a staged process of which this volume is but one step.

Terrestrial national parks are already highly complicated in themselves. As shown in Chapter 1, national parks are about many things. Policy about them runs the gamut from municipal management to wildlife management. Parks also include millions of international tourists annually, multi-million dollar businesses and commercial investments, indigenous people retaining ancient relationships with the land, other local communities, provincial governments, interest groups, scientific communities, and more. It was preferable, therefore, to make sense of these elements with respect to terrestrial national parks and then to use that understanding for a later examination of other parts of the universe of programs that affect protected areas.

Thus, although this book examines aspects of Parks Canada as an organization, especially in the penultimate chapter, it is not intended to be an organizational analysis of that agency. In particular, the analysis does not examine other Parks Canada programs such as the national historic sites or national marine conservation areas. Historic sites have shared administrative space with terrestrial parks for nearly a century and although there are parallel concerns about conservation integrity in both programs, the cultural emphasis for historic sites makes them a substantively different policy area. More closely related to the traditional national park, the marine areas program has not altered the debate about the degree of environmental protection that needs to be afforded to protected areas of any type. More importantly, and complicating an understanding of marine areas, Parks Canada's ambitions for them overlap with policies for similar reserves by the Canadian Wildlife Service and the Department of Fisheries and Oceans. All three agencies' programs are in the process of being harmonized within the federal government. Therefore, it is too early to draw conclusions about how these tri-department arrangements will affect environmental protection or to offer an explanation for policy outcomes that have not yet manifested themselves. Since historic sites are cultural rather than ecological, and since the results of the national marine conservation areas program are not yet revealed, terrestrial national parks remain the most effective unit of analysis for studying the shift toward increased environmental protection within the broad framework of Parks Canada programs.

At the same time, it is worth observing that these parks exist within a complex network of protected areas in Canada; the lessons learned from studying them may be useful for examining other parts of that network or, alternatively, examples drawn from elsewhere may provide insight into terrestrial national parks policy. For example, in addition to the already mentioned programs within Parks Canada, the Canadian Wildlife Service has an extensive protected areas network, both terrestrial and marine, for the benefit of migratory and resident animal populations. Provincial governments also have diverse, complex systems of parks and protected areas. Some places are devoted almost exclusively to human recreation, and thus parallel that part of Parks Canada's mandate, while others are aimed at wilderness protection and wildlife preservation. Some areas, such as ecological reserves, are off-limits to all humans except scientists who need express permission to enter them. The programs in the provinces vary considerably. Some, such as those in British Columbia and Ontario, parallel the national parks system, while others are more limited. An analysis of the politics of these provincial variations would greatly enhance the overall understanding of policy formation for protected areas in Canada.

There are other kinds of protected areas that also deserve attention. Many municipalities provide land (or water) and budgets to protect parts of their territories for ecological purposes beyond human recreation. Privately funded land conservation trusts also protect tracts of land and water across Canada. By complementing public policies these trusts serve public purposes, but little analysis has been done to understand how their activities are facilitated by formal public policy or how they relate to government actions at all levels. Attention to these and other types of protected areas policy would round out an understanding of parks policy in Canada. This book is but one element in a wider universe.

Acknowledgments

I am deeply indebted to many people who gave generously of their time and shared their expertise as I sought answers to questions. Since one of the challenges that confronted me was the paucity of published material on the policy process for parks, the willingness of many people to share their knowledge was an essential foundation for this book.

Numerous Parks Canada officials were enormously helpful, providing the detail, expert knowledge, and insight that allowed me to develop the arguments I offer. In the early stages of my work, two individuals were particularly useful. Harold Eidsvik had been one of two planners in the original planning section for parks in the late 1950s, and he guided me through the documents, ideas, and experiences that led to the 1964 Policy Statement. Bruce Amos, former director of parks establishment, patiently explained that I "could not get there from here" – parks were not quite the instruments I initially took them to be. These two men provided the primer that enabled me to see parks more clearly and build the arguments on which the analysis grew.

Many others at Parks Canada, including several who are retired, explained their roles and experiences in the evolution of policy development. My research was also facilitated by employees in a number of federal departments: the Canadian Wildlife Service, the Department of Energy, Mines and Resources, the Treasury Board Secretariat, and the Privy Council Office. The Academic Access Program of the Privy Council Office was essential for helping me answer questions for which no published sources existed.

Interest group leaders were equally helpful. In particular, the late Gavin Henderson, founder of the National and Provincial Parks Association of Canada, explained the early details and challenges of the parks protection movement. His award as a Member of the Order of Canada recognizes his work for wilderness conservation in this country. In addition, people in the Canadian Parks and Wilderness Society, the World Wildlife Fund, the Sierra

Legal Defence Fund, the Canadian Arctic Resources Committee, and Nature Canada described events, explained strategies, and provided documents.

Thanks are also due to many librarians and archivists whose efforts unearthed obscure and valuable documents. Of critical importance to the early part of this work was the support and guidance of staff at Library and Archives Canada. The interlibrary loans and government publications librarians at the University of Toronto libraries were extraordinarily helpful. The staff of the Documentation Centre, a small library within Parks Canada, were equally generous with their knowledge. Librarians at Environment Canada, the Toronto Public Library, the Vancouver Public Library, and the University of Saskatchewan assisted my work.

I would like to extend special appreciation to two of my former professors, Ronald Manzer and Grace Skogstad, both at the University of Toronto, for their support on this and other projects. I also owe thanks to Randy Schmidt of UBC Press for his encouragement and support during the preparation of this manuscript.

Finally, I wish to thank my lifelong friend Lewis Stiles who read early drafts of this work and offered thorough and thoughtful commentary on every aspect of it. Our conversations about the manuscript were a pleasure among a lifetime of wonderful conversations that are always enriching and stimulating.

The interpretations and the conclusions I have drawn from this information are completely my own. Any errors or omissions are mine.

Abbreviations

ADM	assistant deputy minister
AMB	Archipelago Management Board
AMPPE	Association for Mountain Parks Protection and Enjoyment
APA	Administrative Procedures Act (US)
ARDA	Agriculture and Rural Development Agency
BBVS	Banff-Bow Valley Study
CAP	Canada Assistance Plan
CCMD	Canadian Centre for Management Development
CCME	Canadian Council of Ministers of the Environment
CCREM	Canadian Council of Resource and Environment Ministers
CCRM	Canadian Council of Resource Ministers
CEAA	Canadian Environmental Assessment Act
CNF	Canadian Nature Federation
CPAWS	Canadian Parks and Wilderness Society
CPR	Canadian Pacific Railway
CRASE	Conseil régional d'aménagement du Sud-est
CWS	Canadian Wildlife Service
DFO	Department of Fisheries and Oceans
ELUCS	Environment and Land Use Committee Secretariat
ETO	employee takeover
FEARO	Federal Environmental Assessment Review Office
IPC	Islands Protection Committee
IPS	Islands Protection Society
ITC	Inuit Tapirisat of Canada
IUCN	International Union for the Conservation of Nature and Natural Resources
NCC	Nature Conservancy of Canada
NDP	New Democratic Party
NPPAC	National and Provincial Parks Association of Canada
NPS	National Parks Service (US)

ONC   Office of Native Claims
ORRRC   Outdoor Recreation Resources Review Commission
PCO   Privy Council Office
PPBS   Planning, Programming, and Budgeting System
PSAC   Public Service Alliance of Canada
SCCR   Ski Club of the Canadian Rockies
SLDF   Sierra Legal Defence Fund
SOAs   special operating agencies
TBS   Treasury Board Secretariat
VSCs   visitor service centres
WAC   Wilderness Advisory Committee
WWF   World Wildlife Fund

Taking the Air

1
Introduction: The Meaning of National Parks and the Contexts of Change

Ideas about National Parks

National parks are about meaning. They reflect, for a population, something about itself that it would like to believe. However, these meanings change over time as national, or even international, populations adopt new beliefs about themselves.

Although viewed by many Canadians today in terms of environmental protection, Canada's system of national parks actually reflects more than a century of changing ideas about the natural environment. As meanings change, so does the nature of national parks, and that nature is likewise affected by shifts in who, among the set of policy-making participants, defines new meanings for them. These shifts are not smooth and effortless, and their paths are both obscure and labyrinthine. Because of changing ideas and values, it is difficult to offer a single definition of a national park or even to define, unequivocally, what is national park policy. Canada's own legislation – which was not passed until 1930, forty-five years after the first national park was created – captured the ambiguous position of parks when it declared that they be simultaneously used by the present generation and preserved unimpaired for future ones. This dichotomy between use and preservation is not unique to Canadian parks but is also reflected in definitions such as those used by the World Conservation Union (formerly the International Union for the Conservation of Nature and Natural Resources [IUCN]), a global authority on environmental practice.

By containing this particular ambiguity, national parks policies reflect both past and present meanings as well as foreshadow possible future ones. Identifying actual policy and charting its change therefore comprise a difficult task, which needs to be approached tentatively. Nevertheless, it is clear that policy debates have largely focused on divergent views about the relationship between humans and the natural environment. While this is true in general, over the past fifty years concepts favouring greater protection within national parks have slowly gained ascendancy over those supporting economic use and development. Of course, conceptions of parks are more complex than this dichotomy, and ancillary ideas have been included in one or the other of these divergent views. In order to understand this transition and to identify the associated changes in meaning, it is necessary to explore the various values that are embodied in national parks.

Among the many ideas that today confound national parks policy makers, both inside and outside the state, five frame the meanings that parks reflect to their creators and advocates. First, parks are, both currently and historically, symbolic institutions variously reflecting an ideology of the state or its constituent society (although state and society may not agree on what is being symbolized). Second, parks are instruments of economic development and social (i.e., recreational) policy providing for national, regional, and personal well-being. Third, parks are instruments of environmental policy in that they protect terrain and resident wildlife, selectively represent diverse natural landscapes, and encourage popular nature education. Fourth, parks are human landscapes where people live in an environment and where they also observe and reflect upon their own interaction with that environment. Fifth, parks are heritage artifacts; as social constructions, they are fragments of the mostly vanished Canadian wilderness and, as such, objects of curiosity and wonder.

Parks as Symbols

National parks began in the United States, where, in that country's early decades, there was a sense of cultural inferiority to Europe and a consequent strong desire to show that national greatness, present or potential, existed in the New World too. Roderick Nash, chronicling how early nation builders sought inspiration at home to offset this perceived superiority of Europe, observed that in the early nineteenth century much concern remained about the shortcomings of American culture but that a distinct national personality gradually emerged. Central to that personality was the nature and vastness of the American wilderness. "Romantics," says Nash, "invested it with value while nationalists proclaimed its uniqueness."[1] Later, in the nineteenth century, national parks became both the embodiment and a representation of this new American national character. Alfred Runte, writing specifically about parks, suggests that "cultural insecurity, as the catalyst for concern, speeded the nation's response to the threatened confiscation of its natural heritage" and that the monumental landscapes of the American west were the "cornerstones of [the] nationalistic park idea."[2]

While Canadians are frequently insecure about their place in the world and are proud of the country's natural beauty, nationalism is more often played out in terms of national unity or integration rather than in the expression of national greatness. National integration has been and continues to be the historic project for the federal government and often clashes with provincial ambitions. To pursue this project, a wide variety of policy instruments from transportation through health care has been used in support of the federal government's integrative efforts. The same is true with respect to national parks, which have, in their own way, also been used as an instrument of integration and nationalist symbolism. At the same time, provinces have generally resisted establishment of the federal jurisdiction and the national symbolism inherent in national parks.

For its part, the (national) Parks Branch[3] evinced the federal government's nationalizing philosophy when, in the 1950s, it made tentative steps toward defining a national parks system as one in which there would be at least one national park in each province (even though the national parks plan eventually came to be geophysically, not politically, based). Indeed, exponents of the national parks system, both public and private, now draw attention to the fact that there are national parks in each of the provinces and territories. It is as if a Canadian national parks system would not be complete without representation, regardless of physical merit, in each subnational jurisdiction.

While national parks may symbolize ideas of nationalism and national greatness, they can also express democratic ideas. This democratic ideal reflects a difference in political values between the Old World and the New, at least in the initial decades of parks establishment. European parks were initially the property of royalty. As early as the thirteenth century, the word *park* was used to denote "an enclosed tract of land held by royal grant for the keeping of beasts of the chase,"[4] although royal hunting preserves are thought to have existed even earlier. The term "public park" appeared in the seventeenth century to suggest a place of public recreation as opposed to one reserved for royalty, but it was only in nineteenth-century America that the idea of a park as a place for the common citizen gained prominence. Frederick Law Olmsted, the great landscape architect and advocate of urban public parks, wrote that it is the duty of democratic government to protect natural areas for public enjoyment from obstacles created by the private ownership of land.[5] Indeed, as the explorers of Yellowstone prepared their recommendations to Congress, they explicitly discussed the idea of a national or government-controlled park to allow all people to have access to and enjoy the marvel of Yellowstone's natural wonders. For Americans, in other words, the concepts of citizenship and democracy extended to having the state make available opportunities for outdoor recreation and appreciation of the nation's natural monuments.

These American views deliberately rejected the class philosophy of the Old World, a philosophy expressed by William Wordsworth, who wrote in 1810 that the English Lakes District should be preserved as a national property for "every[one] ... who has an eye to perceive and a heart to enjoy," but that the land would be ruined if "artisans, labourers, and the humbler class of shopkeeper" were allowed to frequent the region.[6] Yet Wordsworth's ideas, whether directly or not, would have found ready listeners in the Parliament of Canada seventy-five years later. In 1885, in a motion to protect the natural hot springs at Banff and thereby establish what would become the focal point of Canada's first national park, Sir John A. Macdonald and other parliamentarians saw Banff as a preserve of the rich and felt that the government should provide opportunities for relaxation to people of wealth. Explicit plans were drawn up to keep "the doubtful class of people" away.[7]

In fact, the democratic ideal of wide public access to parks did not appear in Canadian discussions until well into the twentieth century when car travel became widespread. Surprisingly, this ideal continues to be debated today, although in a new guise. As parks policy has shifted toward increased protection of the natural environment and access has accordingly been restricted, road and other motorized access is increasingly limited in some of the older parks and is not being developed at all in new ones. Some of the new parks are in locations remote from the main bulk of the Canadian population centres and are very expensive to visit. These factors have the effect of making large expanses of the parks system mainly available to the young, healthy, and moderately wealthy. Critics point out that this correspondingly limits enjoyment for the aged, infirm, and less privileged.

While democratic ideals continue to be debated, parks also represent an environmental symbolism irrespective of any tangible protection of the environment, and this symbolic role is a significant aspect of their continuing presence. In a book by the Canadian Nature Federation (now Nature Canada), an interest group deeply concerned about national park policy, this role is explicitly acknowledged: "Countries ... need the symbolism of wild places to remind them of their sources and ... their continued coexistence [with nature] in the world."[8]

Parks as Instruments of Economic and Social Policy
In Canada, national parks were specifically designed to be instruments of economic development when they were first established in the late nineteenth century. As Canada expanded westward, natural resources, in terms of agriculture, mining, and logging, were seen as opportunities for economic and national growth. Parks, in terms of scenic and recreational opportunities, presented a different use of natural resources. By preventing unmanaged agricultural and industrial development of resources in certain areas, parks preserved natural beauty while giving government-appointed managers monopoly control over their natural amenities, which could then be sold (or ancillary services could be sold) to park visitors. At Banff, Canada's first national park, the government expropriated control over the famous hot springs from the original entrepreneurs and then extended virtually monopolistic commercial opportunities to the Canadian Pacific Railway (CPR)

in which the government had so much interest. Following the establishment of Banff, the government created a string of national parks through the mountains along the railway line to provide tourist attractions and economic opportunity for the CPR.

Economic opportunity continued to play a major role in the establishment of other national parks, particularly when they came to be established in the disadvantaged Atlantic provinces. Indeed, Newfoundland's Terra Nova National Park, complete with golf courses and other tourist facilities, was part of the package of enticements that the Government of Canada offered to the then British colony to encourage it to join Canada in the late 1940s. The economic promise of national parks continues to be one of their main features, as they are justified in terms of tourism and other commercial opportunities in order to offset provincial and local concerns about the possible loss of economic activity that might accompany a park's protection of forests and other lands. The federal government has had not only to compensate provincial treasuries for resources situated in provincially located parks but also to assure local people that new economic opportunities will equal or even exceed the commercial value of forgone activities. In short, to gain critical public acceptance, national parks must still be promoted as including economic opportunity.

A relatively recent further manifestation of the economic uses of parks is the inclusion of Aboriginal interests in them. Not only do many new parks (in Canada and elsewhere) allow for continuing traditional indigenous uses of park lands (e.g., hunting, fishing, and gathering), but also paid employment is increasingly a way in which the interests of parks and Aboriginal people are integrated. In many new parks, wardens and interpretive personnel are drawn from local Aboriginal and other indigenous populations. Often there are formal or administrative guidelines requiring such employment.

While direct commercial activity and Aboriginal employment are both past and present factors in national park creation, parks also contain a social policy element insofar as they provide opportunities for outdoor recreation and popular nature education. (In this sense, nature education is an element of both "social policy" and "environmental policy.") In particular, with the increased availability of cars, national parks were promoted by governments as places for healthy, family-oriented outdoor vacations. Through the 1950s and 1960s, national parks focused on campgrounds, hiking trails, and wildlife-viewing locations. The creation of these amenities drew on arguments from mid-nineteenth-century thinkers who held that modern urban industrial workers needed outdoor recreation either in city parks or in the wilderness to maintain their mental and social health. Indeed, in the 1950s, federal park planners considered creating national parks at locations within a short day's drive from Canada's major cities specifically to make outdoor recreation available to the urban masses. This plan foundered on the provinces' own desires to use the provincial land base to make such parks available to what they saw as a provincial constituency.

Parks as Instruments of Environmental Policy

Today, national parks are widely regarded as a means of environmental protection and preservation. In addition, national parks provide two other environmental functions. One of these is to selectively represent samples of the natural environment in a given country or region in order to provide a benchmark for comparison with human-altered environments as well as opportunities for scientific research. The other is that national parks provide a forum for popular nature education.

In most respects, environmental protection has come to be the focus of national parks. Environmental values emerged in western Europe and the United States in the nineteenth century almost concurrently with the development of America's first national parks. These values quickly divided into opposing themes, often distinguished (though not very clearly) in the American debate as conservation and preservation, respectively, which continue to underlie current discussions of environmental policy in general and national parks in particular. More recently, these two concepts have been joined by the perspectives of scientific ecology. Together, these three sets of ideas form the basis on which national parks are considered instruments of environmental policy.

Conservationists are proponents of scientific management and hold that natural resources should be used but used wisely; that is, resources should be managed carefully to avoid waste and to achieve the most efficient production from them. For conservationists, a nation's natural resources should be kept available for present or future production. While conservationists acknowledge that recreation and quiet enjoyment may constitute a kind of use, they argue that these uses do not require exclusive control and need not preclude extractive uses. With careful management, say the conservationists, all these activities can coexist.

Robert Craig Brown's suggestion that Canada's early parks conformed to a "doctrine of usefulness"[9] parallels the conservationist or "wise use" ideas prevalent in the United States in the late nineteenth and early twentieth centuries. The fact that current critics of national parks often argue that parks constitute a single use of resources and a "removal" from production of important forestry or other resources attests to the continuance of the conservationist doctrine.

In contrast, preservationists argue that some parts of the natural environment should be protected completely and kept inviolate from alteration by humans. Human activities, according to this concept, should be limited to observation and contemplation. While preservationist ideas competed with conservationist ones, both remained essentially human centred; that is, preservationists held a transcendental but human view of the natural environment, while conservationists saw the environment purely in terms of human utility.

Since the 1930s, the concept of ecology, wherein the multiple and intricate links among all parts of the natural environment are seen as important, has become an increasingly important part of the environmental and national parks debate. Understanding something about these links introduces a new set of ideas into the discussion of national parks. Thus, while parks policies are still concerned with use versus preservation, the latter concept is given a focused objective in matters of parks selection, definition, and management by the scientific principles of ecology.

Ecological ideas infused concepts of national parks in the post-World War II era as scientists and then park planners began to design parks systems around the perceived need to protect representative samples of all the Earth's major ecosystems for study and reference. While not initially conceived for this purpose, national parks provide a suitable vehicle for these representational objectives. Today there are many small and medium-sized parks that are of doubtful value in actually protecting a functioning piece of an ecosystem but that do provide some (however limited) representation of the pristine environment.

A third element of environmental policy with respect to parks is that, coupled with outdoor recreation, they provide a forum for popular nature education. Parks, both national and provincial, play this educative role by offering various kinds of interpretive and instructional guidance. Trails are designed to take pedestrians to points of interest where plaques, displays, and dioramas enlighten the visitor on matters of geology, botany, wildlife, Aboriginal uses of natural resources, early European explorers, and so on. Summer employment is offered to specially trained interpretive staff to make this perambulatory education even more effective.

Parks as Human Landscapes

Initially, national parks were about the spectacle of wilderness. Despite an 1832 proposal by George Catlin, an early-nineteenth-century American painter, for a park "containing man and beast," the early parks were not about people. In the late nineteenth century, the idea of pristine nature meant that wilderness was almost unencumbered by human occupation and use.[10] In 1872, the legislation creating Yellowstone National Park prohibited settlement upon or occupation by people within park boundaries. This restriction included Native Americans. This was a period in which military conflict continued sporadically between several indigenous tribes and the US government. In 1877, there was a skirmish between the Nez Percé and the government on the territory within the park in which several Natives were killed. In establishing the park, individual indigenous groups were removed to nearby reservations provided for by treaties. In this context of war, treaty making, and relocation, the restrictions on settlement in the new park clearly meant that indigenous people were excluded.

At the same time as Native Americans were prevented from occupying park land, the unregulated nature of the area meant that souvenir hunters gathering animal trophies, geological specimens, and pieces of sculpted hot springs mineralizations were rapidly stripping the park of its attractions. This removal alarmed the park superintendent, who had been given broad powers under the original legislation, and his early reports illustrate his concern for the management of people within the park. Out of these circumstances and from the nineteenth century's romantic ideas of wilderness grew the concept of parks as wild areas free of human occupation. This "Yellowstone model" of parks devoid of people was rapidly adopted around the world and subsequently provided the basis for the internationally recognized definition of a national park. Accordingly, national parks are aimed at protecting ecosystems, which, until about the 1970s, were understood in non-human terms. This definition means that the system of "national parks" in England and Wales is not internationally recognized as such. Those parks, and similar ones in France and elsewhere in Europe, are designated "protected landscapes" (or level five in the six-level scheme adopted by international agreement), whereas "national parks" are level two.[11] For England and Wales, the landscape is really a joint creation of natural features and the long and thorough human occupation that has meant that these areas do not qualify as national parks,[12] although a very similar acknowledgment of indigenous and/or peasant relationships to the land in later decades resulted in changes to concepts of "natural" ecosystems.

In Canada, even though the early parks were essentially about economic development, with townsites established in Banff, Jasper, and elsewhere, Aboriginal people, as they had been in the United States, were initially excluded. When Banff park (then called Rocky Mountain National Park) was created in 1885, the Stoney Indians, who had previously hunted on and travelled over the land, were kept out of the new park. In a report in 1895, the first commissioner recommended that they be kept out permanently.[13] Later, in 1930, when Riding Mountain National Park was being established, government officials forceably removed the Ojibway people, now the Keeseekoowenin First Nation, from their traditional hunting grounds and residential areas in order to include these lands within the park.[14]

However, the conception of parks as unpopulated wilderness increasingly came to be challenged in the post-World War II era, especially in the period of decolonization and expanding human rights ushered in by the 1960s. Based on claims of indigenous rights and on humanitarian grounds,

Aboriginal people in Canada and other formerly colonized countries and hunter-gatherer people around the world demanded recognition. In turn, their co-operation was seen as essential to the ecological protection of parks. Moreover, in some countries, Canada in particular, Aboriginal people established a legal and constitutional claim to the land.

These claims were coupled with scientific recognition that the world's land, save Antarctica, had been peopled for millennia and that, with basic technology, humans were integral to the ecosystems of the planet. The Yellowstone model of parks, based on nineteenth-century concepts, was actually an artificial approach to landscapes. Therefore, increasingly, indigenous people who lived close to the land, including some agriculturalists, were incorporated into concepts of natural ecosystems. Correspondingly, the definition of national parks came to include indigenous people, and these parks were recognized internationally as "national parks."

Parks as Heritage

The idea of parks as heritage is not necessarily a new one. Catlin's 1832 proposal was, in fact, a suggestion to preserve a way of life against the imperative pressures of change. Today, his ideas would be regarded as being about heritage.

"Heritage," says Raphael Samuel, is "a nomadic term, which travels easily, and puts down roots ... in seemingly unpromising terrain." In the United Kingdom, Samuel describes heritage as encompassing widely dispersed matters from the political characteristics of the past, "God, King and the Law, the altar and throne," to language, "the principal element in conveying tradition from generation to generation, to "do-it-yourself genealogists."[15] David Lowenthal makes a similar observation: "Spanning the centuries from prehistory to last night, heritage melds Mesozoic monsters with Marilyn Monroe, Egyptian pyramids with Elvis Presley. Memorials and monuments multiply, cities and scenes are restored, historic exploits are reenacted, flea-market kitsch is elevated into antiques."[16]

For nature conservancy, Samuel says that heritage also refers to "unspoiled countryside and wildlife reserves," although, he acknowledges, this is not limited to "areas of outstanding natural beauty" (as defined in the UK national parks legislation) but includes the entire country, including many urban areas.[17] J.E. Tunbridge and G.J. Ashworth offer five "commonly understood meanings" for the term and, among them, suggest that "natural landscapes [that] are survivals from a past or are seen as in some sense original or typical" constitute a natural heritage.[18]

But Robert Hewison is concerned about the consequences of a concentration on heritage. In his book *The Heritage Industry*, he expresses his surprise that, in the 1980s, a new museum opened in Britain approximately every week, and he wonders how long it would be before the entire country is one vast museum. He further laments that this "industry" seems to be expected to "replace the real industry on which the country's economy depends."[19] He also acknowledges that the term is difficult to define, but he is unequivocal about what it means. For him, the heritage industry produces "fantasies of a world that never was," and at the same time it is "stifling of the culture of the present." As the past "solidifies around us, all creative energies are lost," he argues.[20] Lowenthal agrees, saying that "heritage is held to fossilize."[21] It is this sense of replacement or displacement that raises questions about how parks are heritage rather than environment.

In Canada, the term "natural heritage" has been in use since, at least, the early 1970s. Documents of many kinds frequently use it as a way of expressing one of the values associated with national parks. This usage also helps to link national parks to and distinguish them from national historic sites within their shared administrative domicile in the Parks Branch (Parks Canada). Indeed, one of the dilemmas for the branch was trying to find a way to unify both the conceptualization and the public presentation of the wilderness parks and the historic sites. The search to resolve this dilemma is partly what led to the transfer of the branch from the Department of the Environment to the newly created Department of Canadian Heritage in 1993.

Although the branch, in its new guise as the Parks Canada Agency, was moved back under the responsibility of the minister of the environment in 2003, the 1993 administrative transfer and the shift in emphasis for parks subtly change their focus. Heritage, in all its manifestations, is a spectator activity, even when there are interactive presentations (one is not participating in the past, after all), and not fully a participatory one. As heritage, then, parks are to be looked at. The environment is regarded from a conceptual and emotional distance. Hiking, camping, winter sports, and other outdoor activities remain as opportunities, but the symbolic message conveyed by the administrative location is that parks are reliquaries containing fragments of Canada's wilderness landscape. As such, they are not meant to be realistic presentations of current environmental conditions. Embedded within this message is the signal, for parks personnel and public alike, that parks are no longer policy instruments for environmental protection (except within their own boundaries). Not that national parks, as a federal policy tool, ever did stray far outside their official mandate, but in their new presentation there is a diminished role as an innovative participant in protecting Canada's natural environment.

Defining National Parks Policy

The ideas outlined above are about parks, not about policy (except in passing), although they are often reflected in policy. Policy is, however, equally difficult to define since it has accumulated over a long time and because it contains a wide diversity of ideas. The ideas above are presented chronologically in roughly the order in which they emerged initially in the United States, then in Canada and elsewhere. With the exception of concepts of national greatness, all of these ideas have been part of the history of national parks in this country and are manifest in varying degrees in Canada's national parks today. In the early twentieth century, environmental values were incorporated into administrative practice, and eventually legislation, under the influence of a single senior parks bureaucrat. During that process, an incipient conflict emerged between nineteenth-century ideas about economic development and newer environmental ideas evident in the practices of the Parks Branch. This conflict was interrupted at the national level by the Great Depression and World War II, when virtually all the policy tools of the state, including national parks, were employed to deal with those two immense crises. At the local level, the debates continued.[22]

For a time following World War II, the Parks Branch did not seem to have a focus or direction, and it was not until the mid-1950s that the inherent and arrested conflict between economic development and environmental protection was resumed. From that period to the present, there has been a general policy shift toward increased emphasis on environmental protection in national parks. By the 1970s, this theme became predominant, and national parks were touted as examples of pristine wilderness without human residents. Indeed, it was expected that people would be expelled from new park sites in order to create pure wilderness settings. This view changed in the 1980s when concepts of ecology were elaborated to acknowledge the reality of human presence in natural environments, especially with respect to Aboriginal people. Then, in 1993, with the transfer of the Parks Branch to the Department of Canadian Heritage, the concept of heritage was explicitly and formally attached to parks.

Thus, for over a century, there have been constantly changing ideas about the purposes of national parks, complicated by the fact that some parks already included previous uses coexisting with recent ones. It is, therefore, very difficult to define national parks policy in any general sense. It is only possible to specify it at the margins, so to speak, with respect to certain periods of time. That is, policy emphases, such as outdoor recreation and nature education in the 1950s and 1960s or environmental protection in the 1980s, can be identified as they occur in a specific period or at the margin of the total body of policy. However, the actual accumulated body of policy and practice contains many competing and conflicting ideas, so it cannot be said that parks are singularly about commercial development, outdoor recreation, environmental protection, revenue generation, or national remembrance: they embody all of these aspects and more. Indeed, some parks continue to cater to an urbanized, cultivated use of wilderness even though the general policy is now expressed more in terms of environmental protection.

Current national parks policy, therefore, is an accretion of several policy initiatives, some recent, many long entrenched. The historic purpose of genteel wilderness relaxation with extensive urban amenities continues in the oldest national parks, especially Banff and Jasper (which have become distinct policy problems in their own right). Policy documents must address, therefore, issues such as the nature of human settlements, the types of buildings and built space, and the management of commercial activities. More recently, as parks have become more environmentally focused, policy has had to include criteria for the selection of parks (which mostly emphasize natural characteristics), the degree and method of protection of their natural environments, and the very definition of "natural environment" itself.[23] As the emphasis in parks policy has shifted, there has been an increasing role for public consultation, now institutionalized in Parks Branch procedures, so that policy formally includes a commitment to public participation in policy deliberations. Finally, and most recently, public discussion has included specific concerns about the role of indigenous peoples in national parks, and policy reflects ideas about the extent and nature of their habitation and use of resources there.

Despite this complexity, both historically and currently the contest between environmental protection and preservation movements, on the one hand, and political forces promoting the use of national parks for commercial recreation, on the other, has been at the centre of the policy debate. Since the mid-1950s, the preservation model for parks has gradually prevailed over the development model. In attempting to understand and account for national parks policy, this study explains the reasons and motivations for this trend toward environmental protection.

It is worth a note at this point to distinguish three avenues of exploration in this study. First, since parks are understood to have meaning, one of the tasks is to identify and illustrate that meaning as outlined at the beginning of this introductory chapter. These ideas suffuse the discussion of parks even when they are not the subject of attention. Second, as parks policy is a complex amalgam of a century of decision making, this work offers a way to define and articulate what that policy is, as has been established immediately above. Third, because the principal objective of this book is to explain policy, a theory (or theoretical framework) needs to be identified and shown to assist in understanding policy and its development. The challenge of finding and employing a suitable policy theory is presented in the following section.[24]

The Analytical Challenges

The transition to an environmental focus is difficult to explain because it has included many different participants, has not been a steady and uniform process, and has taken place in four discernible periods. Therefore, an explanation is needed not only for the ascendancy of environmental values over ones favouring economic development but also for why different forces have been influential in each of the periods identified.

In fact, the central problem confronting the student of environmental policy in national parks as it has developed in the past fifty years is that no single theoretical explanation is persuasive over the entire period. To overcome this difficulty, the total time span can be reasonably subdivided into four separate policy periods in each of which political forces bear differently on the policy process. In the first, from (roughly) the mid-1950s to about 1970, the Parks Branch bureaucracy was the central participant in policy development, and policy can be explained by the institutional framework in which the bureaucracy functioned. However, the branch could not institute its proposed policy revisions without the assistance of environmental interest groups, and, even though the branch was the initiator and dominant party, the interaction between the two was essential to the progress of policy formalization.

As the second period began in the late 1960s and early 1970s, the balance between the institutionalized bureaucracy and environmental interests shifted toward approximate parity, wherein both sides initiated as well as responded. In this period, the institutional framework was opened to an ill-defined public participation process in which the effects of governing institutions were very fluid. Ideas about environmental protection and ones about public participation, both current at the time, infused both sets of actors and thereby offer an important element of the explanation for national parks' environmental emphasis through to the end of the 1970s.

The third period, after a brief lull at the beginning of the 1980s, began in earnest with the Mulroney Conservative government era. In this period, environmental interest groups were able to take a critical lead in advancing the environmental character of national parks policy largely because they had learned how to use the institutions of the state, including the courts. Ideas were also important, however, because some institutions had changed in response to new ideas about the role of the public in policy development and in the courts. Thus, an understanding of the interaction among institutions, interests, and ideas in this period is necessary to explain the consolidation of policy.

In the fourth period, state officials, particularly appointed ones, once again became the dominant participants, and again policy can be best explained by understanding the management needs of the bureaucracy and the institutional framework in which it operated. Ideas were also important since neo-conservative concepts occupied much of the broader policy debates, which influenced the choices available to policy makers. However, the bureaucracy was selective about which elements of the business-oriented framework to adopt and how to use them to pursue the goals of the parks program.

Thus, the argument presented in this analysis is that national parks policy can be explained best by examining the institutionalization of ideas within a context of constant change and interaction among environmental interest groups and state institutions. It will show how the interaction of groups and state institutions has led to greater emphasis on environmental protection in national parks. In addition, however, it will show that policy contexts are not static and that the interaction will change over time. In turn, the presence and dynamic of contextualizing ideas, strongly influencing the relationship among policy participants, explain that change.

The Workability of Policy Theories

Numerous theories seek to explain some feature of parks policy, and several might be given consideration. However, most have some limitation that prevents them from providing a convincing explanation. For example, a Marxist or class-analysis model might be used to show how the first parks provided important opportunities for capital accumulation and were developed to enhance the profitability of the CPR and other early railways in Canada. Such a model does not, on the surface, seem to be a likely one for explaining national parks policy since it is, essentially, about class conflict between capital and labour. Therefore, this approach does not explain the shift to stronger environmental protection.

Similarly, a public choice theory might explain how individual actors, politicians, and bureaucrats, in particular, employ self-interested, utility-maximizing criteria as they decide about parks questions. These ideas are initially very attractive for an analysis of the development of national parks policy since budgets and bureau size have expanded over recent decades (until the beginning of the 1990s), but it would be nearly impossible to show empirically how self-interest affected behaviour differently than commercial interests. Arguably, self-interest would be rewarded more by following a development-and-use policy for parks.

In the 1980s, numerous scholars identified the triumvirate of ideas, interests, and institutions as an explanation for policy where ideas and interests interact within established (mostly state) institutions. While incorporating the principal arguments of interest group theory, this approach recognizes that policy is made within an institutional framework, and the structures and processes of institutions will affect how groups function and how they interact with the state.

Ideas and Public Policy

Ideas are central to any explanation of policy. According to Ronald Manzer: "Ideas are important as determinants of public policies because participants in politics and policy-making depend on ideas in order to know what are public problems, understand potential courses of action, decide which policy is best for them in the circumstances, and later evaluate the overall results."[25] In a similar vein, Judith Goldstein says that ideas serve as "road maps, providing guidance to leaders."[26]

Margaret Weir earlier commented that too little attention had been given to "how ideas become influential, why some ideas win out over others, or why ideas catch on at the time that they do."[27] Manzer, however, identifies the critical element by discussing "policy makers," "political rivals," "participants in politics," "interest groups," and "political opponents" because, of course, ideas are brought into and are present in the policy process by and within the political actors also present.[28]

Ideas are not only present in the participants, however, but are also extant in the many institutions of government and the state. They exist within legislation, practices and procedures, formal rules and orders. Within government and the state, therefore, ideas of a former period are themselves institutionalized, and government itself thus reflects historic ideas.

In terms of explaining policy, therefore, ideas have several possible roles. First, they can be constitutive of meaning whereby they form the basis of individual and collective identities in both fundamental and ephemeral ways (in this case about parks). Second, there are substantive ideas that constitute the specific content of policy – whether, for example, it should be stringent or relaxed, universal or individual, accommodative or punitive. In addition, substantive ideas are about the choice of policy instruments to be used, such as taxation, expenditure, or regulation. Third, ideas are about cause-effect relationships, about what works and what does not. Fourth, ideas encoded in institutions, rules, and practices determine, or at least influence, who may be involved and under what circumstances. Fifth, ideas guide or condition the often rapidly changing policy process. In particular, there are short-lived ideas, sometimes experiments, sometimes simply fashions or trends, about how policy development is to be conducted and who may participate in it. These more fleeting and transitory ideas are the focus of this book.

Interest Groups and Policy
Considerable Canadian scholarship concerning groups has analyzed them within the context of the policy community model, where that community consists, on the one hand, of a subgovernment with a leading bureaucratic agency having a statutory mandate over the policy area, together with (mostly) institutionalized interest groups, and, on the other hand, an attentive public of interested but not actively participatory parties. Related to policy communities, work on policy networks has provided detail about how groups interact with each other and with the state. William Coleman

and Grace Skogstad and others have elaborated upon this latter framework by distinguishing three broad categories of policy networks found within a policy community:[29] pluralist, closed, and state-directed.

The differentiation of the policy community into networks enables distinctions to be made among the separate processes concerning the creation or management of each of nearly forty existing national parks, several designated regions awaiting parks, and the general policy debate at the national level – all of which may, at different times, constitute different policy loci. Another insight into national parks policy development, and the most important in terms of the thrust of this analysis, is the fact that the policy network model describes the several different relationships that have characterized the interaction between the Parks Branch and organized groups over the past five decades.

Despite the undoubted value of the policy community framework, there are several respects in which the model is not helpful. First, because of the resources that they can bring to bear, institutionalized groups are seen to dominate policy communities, and groups with less capacity are relatively insignificant in comparison.[30] However, in the contest between preservation and development in national parks, for much of the period under discussion, the preservationist groups were issue oriented or, at best, fledgling groups (in the terms of this literature), while the development interests were organized into local or national institutionalized groups. The relative success of these weaker (environmental) groups in shifting policy toward environmental protection is therefore unexplained by the policy community model with its attention to the advantages of institutionalized groups.

A second concern is that at its most fundamental level the policy community model is conceived in terms of different interests competing with each other for influence over policy ideas and outcomes. However, groups favouring commercial development in parks are mostly not evident in the policy process at the national level. Development interests are reflected in policy formulation in highly abstract, almost invisible, ways at this level. The details of policy networks are valuable, but groups successful at influencing parks policy conform only weakly to these configurations described by network models. For example, groups challenge the state not by "drawing on an inclusive, hierarchical associational system"[31] but by being able to use state institutions such as Parliament, the Constitution, and the courts.

For national parks, the most significant shortcoming of the policy community model is that it does not, at its present level of development, explain change over time. Whereas the parks policy network in the 1950s and 1960s might be described, with modifications, as a state-directed network, by the 1970s this had become more like a pressure pluralist one and by the 1990s had acquired some characteristics suggesting a limited form of concertation.

Taken together, these observations about the policy community model show that, while it is essential to understanding changes in national parks policy, it needs to be buttressed by additional analytical concepts.

Institutions in Policy Analysis

James March and Johan Olsen,[32] Theda Skocpol,[33] Peter Hall,[34] and others have argued that policy is not simply the aggregation of the bargains among competing individuals and organized interests but also the result of the organizational or institutional framework in which competition takes place. For them, an understanding of the combined effect of institutions together with interest groups and ideas is necessary to more fully explain policy outputs. By making some policy options available and precluding others, institutions structure or channel the competing interests and the ideas that these individuals and organizations convey.

One of the many diverse issues in the literature on institutions is the debate between rational choice and historical institutional approaches to institutional analysis. For rational choice theorists, institutions are no more than the constraining and channelling contexts in which participants seek, under conditions of rationality, to maximize their self-interest in pursuit of goals exogenously determined. In contrast, historical institutionalists see the matter more broadly, arguing that institutions shape the goals of participants as well as their strategies and relationships. Equating organizations and institutions as he does, Hall says that "organizational position ... influences an actor's definition of his own interests, by establishing his institutional responsibilities and relationship to other actors."[35] This self-definition by policy actors leads historical institutionalists to be more inductive than rational choice theorists since the goals of participants must be determined during the analysis rather than being taken a priori into it.

The distinction between the concepts of rational choice and historical institutionalism is relevant to national parks because the development of policy has been strongly influenced, both constrained and facilitated, by the central institutions of the Canadian state, such as federalism, parliamentary government, ministerial authority, and the courts. At the same time, participants' goals concerning both policy and their relation to it have arisen partly from the institutions within which national parks are situated. In this context, it is important to note that national parks and the National Parks Act (1930) are themselves institutions and that their very existence influences the kinds of goals that various participants develop with respect to them.

Relatively little of this literature has addressed changes in these variables over time. Because the interaction (like the ideas, institutions, and interests themselves) is not static, it is necessary to explain the changing contexts in order to fully explain the policy itself. Thus, this analysis of how the policy contexts change over time will add to existing understandings about institutions and enrich general theoretical explanations of policy analysis over extended periods of time.

The Role of Contextualizing Ideas in Understanding Change

Canadian national parks policy presents a series of challenges to attempts to explain its development over the period from the mid-1950s to the early twenty-first century. One, as outlined above, is to define the policy, given its multiple components, in such a way that it can be analyzed and explained at all. Another is to choose a theoretical perspective that can provide a persuasive explanation for the policy. Since no one theoretical approach is consistently effective when applied over a fifty-year period, this presents a third and general challenge. This one is that, while standard theoretical perspectives on the one hand, or the composite approach of looking at institutions, interests, and ideas together on the other, may be persuasive for one period, neither any single approach nor any particular configuration of several will be uniformly convincing in all periods. The challenge is therefore twofold. The first part is to offer an explanation for the policy output in any particular period. The second is to understand changes in the factors relevant to the explanation of that policy output.

There is a vast literature on national parks, most of it describing their natural features or narrating their human histories. Few studies address policy except in descriptive or prescriptive (usually in highly normative) terms. Limited attention has been given to explaining parks policy in terms of theories of public policy in general. Without much previous analysis, the study of parks policy must begin without reference points, a situation that is complicated by the many political influences that affect the development of policy.

In the beginning of national park development, railway interests were a significant factor, a fact that might suggest that some form of Marxist or elite-accommodation model would be useful in explaining the pre-World War II period. Ambitious politicians have also, on occasion, played a major role in the expansion of the parks system, which suggests a public choice approach wherein self-interest is determinative. In the current period, interest groups have been central to the policy process, and this involvement suggests either a pluralist or a policy community explanation. Each has some relevance, but each is also insufficient to explain either the century-long development of national parks or the relatively recent shift toward strengthening environmental protection. In place of these explanations, or combining them, an explanation is sought that can unify the multiple political factors and the transformations through time.

Contexts, Ideas, and a Theory of Policy Change

Heraclitus, the sixth-century-BC Greek philosopher, observed that "one cannot step twice into the same river";[36] everything is in flux. Institutions, ideas, and interests exist in constantly changing contexts, and the intersection among these political factors, which may help to explain policy, will not necessarily be stable. Hence, to understand more fully the various influences on policy, it is essential to understand how changes in the policy-making context affect the ways in which institutions, ideas, and interests may come to bear on policy decisions.

Contexts are widely recognized as influential in political life. Kenneth Dyson, for example, in his work on the development of the state in western Europe, posits that "concepts and contexts are inseparable."[37] Robert Putnam, in his twenty-year study of Italian regional government, suggests that "the practical performance of institutions ... is shaped by the social context within which they operate."[38] In a similar vein, Kent Weaver and Bert Rockman comment that institutional "capabilities are inherently situational: they involve a relationship among government objectives, efforts and perceived problems that are never completely comparable across individual countries."[39] James Farr takes this view further and proposes what he calls "situational analysis."[40]

Most of these comments refer to a short-term, static situation, but the relevance of differing contexts in different periods is also frequently acknowledged as politically influential. Douglas Ashford, for example, draws attention to the importance of timing and the context of the moment when he suggests that policy case studies describe a particular setting and give "an account of prevailing ethical and moral standards at work in political and social life at some moment in history."[41]

Similarly, Carolyn Tuohy acknowledges the importance of context for Canadian health policy when she suggests that health policy will vary depending on the "climate" of federal-provincial relations or what she calls the intersection between institutions and ideas. Expressed somewhat differently, as the intersection changes, so do the ideas that are incorporated into the developing policy. For Tuohy, "shifts in the climate of federal-provincial relations over time" will affect health policy outputs.[42] Moreover, changes in "the dominant theme of the international climate of policy ideas" have shifted the emphasis from "access" to "cost control" in Canadian health policy and changed policy outputs.[43] These shifts in climate are not changes in institutions or even, for that matter, in substantive ideas about policy content; rather, they are shifts in the manner in which institutions function or in the background against which certain (substantive) ideas are adopted.

In another area of Canadian social policy, Rodney Haddow has drawn attention to the importance of changing contexts over time. By comparing the postwar development of the Canada Assistance Plan (CAP) in the 1960s and the later failure of the Social Security Review in the 1970s, Haddow argues that the difference in context between these two periods was influential in the success of one policy initiative but not the other: "A singular merit of the period spanned by the two reforms ... is that it witnessed a significant transition in [the] internal arrangements of the Canadian state, which altered the organizational context of policy making but not necessarily the fragmented nature of the state. The cases examined here therefore provide an excellent opportunity to document the impact of distinct forms of state organization on policy making."[44] Haddow reiterates this point later when he says, "Changes in the structure of the Canadian state account for the most striking differences between the CAP and the [Social Security] Review."[45]

In a more detailed approach to differing temporal contexts, George Hoberg offers a framework for what he calls regulatory "regimes." By examining environmental regulation in the United States from 1933 to the early 1990s, he distinguishes between two such regimes, the New Deal (1933-69) and the Pluralist (1970-92). In his analysis, Hoberg identifies a series of characteristics and shows how they changed between the two regimes. For example, procedures in the New Deal regime were "informal, nonlegal and consensual," but in the Pluralist regime they were "formal, legal and adversarial."[46] Similarly, supporting norms in the earlier regime were characterized by agencies representing the public interest, whereas later the public interest was represented by a balance of interest groups mediated by the courts.[47] By describing the features of each regime, Hoberg reveals a focus on institutional factors.[48] However, by paying attention to both "policy objectives" and "supporting norms" his analysis also incorporates some attention to prevailing ideas that help to establish the differing contexts in which policy develops and that are therefore influential in policy development.

In much the same way that Dyson, Putnam, and Farr recognize that contexts are important, Tuohy, Haddow, and Hoberg acknowledge that contexts change and that the altered ways in which institutions function affect policy processes and outputs. Forms of and differences in state organization or intrastate relations do not arise spontaneously, however, and one therefore must look at ideas concerning the practice of intrastate relations (i.e., both intergovernmental, in a federal state, and intragovernmental) to explain them more fully. The changes to institutions or to institutional factors might themselves be interpreted to acknowledge that ideas, to paraphrase Manzer, are important as determinants in institutional change because institutional participants depend on ideas to decide which changes are best for them in the circumstances.[49]

One final author whose work supports the importance of both context and changes in context is Hugh Heclo, whose analysis of social policy development in Britain and Sweden during the late nineteenth and early twentieth centuries is valuable to the current analysis in two respects. First, Heclo argues that most policy studies tend "to consider the role of political factors in isolation rather than in interaction through time."[50] Social policy in Britain and Sweden developed over many decades and is, according to Heclo, "too complex to be explained simply"[51] as the result of a single political factor (or perhaps a limited few) such as political parties, interest groups, and the like. Combining several influences, however, raises questions about the nature of their interaction that, Heclo urges, should lead one to inquire into how problems are worked out over time. The influence of time on ideas, for him, lies at least partly in the succession of generations: "In time ... generations of policy makers may rise to positions allowing them to express in policy their own generational views of the issues and presumptions for action (as Edwardian poor law opponents, Keynesian reformers, anti-means-testers from the 1930s and so on). Social policy in any period acquires a molar quality through these bodies of common interpretation."[52] Heclo's suggestion of idea change as a result of cohort succession does not explain the more rapid sequence of contextualizing ideas with respect to national parks (each segment of which is more brief than a generation), but it does draw valuable attention to the knowledge that policy factors interact differently at different times.

Second, Heclo eschews the conception of politics as being exclusively about conflict and power. For him, "governments not only 'power' (or whatever the verb form of that approach might be); they also puzzle. Policy making is a form of collective puzzlement on society's behalf; it entails both deciding and knowing."[53] This viewpoint is instructive for analyzing national parks policy because, while there were, at times, obvious conflicts, and often the application of power, many of the significant decisions were made by bureaucrats seeking clarity in their jobs and by co-operative participatory relations between the Parks Branch and the various members of the policy community. A principal difference between Heclo's argument and the present one is that Heclo locates a significant portion of the explanation for early-twentieth-century British and Swedish social policy in those countries' bureaucracies, whereas for Canadian national parks no single factor stands out over the four decades addressed herein.

Contextualizing Ideas

This brief review illustrates that contexts taken alone and changing contexts over time have already been presented by several authors as having an influence in policy development, although there have been varying degrees of emphasis on the aspect and importance of change. While changing ideas have been recognized, they have been seen either as differences in substantive ideas (through generational succession, for example) or simply as one of several factors (as in regime change) rather than being distinguished as a separate and significant variable. For national parks in Canada, the substantive idea of environmental preservation has been present since the early twentieth century and included in official policy since 1930. However, it did not become an effective part of policy until the 1960s and subsequently. The reason for the change from formal but ineffective to manifested policy through the postwar era can be explained by different factors at different times, and the underlying, and thus critical, factor is that some ideas altered the context of the policy environment and therefore affected which variable would be influential in different periods. Ideas that affect the policy-making context in this way have been called "contextualizing ideas" for the purposes of this study.

Contextualizing ideas shape and condition the policy-making environment in which discussion takes place and in which substantive ideas, interest groups, and institutions interact. Where policy development is, to invoke Heclo, more about puzzling than about powering, contextualizing ideas provide a logical argumentative advantage to some policy participants in contrast to others. The leverage gained through the presence of these ideas influences which groups or agencies may achieve prominence in deliberations, which institutions may be brought to bear on issues, and the manner in which the institutions may be used. This leverage and the organizations thus favoured, in turn, benefit some substantive ideas over others. As they change, contextualizing ideas create new opportunities for policy entrepreneurs and therefore favour change relative to the status quo. Nevertheless, these ideas interact with existing ones, both contextual and substantive, to shift rather than revolutionize policy direction. Hence, the corpus of national parks policy today contains most of the ideas ever incorporated into this arena, making it highly complex.

Contextualizing ideas bear more directly on the form of policy than on its substance, but by affecting form they also, indirectly, affect substance. For example, rationalism in government was not intended to make national parks policy more explicitly environmentalist, but by motivating a particular (rationalist) framework it also favoured a wilderness and preservation conception of parks. In affecting policy in this way, contextualizing ideas leave an imprint but are not the manifest subject of policy. These ideas are also relatively transitory in that they tend to be influential for, perhaps, ten to fifteen years and are subsequently replaced by other prominent ideas. They appear to arise from more deeply rooted conceptions such as those about democratic participation or Aboriginal rights. But they may also be satellites to other currently hegemonic ideas or paradigms in the way that market orientation in parks is currently a spinoff from a more broadly based, neo-conservative, monetarist paradigm. By conditioning, perhaps even establishing, the context in which policy discussion takes place, contextualizing ideas privilege some participants and their substantive ideas and thus channel the direction of policy change.

2
Background to the Postwar Era: A Brief History of Canada's National Parks

The debates and decisions of the nineteenth and early twentieth centuries determined the events surrounding national park development in the post-World War II period. In this earlier period, the framework of parks as a policy arena was established and the dichotomy between the substantive policy ideas about preservation on the one hand and resource use on the other infused the deliberations around parks. This dichotomy was in turn institutionalized in parks legislation in 1930 and has animated the public debate ever since. The early period of parks establishment and policy development was the result of the context of nation-building and economic development ideas that were interwoven in and that characterized the era. To understand and give context to the events of the post-World War II period, it is necessary first to trace the origins of national parks. This history will show how the initial decisions and events were institutionalized in parks and came to bear such influence on later policy debates.

Early American Influences on National Park Development
The national park idea arose in the United States and was quickly adopted in Canada and eventually in many other countries around the world. Two major influences affected park development in Canada and elsewhere. First, the basic idea of the national park emerged and was established in the United States. Second, somewhat less evident, is the body of environmental values that informs not only parks policy but also many other aspects of modern environmental thinking.

Yellowstone National Park, established in 1872 in Wyoming, is commonly held to be the first national park, although Yosemite, created in 1864 in California, was also defined and legislated by the US Congress. Yosemite, however, was within an existing state and shortly after its creation was transferred to California as a state park. In contrast, Wyoming was still only a territory fully under Washington's jurisdiction when Yellowstone was established and did not receive control of the park when it became a state in

1890. Therefore, it was in the period between 1864 and 1890 that the national park idea, the idea of protecting special areas of land under federal jurisdiction, was born.

Yellowstone and other early national parks were not designed to protect the environment but were almost entirely the result of nationalism and feelings of national prestige, both supported by commercialism. In these terms, Alfred Runte has persuasively argued that both Yosemite and Yellowstone were the result of an American sense of inferiority to the cultural grandeur of Europe. Early Americans, he suggests, were separated from European traditions after their independence from Britain and sought reassurance for a glorious American future from their own landscape.[1] At first, their efforts east of the Mississippi were unconvincing, but with continued westward expansion after the 1840s American cultural nationalists were finally provided with the kind of natural grandeur that suggested national greatness. In the Pacific Northwest, for example, there was "mountain scenery in quantity and quality to make half a dozen Switzerlands," and in California, Yosemite Falls was described as without parallel anywhere in the world.[2] As for antiquity, the discovery of the Sierra Redwoods, which "began to grow before the Christian era"[3] and flourished well before European civilization, suggested to early nationalists America's greater link with the past.

But when Yosemite and the Sierra Redwoods were set aside as the first wilderness parks, the reserved lands were small by modern national park standards, comprising the Yosemite valley and a mere four square miles of redwoods, only forty square miles in total. In other words, specific elements of dramatic scenery were protected rather than those areas later regarded as vital by application of yet-to-be-developed principles of ecology. "Monumentalism," says Runte, "not environmentalism, was the driving impetus behind the 1864 Yosemite Act."[4]

Yellowstone, on the other hand, at 3,300 square miles, was not small. When it was established, there were no roads or railways into the region. The legislation establishing Yellowstone is comprehensive in its protection of the lands within the park. The pristine nature of the area was, however, the result of an act of God, not an act of Congress. Runte argues that, despite its size, Yellowstone was also about monumentalism. Little was known about the Yellowstone area in 1872; the decision to go ahead with the park was based on only one expedition into what was an isolated region. While modern writers frequently cite the vast size of the park as evidence of an environmental vision behind its creation, Runte concludes that "had more been known about the region ... in all probability Yellowstone ... would have been established as a series of parcels [each] encompassing little more than its major attractions."[5] Other writers on the early US national parks generally support this view. John Ise remarks, for example, that in 1872 "Congress had no conception of a national park as we think of it today,"[6] while Marilyn Dubasak writes that Yellowstone National Park "was created for several reasons, none of them specifically the preservation of wilderness"; this was, rather, a "byproduct" of the park.[7]

Environmental values were the second major influence on national park development, but they emerged independently of the park idea itself in nineteenth-century America and were later grafted both onto the national parks concept and onto existing parks. While these values almost certainly did not motivate the creation of national parks in this early stage, they did quickly become a major focus in the longer-term development of the parks system. The precise origin of American environmental values is unclear. They no doubt owe some debt to American transcendentalist writers such as Henry David Thoreau and Ralph Waldo Emerson as well as to ornithologist J.J. Audubon and wilderness painter George Catlin.[8] But it was John Muir who catalyzed earlier ideas into a more unified body of environmental thought, promoted national parks as vehicles for environmental protection, and established the long-standing environmental group, the Sierra Club.

The efforts of Muir contributed to the confluence of environmental values and the national parks idea. In 1890, the US Congress established Yosemite National Park, encircling the smaller (and previously created) California state park, "largely due," according to Ise, "to the persistent efforts of John Muir."[9] Roderick Nash marks the significance of Yosemite National Park as the "first preserve consciously designed to protect wilderness,"[10] although Runte suggests that it was not "until the 1930s [that] wilderness preservation [would be] recognized as a primary justification for establishing national parks."[11]

While Muir and his supporters were successful in introducing the idea of wilderness preservation into the national park discussion, a schism was developing between two kinds of environmental values. On one side were the preservationists, including Muir and his supporters, who believed that some sections of wilderness should be protected absolutely from significant human alteration. Conservationists held, on the other side, that resources should be protected and the environment respected only so that they could be used in more efficient ways, if not at that time, then at some future time. For conservationists, "use" generally meant some form of agricultural or industrial production, and parks, as conceived by the preservationists, therefore constituted a waste of the resources contained in them. The contest between these two sets of ideas dominated early discussions surrounding national park development in the United States and, perhaps more significantly, set the stage for a continuing debate about resources, parks, and a wide range of environmental questions lasting through the twentieth century to the present.

This debate quickly spilled into Canada, where the contest between preservation and conservation (or "wise use"), though somewhat slower to get under way, continues today. In the late nineteenth century, the wise-use idea complemented Sir John A. Macdonald's "National Policy" and Canada's own ambitions of national expansion. Preservationism did not arrive until much later.[12] The first idea to cross the border, however, was that of the national park itself.

The Beginnings of Canada's National Parks

National parks began in Canada in 1885 when a small park was established at Banff, with the now famous hot springs as its centrepiece. Other parks in western Canadian federal lands quickly followed, and at the beginning of the twentieth century there were seven national parks. Early legislation did not provide any policy mandate, however, and did little more than enable the government to set aside and reserve Crown lands for the purposes of parks (whatever those purposes might be). Non-legislated policy, on the other hand, made it clear that the first priority for parks was the provision of economic development opportunity and, where possible, increases in government revenues. Although the idea of national parks was adopted from the United States, neither of the motivating concepts (monumentalism and, later, environmental protection) that were influential there inspired the first Canadian examples. In Canada, as Robert Craig Brown and others have noted, national parks were part of the federal government's "National Policy" to promote economic growth and the expansion of Canadian territory. More specifically, early Canadian parks were seen as an opportunity to generate government revenues and to provide passengers and hotel patrons for the Canadian Pacific Railway, whose economic fortunes were of special interest to the government. Although the grandeur of the Rocky Mountains was noted, that notice was limited to advertising campaigns to attract tourists and was not part of the public or intellectual discussion about the nature of society, as it had been in the United States. Nor were the first national parks seen as a means of environmental protection since this concept did not enter official consideration until after 1911, and then only slowly.

Development of Canada's Early National Parks

Thus, parks in late-nineteenth-century Canada, unlike those in the United States, were not the subject of a debate on early environmental policy. Robert Craig Brown has suggested that "the origins of Canadian national parks policy are to be found in the expansionist, exploitive economic programs of the National Policy of the Macdonald Government after 1878. In contrast, there is little evidence to suggest that national parks policy originated in any conviction about preserving the 'wilderness' on either aesthetic or other grounds."[13] Leslie Bella has further argued that Canadian national parks, in the late twentieth century, were still not "removed from economic development" but remained "the focus of that development."[14] As mentioned, one of the economic purposes of the early national parks was to provide resorts that would attract tourists as passengers to the CPR and customers to the hotels and other facilities in the park. This activity would, in turn, provide revenue for the government treasury. Speaking to Parliament, Sir John A. Macdonald said about the park reserve at Banff that "it has all the qualifications necessary to make it a great place of resort ... There is beautiful scenery, there is prairie sport and there is mountain sport; and I have no doubt that will become a great watering-place ... [T]hat is a perennial source of revenue, and if carefully managed it will more than many times recuperate or recoup the Government for any present expenditure."[15] The government expenditure referred to was, of course, needed to "make a park of this tract of land ... to improve on it to a certain extent."[16] In other words, Banff was not meant to be a nature preserve or a wilderness park.

Thus, rather than protecting environmental values, the park created a monopoly to protect the commercial values associated with the hot springs and the mountain scenery. The discoverers and early entrepreneurial developers at the hot springs were told to leave the land reserved for the park,[17] while the government granted extensive commercial privileges to the CPR, including the opportunity to build hotels and other tourist amenities within the park boundaries.[18]

Since the early national parks were seen as revenue-generating resorts, it is not surprising that their park status was not meant to prevent the continued extraction of all manner of natural resources. Bella and others have chronicled the coal mining and limestone quarrying that continued in Banff National Park until 1930, when they were discontinued by the simple expedient of redrawing the park boundaries so that the mines fell outside the park. Logging, mining, and gravel extraction continued in other parks until well after World War II.[19] Indeed, logging in Wood Buffalo National Park[20] and waterfowl hunting in Point Pelee National Park[21] continued until 1989.

Brown's suggestion that Canada's early parks were simply part of the broader "doctrine of usefulness" parallels the conservationist or wise-use ideas being discussed in the United States in the late nineteenth and early twentieth centuries. In fact, Canadians had been following the American discussion and in 1906 invited Gifford Pinchot, the US chief forester and the intellectual leader of the conservationist school of thought, to the first Canadian Forestry Convention in Ottawa.[22] Although Canada's early parks officials were aware of John Muir and his preservationist ideas,[23] the wise-use approach to resources, including parks, dominated Canadian policy making throughout the first half of the twentieth century.[24] Marilyn Dubasak, in comparing wilderness preservation in Canada and the United States, has argued that the preservationist ideas did not seriously influence Canadian political culture and policy making until the 1960s.[25]

Early National Park Legislation and Organizational Development
Environmental protection clauses were not included in Canadian national park legislation until forty-five years after the first reservation of land at Banff in 1885. That initial reservation was made by an order-in-council that remained in force until it was superseded by the first park legislation (the Rocky Mountain Parks Act, 1887), which did no more than establish the government's authority to set up and manage the parks. Later the Dominion Forest Reserves and Parks Act (1911) made only modest changes toward protecting park lands, although it did make a significant contribution to the future course of national parks policy by establishing a separate agency for the administration of parks. But the National Parks Act (1930) finally articulated a purpose for national parks and gave some legislative expression to the idea that greater environmental protection was needed to retain the (economically valuable) wilderness character.

While the National Parks Act was thus more important in defining the purposes of national parks, the 1911 Forest Reserves and Parks Act did lay the foundation for the later legislation and reflected the growing importance of national parks as a distinct policy area. Significantly, the debate accompanying its passage and the terms of the act itself indicate a modest shift in policy toward environmental protection, especially for increased protection of wildlife within park boundaries, and away from resource extraction.[26] The most important feature of the act from the parks perspective, however, was creation of the Dominion Parks Branch, an agency exclusively dedicated to the management and administration of national parks, thus taking them out of the forestry and resource development framework in which they had previously been situated and allowing for the development of policies specific to them. This development made Canada the first country in the world, preceding the United States by five years, to establish an agency solely for this purpose.[27] Equally significant was the appointment of James B. Harkin as the first commissioner of dominion parks (as national parks were then called). In contrast to John Muir, who, with bushy beard and rugged clothing, was a "mountain man," Harkin was a primly dressed Ottawa mandarin. Although starkly different in personal style, Harkin was as central, in his way, to wilderness protection in Canadian national parks as Muir was, in his way, to those in the United States.

J.B. Harkin, Commissioner of National Parks
When he was appointed to the post of commissioner, Harkin admitted that he knew nothing about parks[28] but quickly set about to change that by travelling to western Canada to see the existing parks, by assembling information about them, and by forming contacts with Americans who, though not yet operating through a formal agency, had considerable experience in

parks administration. In particular, Harkin became familiar with the writings of John Muir, recognizing his contribution to the redefinition of the role of national parks in American life. Some observers have remarked that Harkin, like Muir, held an almost mystical view of the wilderness, but that did not prevent him from recognizing the need to promote the revenue-generating and other economic potential of parks to parliamentarians who sought economic expansion.[29]

Alan MacEachern is less willing to give Harkin sole credit for instilling a preservationist ethos into parks policy and suggests that it is safer to see him as a product of the collective attitudes of the branch, that "he relied on his staff to help draft policy, and so served as a conduit for the philosophy germinating within the Branch."[30] This view is consistent with the argument raised in this book and is probably right to deflate the hagiography that has grown up around Harkin. Nevertheless, Harkin was a senior administrator who presided over the initial formation of the Parks Branch and its management for twenty-five years. Under his direction, the organization increased from a mere seven staff members to over eighty, while the parks themselves increased threefold both in number and in area. Despite the paucity of writing unequivocally credited to him, the administrative achievements are beyond doubt. Few public servants, even in Canada's early years, can claim a quarter-century of tenure and associated organizational growth.

Notwithstanding his importance in the early organizational formation of the Parks Branch during his years as commissioner (1911-36), Harkin's most significant contribution was his influence on the preparation of the National Parks Act (1930). The wilderness protection features of the act owe themselves to Harkin, who, like other civil servants, was responsible for policy development on what we now call environmental issues (whatever advice he may have received from his staff). According to Janet Foster, in the related area of early wildlife policy, "one searches through voluminous ministerial records and manuscript collections ... in the hope of finding evidence that prime ministers or cabinet ministers initiated programs for wildlife conservation. But one searches in vain. The concept of wildlife conservation neither originated nor evolved at this high level of government. Rather it was at the level of the senior civil servant that the awareness was born and that new concepts emerged and took shape." Foster goes on to say that Harkin, in particular, had "a clear and unfailing vision of what wilderness, parks, and wildlife signified for the Canadian people in terms of both aesthetic and economic importance."[31]

In the early years of his office, Harkin realized that the dual mandate of the Forest Reserves and Parks Act was not the best framework for the development and management of national parks as such. New legislation exclusively for parks was therefore drafted in 1919, but it was not introduced to Parliament for several years, and it was not until 1930 that the National

Parks Act finally became law.[32] The new act made many important changes to the two preceding pieces of parks legislation, but perhaps the most critical was the wording of the preamble. While the two earlier acts had described land as "reserved and set apart as a public park and pleasure ground for the advantage and enjoyment of the people of Canada," section 4 of the National Parks Act introduced the idea that national parks should be protected and preserved nearly in their pristine state: "the parks are hereby dedicated to the people of Canada for their benefit, education and enjoyment [and] ... shall be maintained and made use of so as to leave them unimpaired for the enjoyment of future generations."[33] The word *unimpaired* reflects ideas found in Harkin's own writing, for example when he described national parks as "vast areas possessing some of the finest scenery in Canada in which ... primeval nature [is] retained."[34]

Janet Foster's assessment also suggests that Harkin was influential in introducing these preservationist sentiments into the legislation. Leslie Bella more directly credits Harkin's efforts, together with those of some early interest groups, for "sav[ing] the national parks from [resource] exploitation."[35] This view of Harkin's role is supported by comments during debate about the new legislation in Parliament when opposition member R.B. Bennett (later prime minister), in arguing against greater protection for parks and reflecting criticisms of the new act emanating from his home province of Alberta, credited Parks Branch officials with the wording of the act. "The permanent officials," charged Bennett, "have added to section four these words, ... 'so as to leave them unimpaired for the enjoyment of future generations.'"[36] The vague "permanent officials" mentioned at this point became "Mr. Harkin" later when his name was brought specifically into the debate.[37]

Despite his efforts toward using national parks to protect Canadian wilderness, Harkin also recognized that, on the political side of government, parks were still seen as sources of revenue and private-sector economic opportunity. To justify the maintenance and expansion of parks, Harkin promoted them in these terms. Indeed, numerous early conflicts over resource use, such as coal mining or hydroelectric developments in the parks, were resolved simply by redrawing the boundaries of the parks. The policy message was clear. Parks were there as resorts and, as such, could afford a modest protection of the landscape as long as commercially valuable resource exploitation was not prevented.

While his balancing of commercial interests and his own efforts to protect wilderness enabled Harkin to increase the number and area of national parks during his tenure, it also firmly established economic activity and commercial interests within them. Therefore, although Harkin was instrumental in instituting a legislated basis for wilderness protection, he also presided over the development of a parks system that contained within it, like the legislation itself, an ambiguity that was not resolved in the 1930s and came back to trouble the branch in the 1950s and 1960s. In some parks, it still bedevils policy makers and administrators.

Resources Transfer Acts and the National Parks Act
Ironically, passage of the National Parks Act was simply the end of the first period of national parks policy development rather than the beginning of the second. Until 1930, the federal government could create national parks unilaterally in western Canada, without specific reference to provincial governments or legislatures, since Ottawa held jurisdiction over land and other natural resources in the three Prairie provinces and in the railway corridor through British Columbia.[38]

With the acquisition of Rupert's Land from the Hudson's Bay Company in 1869, Canada had taken control of what was, essentially, a colonial possession in western Canada. Although the Province of Manitoba was soon created, it had little power, and, although a rudimentary territorial legislature followed for the rest of the Northwest Territories,[39] the government in Ottawa had full control over the disposition of land and resources and with that control established the first national parks in them. Creation of the Provinces of Saskatchewan and Alberta in 1905, and expansion of Manitoba's borders in 1912, did not affect that federal discretion since the new provinces were not given control over land and other natural resources at the time of their creation.

This differed from the situation of other provinces, which held full territorial control of resources on their entry into Confederation and which were (and still are) compensated for surrendering land for national park purposes. Unlike the others, the three Prairie provinces have never had the same opportunity to negotiate the existence or extent of the early national parks within their territories. In effect, therefore, national parks established in them before 1930 represent a remnant of the old Northwest Territories.

However, concurrent with passage of the National Parks Act, and closely linked to it, Parliament passed a series of other acts that transferred jurisdiction over land and other natural resources from the federal government to the respective western provinces. These resources transfer acts did not end significant federal involvement in western resources development, but they did end the federal government's ability to create national parks without provincial consent. Since the federal government had not yet conceived of parks in the north, provincial governments were, by the early 1930s, in effect, essential actors, along with the federal government, in the creation of national parks.

The national parks and resources transfer bills were developed in tandem, and, because parks are themselves an aspect of land and resource use, the legislation for the former could not be concluded until an understanding had been reached on the latter – but that took more than a decade. Indeed, one of the elements of that debate was the issue of the parks themselves. Although the provinces (Alberta in particular) argued that they should be under provincial jurisdiction, the federal government sought to retain them. This refusal to relinquish control sparked considerable debate at the time and still occasionally causes resentment, especially in Alberta. That province, which had (and has) the largest area of national parks within its boundaries, and which had probably suffered most as a result of the time taken to transfer resources,[40] was the most vocal in criticizing the National Parks Act. R.B. Bennett, then leader of the opposition, berated the government for allowing control of national parks to be held in offices thousands of miles from the parks themselves. This criticism continues to be made today, particularly with respect to Banff and Jasper National Parks.

The National Parks Act itself is a modest document; its main substance takes up only six small pages, while an additional nine pages (a "schedule") specify the legal boundaries of four parks and one historic site. One of the main purposes of the legislation was simply to create a separate act for parks, thereby removing them from the Dominion Forest Reserves and Parks Act, which had previously provided their authority. The principal clause of the act is section 4, the statement of "general purposes," which says, as cited above, that "parks shall be maintained and made use of so as to leave them unimpaired for ... future generations." The exact wording of this clause has been retained in subsequent legislation, thus continuing to be the guiding principle for policy and management. However, it is ambiguous in proscribing impairment while at the same time encouraging use. This ambiguity has haunted policy development and, at the beginning of the twenty-first century, has interest groups organized around its competing ideas. Awkwardly, the act does not specify the degrees or types of use or the criteria to assess impairment; the definition of these matters has been a significant task for policy makers for over half a century. At the same time, the requirement to leave parks unimpaired has been seen by many as the foundation upon which all subsequent ecological protection has been based. Even at the time, this was seen as a significant statement for national parks.

In addition to this clause, the act ensures that all park lands will remain in Crown ownership (section 6). Land may be sold to railway companies for rights of way and station grounds but must be returned to the Crown if no longer used for those purposes. While the management of lands within parks has been more difficult than the simplicity of the act may suggest, the Crown has nevertheless been able to retain greater control than it would in a private-ownership setting. Additional authority permitting (but not requiring) preservation of environmental features is granted to the governor in council for the issuing of regulations (section 7) to protect flora, wild animals, and fish and to prevent water pollution. This authority is under-pinned by police powers given to park wardens and by the provision of specified penalties for offences.

In addition to terms granting authority for the protection of parks, the act conducts several straightforward tasks for the overall management of parks, such as the creation or redeclaration of an administrative organiza-tion (a commissioner of parks, wardens, wardens' duties, and authorities). It acknowledges the position of railways in the parks and provides for the management of the resident human communities.

Despite its brevity and limited details, the National Parks Act made im-portant contributions to the early protection of park ecology and provided a significant foundation upon which later additions were built. However, the act was not aimed solely at protection. One of its more controversial aspects was the boundary definition for Banff National Park, which occurs in the nine-page schedule. For Banff, these boundaries constituted a sub-stantial decrease in size as several pieces of the former park were cut off because they contained economically valuable resources. Notable among these cuts was the Spray River valley, which contained hydroelectric poten-tial of interest to the Calgary Power Company. Other areas that included coal mines and the cement plant at Exshaw as well as extensive forested areas were also taken out of the park.[41] The areas that remained in Banff were those with particular scenic importance but, it was thought by some, little other value. Much of the debate about these exclusions revolved around the concept of a park and whether scenic values should be the only criteria. Ecological protection, even if not expressed in those words, was recognized by some of the advocates for the larger park, but it was not persuasive in Parliament, where arguments about economic potential were stronger. An-other issue in the legislation, in terms of ecological protection, was the wide discretion given to the governor in council. Considerable political energy in the post-World War II era would be devoted to constraining that latitude and shifting authority to the more open forum of parliamentary debate and to structured relationships between the state and the public, especially Ab-original people.

The Interregnum

It is impossible to know what effect the resources transfer legislation, on its own, would have had on the expansion of national parks because 1930 also marked the beginning of the Great Depression, which was then followed by World War II. Those two catastrophic events consumed the principal ener-gies of the country, and national parks were a minor issue on the govern-ment agenda. For whatever reasons, the themes of development versus preservation that were adumbrated in the preamble to the National Parks

Act were muted in the two decades or more that followed. It seems reasonable to describe the period from 1930 to approximately 1955 as an interregnum. In that period, indeed until 1970, only four new national parks were established, all in the Atlantic provinces and all, at least partly, with the justification of economic development and the transfer of federal money to the economically depressed Atlantic region. The most overtly political of these parks was Terra Nova National Park, established in Newfoundland in the mid-1950s as part of the Confederation deal in 1949.

The relatively low rate of park establishment was not the only feature that characterized the depression and war years as an interregnum. In this period, national parks were used for purposes dramatically different from those featured in any of the conceptions of parks before or since: they were used as work camps and prisons.

The use of national parks as sites for internment camps for foreigners with suspected enemy sympathies had first been implemented in World War I when James Harkin saw an opportunity to offset his budget reductions with cheap labour,[42] and this practice of augmenting parks budgets was used intermittently through the 1920s to deal with localized unemployment problems. However, with massive unemployment in the 1930s, the establishment of work camps and the use of cheap labour for road construction, land clearing, and building park facilities became more common in the western national parks. With the beginning of World War II, parks were again pressed into service for prison camps, particularly for internees of Japanese ancestry forcibly removed from the coastal areas of British Columbia.[43]

Conclusion

With the end of World War II, the prison and internment camps were emptied, closed, and virtually all the fixtures removed. While formal parks policy was not officially altered in the 1930s and 1940s, little attention had been paid to the implementation of the ideas about parks discussed through the 1920s and represented in the National Parks Act. The 1930s and the war years were almost entirely a vacuum in policy making. At the end of the war, the Parks Branch was administering the existing parks but appeared to have lost its direction and focus concerning a clear purpose for them. In 1945, the act was not in fact providing policy objectives to the branch, and for nearly another ten years it was not clear what the practical character of parks policy would be. The renaissance of national parks ideas and a renewed vigour directed at the development of a truly national system of national parks had to wait. When this renewal did begin, the past became part of the new context of ideas since the strong economic development thrust of the early parks continued to motivate provincial and local politicians even while the environmental ideas of John Muir and J.B. Harkin had been institution-alized in the National Parks Act.

Therefore, when the Parks Branch attended to policy questions in the 1950s, it began more or less where Harkin and Parliament had left off in 1930, trying to determine how to implement the legislation and how to cope with the ambiguities that it contained. But the postwar era was also a new one, in which federal power over land use was significantly reduced and in which governments themselves would form new relationships with their citizens.

3
National Parks and the Era of State Initiative, 1955-70

During the period from the mid-1950s to the early 1970s, two principal policy developments took place for national parks. Both occurred almost entirely within the Parks Branch, and both were seen, essentially, as "management tools" by branch officials. The 1964 *National Parks Policy* was a means of informing the public about how the branch intended to carry out the national parks mandate, and its preparation was seen by the branch as strictly an internal responsibility. No role was envisaged for the public in the preparation of the document, although public support was actively sought for the policy's formalization in Parliament. Similarly, the System Plan was designed, for management reasons, for the identification and selection of potential park sites. It was not seen initially as a definition or conception of national parks for policy purposes.

In the mid-1950s, when these policy developments were yet in their nascent stages, the national parks of Canada, despite seventy years of existence, were without an effective policy. The National Parks Act had been passed in 1930 but had never been effectively implemented since its passage had been immediately followed by the Great Depression and World War II.

In the aftermath, the Parks Branch was able more or less to return to its previous activities. Now, however, it faced a new political and social environment. The federal role in parks had been significantly altered by changes in intergovernmental relations. Governments themselves were changing too as there were pressures to revamp the functioning of cabinet, the bureaucracy, and the nature of policy development. Society had also changed. Canada was more urban, incomes were higher, and the population, with a burgeoning number of cars, was more mobile. Finally, public attitudes toward the parks themselves were beginning to reflect a growing environmentalism as new values emerged among Canadians.

In this context of social and political change, the Parks Branch began to fill the gap in policy that had been left by economic depression and war and to reconsider parks under the terms of the National Parks Act. The process of redefining policy continues into the present, but there was a distinct period from about 1955 until the early 1970s in which the Parks Branch held the initiative for policy ideas, and it is there that one looks to examine the origins of postwar parks policy.

Out of the numerous ideas discussed during this fifteen-year period, the two documents under consideration here established a renewed vision for national parks. First, in 1964, after nearly seven years of discussion, the minister responsible presented a formal policy statement to Parliament. This statement reiterated the act's attention to environmental preservation but without radically departing from earlier concepts of development in parks. Second, in 1970 the Parks Branch developed a system-wide plan that provided, for the first time in their history, a unifying theme for national parks and made them more than a coincidental collection of protected lands.

Neither document fully addressed the inherent conflict between preservation and development, and it remained then, as today, the challenge for drafters of park policy to find a balance among conflicting ideas about the purposes of national parks.

The emergence of these two documents from a complex mix of competing ideas can be partly explained by understanding concurrent changes in the character of the setting in which governing institutions functioned. In the particular circumstances of that setting, new ideas about government organization and policy development were being considered in order to address policy concerns that originated in the Depression and the war. Three of these new ideas had an important effect on national parks. First, an expanded role for environmental interest groups changed the balance of societal influences in relation to government and gave an opportunity for preservationist ideas to be incorporated into parks policy. Second, the advancement of ideas about the rational development of policy enabled park planners to transcend the local brokering that earlier had motivated parks establishment and to apply scientific principles to the process. Third, changing intergovernmental relations and the changing pattern of co-operative federalism nudged federal parks policy away from preoccupation with tourism and recreation and toward a greater attention to wilderness and natural features.

The 1964 *National Parks Policy*

Following the war, the Parks Branch continued with routine management more or less as it had been doing for two decades. By the mid-1950s, however, it was apparent that a more co-ordinated approach was necessary, and the Parks Branch began to consider long-term planning for uniform management and expansion of the parks system. Among the many tasks that needed to be done was the development of a coherent policy and a consistent interpretation of the National Parks Act for the administration of the parks. The branch acknowledged that, although policies existed, they had "been developed piecemeal and [were not] adequate to assure that the real objectives [were] reached or maintained."[1] To remedy this, a single consistent policy statement was drafted for internal discussion and circulated within the branch in November 1957. However, it would not be until September 1964, after seven years and a change of government, that this draft document[2] was presented to Parliament and became a formal statement of policy.

As the first step toward redefining the national parks mandate, this document was a cautious one. Its major significance, in terms of environmental protection, was that, in even reiterating the balance between ideas about development and preservation, it publicly restated the preservationist ideas already contained in the act. The policy statement is not easy to summarize as it contains eighty-five numbered points, with half as many subsidiary points, in fifteen sections that range in scope from forestry to private dwellings and from items as specific as camping permit fees to ones as general as the criteria for future national parks. The first section, however, about the purposes of national parks, sets out two broad policy points:

1   The basic purpose of the National Park System is to preserve for all time areas which contain significant geographical, biological or historic features as a national heritage for the benefit, education and enjoyment of the people of Canada.
2   The provision of urban type recreational facilities is not part of the purpose of National Parks. Such recreation facilities in harmony with the purpose and preservation of a park may be introduced as required to meet recreational needs; but always so as to minimize impairment and not at all if substantial impairment is inevitable.[3]

The central theme of allowing recreation that was in harmony with environmental protection while at the same time recognizing the need for access to parks was reiterated throughout the document. For example, on the subject of roads, the policy statement accepted them as a necessary means of access but stated that their "location, design, and construction ... must keep impairment of the landscape to an absolute minimum and avoid interference with special park features."[4] Similar positions were taken with respect to boats and boat facilities, visitor accommodation, camping and campgrounds, and even recreational activities themselves, where "only the wholesome outdoor types of recreation which are compatible with that natural atmosphere will be permitted."[5] Towns and permanent residency were, according to the policy, an intrusion and should be allowed only if they assisted the visitor's enjoyment of the park "for what it is,"[6] but even then residence was to be encouraged outside the park where practicable. The policy also suggested that new parks should be selected strategically in order to avoid the possibility of future conflicts between national park values and industrial and transport activities.

Under each subject heading, the policy acknowledged the existence and indeed the need for roads, visitor accommodation, services, and recreational opportunities, but it also stressed the need to minimize their effect and to limit impairment even though that might mean dismantling some facilities and constraining commercial potential. Thus, the general thrust of the policy statement was to recognize the existence of human activities within parks but more strongly to emphasize the need to maintain their natural integrity. Therefore, while the policy attempted to moderate and contain commercial interests and activities, it did not do so in profound or radical ways. By recognizing that the act gave only a general statement of purpose, the policy defined the act's objectives more clearly and in so doing redirected the attention of both management and the public toward protection of a park's natural environment and away from commercially based entertainment.

Ideas and National Parks
Chapter 1 discussed ideas in terms of how they guide the behaviour of political participants, how those participants convert ideas, and how ideas themselves become congealed in the rules and practices of institutions.

In these terms, political ideas can be seen to have influenced the 1964 *National Parks Policy* in two important ways. That is, both the content of policy and the process of policy development were affected by political ideas in this period. The ideas that influenced the definition of the problem were those already contained within the state. But new ideas about the role of societal interests and ideas that motivated the organization of interest groups outside the state affected the policy process by giving rise to new participants.

Thus, the 1964 policy derived its central ideas from the National Parks Act and the management ideas that had been put in place by J.B. Harkin three decades earlier. The concepts of protection and use and their divergence were already reflected in the act but it did not elaborate on them or on how each would be reflected in parks management. Its contradictory preamble left, as the 1964 policy pointed out, "ample grounds for varying opinions as to exactly what the legislators had in mind."[7]

This dual position in the act was also reflected in the individual parks themselves. They had evolved as resorts where nature was modified and artificial recreation was provided for the entertainment of visitors. At the same time, increasing attention to preservationist concerns through the early years of the twentieth century had led to more emphasis on parks as a medium for outdoor education and recreation based solely on the natural environment. These contradictions were carried forward into the 1950s and 1960s, not only because of the wording of the act, but also by management practices that had become part of parks administration.[8]

Not only the act, but also the existing situation, therefore provided important ideas for the 1964 policy statement. More subtly, however, the act had been interpreted in two new ways that had influenced park planners. First, it stipulated that national parks are for all Canadians,[9] not only for "the better class of people," as Sir John A. Macdonald had contemplated in 1885; second, the act referred to the interests of future generations whose needs must therefore be anticipated and included by contemporary policy makers and planners. Thus, it is evident that the planners were not seeking a new and grand orientation; rather, they saw their task simply as developing a management tool to guide administrative decisions in carrying out their existing mandate.[10]

Despite the relatively limited ambitions of officials concerning the policy statement, there were new ideas afoot about the policy process itself. Both inside and outside the branch, there was a gathering belief that societal interests had an important role to play at least in the promotion of any policy, if not in the development of its substance.

In the 1950s and 1960s, public participation took on a tone different from that of earlier decades as the Parks Branch began actively to seek new partnerships with interested groups and to rely on them for help in promoting the developing policy statement. These new alliances were in contrast to the historical predominance of business interests in direct relationships with ministers and other politicians. The new partnerships, however, did not affect the content of policy, which remained entirely within the determination of the branch. Thus, emerging environmental interests became important in this period only for the political support that they were able to provide the branch, and eventually the minister, as it endeavoured to have the policy authorized.

In the 1950s, there were no truly national environmental interest groups and, in fact, few such groups at all. When the initiative was taken, in 1963, to establish a national organization to promote environmental protection in parks, what became the National and Provincial Parks Association of Canada (NPPAC, now CPAWS), only four existing groups were available to lend support and all of these had relatively limited regional focuses. Two of them, the Conservation Council of Ontario and the Federation of Ontario Naturalists, were, as their names suggest, active in Ontario, although in principle they supported environmental protection efforts elsewhere in Canada. The Alpine Club of Canada, which had backed J.B. Harkin in the 1920s, was largely confined to the Rocky Mountains in Alberta and was interested mostly in mountaineering issues, although it, too, generally favoured environmental protection across the country. The Canadian Audubon

Society (later the Canadian Nature Federation and now Nature Canada), a branch of the famous American group, had been formed in the 1930s but in the 1960s was not yet a fully national organization. There had been at one time a National Parks Association, but in the early 1960s it seemingly had disappeared. The 1960s themselves witnessed significant growth in environmental organizations, beginning with NPPAC in 1963, the World Wildlife Fund (in Canada) in 1967, and Greenpeace and others in 1969. This growth continued into the 1970s and 1980s.

These new interest groups owe their origins to two sets of forces. First, relatively new state-society relationships resulted from the rise of the administrative state, which created new opportunities for interest group participation. Second, changing attitudes toward the environment motivated individuals to form new environmental organizations. Although there had long been some degree of congruence of ideas between environmental groups and the Parks Branch, the newly organized interests began to manifest ideas concerning the policy process even though they had not yet contributed their own ideas to policy content.

Both the influence of interest groups in general and the salience of environmental issues in particular have antecedents reaching back to the early part of the twentieth century and before. However, only in the postwar period did these phenomena begin to take a prominent role in policy deliberation. Even though the basis for organization had been there for several years, organized environmental interest groups developed slowly. And even when organizations did emerge, it was often due as much to state initiative as to private response to perceived problems. Nevertheless, the state provided no organized process for public involvement, and there is little evidence of direct public input. Although such input was not entirely absent, it was strictly filtered through the parks bureaucracy.

This had not always been the case. The idea of national parks had begun in Canada, after all, in conjunction with building the Canadian Pacific Railway, and that company had played an important role in establishing the first parks. On the other side of the parks vision, the Alpine Club had worked vigorously to support J.B. Harkin's efforts in the 1920s to provide more protection for the natural character of parks in policy and legislation.[11]

This early participation by societal interests had largely dissipated by the 1950s. Railway interests in parks had diminished by this time, particularly with the rise in popularity of the automobile. This change, in turn, led business interests to become less concentrated as the automobile industry and the various services to the travelling public were not part of a single integrated organization in the way that the railway industry had been in the nineteenth century. In addition, the Alpine Club and other public interest groups were quiescent, perhaps feeling the effects of the long years of depression and war.

Despite the relatively slow start in the growth of organized interests, the number, sophistication, and societal scope of groups began to expand significantly in the late 1950s. The basis of this expansion, Paul Pross has suggested, lies in the changing relationship between state and society that began as early as the 1920s. According to Pross, the growth in the size and complexity of government enhanced the role of professional advisers and shifted the policy-making capacity from the executive to the bureaucracy. The bureaucracy, in turn, had a symbiotic relationship with private interests in what J.K. Galbraith has called the "technostructure."[12] As the Canadian economy became more sophisticated, an increased responsibility fell on the state to manage the supply and demand of economic inputs such as skilled labour, natural resources, and energy. The professional and technical expertise necessary within government to provide these resources led to links being formed with similar professional expertise in the private sector and thus to the development of professional and technical associations. These associations supported the use of technical criteria in policy formation and a shift away from "political" criteria, especially the application of a spoils system. Through the 1920s and 1930s, this development evolved into "a sophisticated network that [cut] across the lines dividing government and business."[13]

This process of change was well advanced by the 1950s, but for parks the nature of the technostructure was more a potential than an actual determinant of state-society relations. That is, the professional and technical expertise in parks management and planning existed almost exclusively within (mostly federal) government agencies. The scientific tasks of biophysical mapping, ecological management, and environmental protection, which were to become themes in parks planning in subsequent years, were only beginning to be considered in the 1950s. What little expertise existed in those areas was divided mostly between government and academia. While the academic expertise was potentially available to interest groups of the time, these groups did not have the organizational capacity to find and coordinate a body of expertise parallel to that in government. Nevertheless, there existed within the general policy arena the potential for social expertise to be called upon in policy development. Initially, on the government side, national parks had been administered by a staff of trained wardens and superintendents experienced in managing the interaction between the public and the natural environment, but as management's focus shifted to biophysical and ecological concerns the public expertise in these subjects (in universities, for example) began to be organized by interest groups, thus establishing a professional and technical relationship that bridged the gap between government and environmental groups.

The relatively autonomous position of the Parks Branch within government facilitated the growth of this relationship. While it was not, at the time, a department in its own right, the branch operated somewhat independently within the structure of the Department of Northern Affairs and Natural Resources, and the director of national parks had, in terms of policy advice, a relatively direct relationship with the minister. The branch, therefore, fit the description of an "agency" associated with what Stephan Dupré has called a "departmentalized cabinet," in which "the ministers are endowed with a substantial measure of decision making autonomy."[14] However, departments, and presumably some subdepartmental agencies, "are the prime depositories ... of special expertise,"[15] and in order to proceed with policy formulation and implementation ministers must rely heavily on the bureaucracy that holds such expertise. This situation provides the agency with the opportunity to forge the kind of relationship suggested by the conditions of the technostructure in which government expertise interacts with private-sector knowledge. These characteristics of the departmentalized government agency make it, rather than the minister, the focus of interest group attention where these groups interact with the department's own experts.[16]

The rise of environmentalism is more difficult to explain. One of the prominent attempts is Ronald Inglehart's theory of value formation and culture shift in advanced industrial societies. Inglehart, and most analysts using his framework, examine the formation of new values in the 1960s and later. Nevertheless, though nascent, environmental protectionist values were already evident in Canada in the 1950s, as illustrated by the existence of organizations such as the Conservation Council of Ontario and the Canadian Audubon Society. Perhaps the values and mechanisms that Inglehart posits were already influencing the middle class in Toronto, or urban Ontario more generally, and this population constituted a leader in the (hypothesized) social transformation, followed, in succeeding decades, by those in other parts of Canada. Although it may seem premature compared to other analysts' approach to value shift, in the absence of an alternative explanation, Inglehart's reasoning may be offered to account for these early environmental ideas. The social adjustments that his argument purports to explain may already have been in progress in the limited social and geographic space of urban southern Ontario in the middle to late 1950s.

Inglehart's theory is based on Abraham Maslow's five-stage hierarchy of human needs, which are translated into a dichotomy between materialist and postmaterialist values. Materialist values reflect the priority of what Maslow described as physiological and safety needs, while postmaterialist ones are concerned with his remaining three categories: belongingness, esteem, and self-actualization. This division between materialist and postmaterialist values in relation to Maslow's hierarchy and the items used in Inglehart's initial research surveys is shown in Figure 3.1.[17]

Figure 3.1

Items used in Inglehart's 1973 survey and needs they were intended to tap

Inglehart's dichotomy	Maslow's typology of needs	Inglehart's survey subjects
Social and self-actualization needs (postmaterialist)	Aesthetic	Beautiful cities/nature
	Intellectual	Ideas count Free speech
	Belonging and esteem	Less impersonal society More say on job, community More say in government
Physiological needs (materialist)	Safety	Strong defence forces Fight crime Maintain order
	Sustenance	Stable economy Economic growth Fight rising prices

Source: Ronald Inglehart, *The Silent Revolution: Changing Values and Political Styles among Western Publics* (Princeton: Princeton University Press, 1977), 42.

Inglehart has postulated that, as economic circumstances improve, individuals or categories of individuals (such as age cohorts or social classes) in new generations will be more likely to have postmaterialist values than will preceding generations. Generational change will thus result in a cultural shift toward an increasingly postmaterialist society. As Inglehart puts it, "those who were economically secure during their formative years will be more likely to have Post-Materialist value priorities."[18]

This proposition has received significant attention since it was first published in 1977. While the argument connecting confident economic attitudes and generational change has received some critical analysis,[19] other ideas have been advanced that offer alternative or parallel explanations. In Scandinavia, for example, Oddbjorn Knutsen argues that "education is the socio-economic variable which is most strongly correlated with MPM [materialist-postmaterialist] values."[20] At the same time in Germany, Hans-Georg Betz agrees that the rapid rise in education in the 1970s and 1980s is correlated to support for the Green Party (in fact, material insecurity seems to be even less a factor; that is, Green Party supporters are highly educated but materially insecure).[21] Unlike Inglehart, Knutsen and Betz do not find postmaterialist values strongly linked to higher income or otherwise improved economic circumstances. In Canada, Herman Bakvis and Neil Nevitte have concluded that "postmaterialism remains both elusive and abstract [but] useful in forcing us to think about the changes that have been wrought in the economic, social and psychological fabric of modern industrial societies."[22]

The tentative nature of Bakvis and Nevitte's conclusion is appropriate. Although empirical support for Inglehart's original thesis has been elusive, there does seem to be some generalized relationship between social and economic changes in society and the rise of postmaterialist values such as environmentalism. These changes would not have been strongly evident in the mid-1950s because the predominant generation was that which had lived through the Depression and World War II, but some evidence suggests that adoption of postmaterialist attitudes may already have been underway. In fact, as the 1950s drew to an end, increasing attention began to be paid, not only to societal groups' participation in policy issues, but also to postmaterialist values such as environmentalism. Thus, while the Parks Branch may have begun its deliberations on the policy statement as a management tool, there were already forces at play that would place that policy in a very different context.

The Role of Bureaucracy

Neither the rise of interest groups nor the emergence of environmentalism directly affected the ideas included in the preparation of the 1964 policy statement. That process occurred entirely within the Parks Branch, and the ideas involved came from the existing parks mandate.

In considering the role of bureaucracy in the creation of the 1964 policy, two questions arise. Why was the policy developed at all, and why did it represent such a relatively modest change from what preceded it? Since the Parks Branch was the principal (largely autonomous[23]) agent in the development and writing of the policy statement, to answer these questions it is necessary to examine the branch's circumstances in order to explain the timing and the nature of this part of the policy process.

The timing of the draft policy is partly the result of changes and developments occurring in and around the Parks Branch itself. From the mid-1930s through the 1950s, the branch experienced a series of frequent reorganizations and evaluations that were both part of the ongoing process of government and part of a preparation for the future. In 1935, four departments, including the Department of the Interior, in which the Parks Branch was then located, were merged into the Department of Mines and Resources. This consolidation had the effect of reducing the overall status of the Parks Branch and led directly to the retirement of J.B. Harkin after twenty-five years as commissioner of national parks. Following the war, the unit that included national parks was abolished, and a new one with a different collection of functions, including parks, was created. Two years later, in 1949, the Department of Mines and Resources was eliminated, and national parks went to the newly created Department of Resources and Development. There it was grouped together with wildlife, water resources, land, northern administration, engineering and construction, and the national museum – all in a single branch. This arrangement did not last, however, and in less than a year national parks were located in their own branch within a reconstituted Department of Resources and Development with a narrower mandate, including only national parks, national historic sites, wildlife, and the national museum. Then, in 1955, a further reorganization of the department, now renamed the Department of Northern Affairs and National Resources, expanded the Parks Branch by putting the former engineering and architectural services under its mandate, although the museum was moved to its own branch in 1957.[24] If the branch lacked focus and the ability to formulate a coherent policy during these two decades, it seems likely that these frequent changes in its organizational setting were at least partly responsible. By contrast, the changes in the late 1950s seem to represent, at last, a focusing and refining of the organizational framework itself, which may have been the necessary precursor to efforts to define policy.

The external setting of the Parks Branch was not the only problem, however. In the immediate postwar years, the internal workings of the branch were also subject to increasing pressure and eventually to evaluation and reorganization, which continued through the late 1950s. By the middle of the decade, the branch was having difficulty carrying out its basic functions and responsibilities at a suitable level because of demands emanating from the rapid growth in the number of visitors to the national parks. These difficulties led to an overall review of the organization and methods of the branch by J.I. Nicol in 1961. According to W.F. Lothian, the semi-official historian for national parks, the "specific objectives of the study included the improvement of administrative and financial procedures; decentralization of responsibilities and authorities; more efficient use of staff; reduction of routine work undertaken by senior officers of the Branch; and the elimination of overlapping [sic] not only between divisions but between divisions and field offices."[25] Nicol's report, after being vetted by the department and the Treasury Board, led to a reorganization within the Parks Branch by the new Liberal minister of northern affairs and national resources in 1963. Moreover, the conclusions of Nicol's report occurred simultaneously and concurred with the recommendations of the report of the Royal Commission on Government Organization (the Glassco Commission). J. Grant Glassco had investigated many functions and facets of the federal government in general and, after careful evaluation of administration and land management practices of the Parks Branch in particular, recommended that "a review be made of national parks policy and a comprehensive statement of future goals be incorporated in the relevant legislation."[26]

In this context of change, evaluation, and reorganization from 1947 to 1963, concepts emerged for planning and preparing a coherent unified national parks policy. This process began very gradually when a nascent planning section was established in 1955. The initiative was consolidated in 1957 with the appointment of three people – an engineer, a draftsperson, and an administrator – to carry out a planning function. This configuration of personnel reflects the heavy emphasis in park activities on engineering concerns; about this time, for example, a major portion of the national parks budget was devoted simply to building highways. Relatively less concern was given to a comprehensive review of the act and its meaning, but in 1959 the planning, as opposed to the engineering, function of the Planning Section was strengthened when two specialists in parks management replaced the engineer.

From such small beginnings, a national parks policy proposal was drafted and sent, in 1957, to senior officials for the first internal discussions. From 1957 until the proposal was formalized in September 1964, while the policy remained in draft form, active discussion involved only officials within the Parks Branch, despite growing public interest in environmental matters in general and in national parks in particular.

A Change in State-Society Relations
While the Parks Branch was able to act independently in the drafting of the policy statement, it was not able to push the proposal through to adoption without external help. Just as the Alpine Club had campaigned to support J.B. Harkin's initial proposal for a national parks act in the 1920s, so too the Parks Branch benefited from political efforts by several naturalist groups in the 1960s. These groups aimed to have the proposed 1964 policy statement adopted while having to contend with business groups that had rallied to criticize it.[27] This increased activity by environmental groups was part of a long-term change in state-society relations in Canada. For national parks, it also reflects the direct effect of the Resources for Tomorrow Conference held in Montreal in 1961. In the short term, these changes in state-society relations were important for achieving adoption of the proposed policy statement; in the long term, they also marked the beginning of a broad transformation in the structure of state-society relations in the national parks policy arena.

In the mid-1950s, when the Parks Branch first drafted its proposed policy statement, it did so within the departmentalized framework that Dupré has described and did so with considerable autonomy. What the branch was seemingly unable to do, however, was advance the policy to a stage of formalization where it would be authoritative. For this, it needed the minister's agreement, which, apparently, was not forthcoming until after the change in government in 1963. Until that time, Alvin Hamilton, the minister responsible for national parks through part of the Diefenbaker period and who viewed conservation in terms of "using our resources as rationally as we can [and,] ... whenever possible, a multiple use of our resources,"[28] would not bring the draft policy forward for official approval. Without the sanction of the minister and of Parliament, the chief of the Planning Section urged, as late as 1962, the de facto use of the policy statement even though it had not been formally approved by cabinet.[29] It was at this time that the Parks Branch began actively to seek societal partners because, from the perspective of branch officials, there were already numerous organizations to support the "use" side of the national parks mandate, but there was a paucity of voices in favour of the "unimpaired" side.

The formative event in advancing societal interests and thereby in supporting the preservationist ideas in the proposed policy was the Resources for Tomorrow Conference. This conference was the result of the Diefenbaker "Vision," which sought increased development of northern Canada and a more effective use of the country's natural resource base as a way to raise the national income and, by using that expansion in national wealth, to improve social justice.[30] National parks were included in the Vision (and therefore in the conference) since parks, as tourist destinations and playgrounds, were, at the time, seen as one of several means of exploiting natural resources.

Prior to 1961, those environmental interests that did exist, such as the Canadian Audubon Society and the Alpine Club of Canada, had urged various ministers to safeguard environmental values in national parks, but none had made it the focus of their activities, and their support for national parks protection was rather weak. Indeed, as Alvin Hamilton, despite his views on conservation generally, had asked, "How can a minister stand up against the pressures of commercial interests who want to use the parks for mining, forestry, for every kind of honky-tonk device known to man, unless the people who love these parks are prepared to band together and support the minister by getting the facts out across the country?"[31] Parks Branch officials had already begun to advance the idea of an interest group to speak for preservation in the late 1950s, and they continued to support the formation of such a group during and after the conference.[32] At the conference itself, the idea that a specific organization should be established for safeguarding parks was first publicly discussed. However, there was no strong organized environmental group to support Hamilton and Walter Dinsdale, Hamilton's immediate successor through the remaining period of the Conservative government.

The idea lay dormant for almost two years, during which the Parks Branch continued to express the hope that an organization would form to support the environmental side of parks. Finally, in 1963, William Baker, a private-sector consultant who had worked closely with the Parks Branch,[33] approached Gavin Henderson, executive director for the Conservation Council of Ontario, to discuss the need for such a group. Henderson pursued the idea and managed to get enough support (though ambivalent and uncertain) to form an organization, the National and Provincial Parks Association of Canada (NPPAC). Existing naturalist and conservation organizations (for example, the Conservation Council of Ontario, the Canadian Audubon Society, and the Federation of Ontario Naturalists) participated in formative discussions of the new association, but some were concerned that another organization would merely dilute the conservation community, even though none of these groups was itself able or willing to undertake the task of speaking for national parks. In addition, NPPAC was able to get some support from well-placed members in Toronto business and professional circles and to establish a blue-ribbon board of trustees. This support turned out to be rather tepid, however, as the trustees, charged with fundraising by the organization's charter, were unable to raise significant amounts of money.

Once again the Parks Branch moved to support the environmental side of parks by giving financial assistance of $20,000 to get the NPPAC started, enabling it to become a nationally chartered organization in 1963. The decision to make this money available had the highest approval in the branch, including the new Liberal minister, which reflected the importance placed on gaining societal support for a more preservationist agenda. Thus, rather than having strong popular support, the creation and early existence of NPPAC was mostly the result of the dedication and organizational skill of Henderson, who became its first executive director, and the timely, tactical support of the Parks Branch. Finally (in September 1964), with the active support of NPPAC, the new minister in the Pearson Liberal government had sufficient confidence to present the draft national parks policy to Parliament for formalization despite strong opposition from commercial interests.

The Effect of Party Politics

Some of the time needed to push the policy forward during the six years of Conservative government was due to the process of internal Parks Branch discussion and to the diffidence of the branch itself, but the delay in publicizing the policy while the Conservatives were in power, and its consequent advancement after the return of the Liberals, owe much more to the differences between these two political parties. In general philosophy and in the composition of their governing caucus, the Liberals were more disposed to support the national parks policy than were the Conservatives.

For the Conservatives, their general philosophy of economic development combined with the composition of their caucus, with its strong representation from Alberta, where national parks were (and still are) viewed with suspicion, served to maintain an emphasis on use and economic development for parks. Their broad philosophy of economic development, as articulated in Diefenbaker's Vision, led to (in addition to the Resources for Tomorrow Conference) the Roads to Resources program launched in 1958.[34] Since parks were seen as a recreational resource, this program was used to build roads to and within parks and to encourage provinces to provide land for parks in return for the federal funding of provincial road construction. Another economic development program sponsored by the Conservatives, and relevant to parks, was the Agricultural and Rural Development Agency (ARDA),[35] a joint federal-provincial program designed to alleviate rural poverty and to improve the efficiency of Canadian agriculture. One aspect of ARDA was the provision of aid to farmers on agriculturally marginal land, allowing them to leave and allowing the conversion of that land to other uses, such as, potentially, parks and recreation.

Taken together, the Roads to Resources program, ARDA, and the Resources for Tomorrow Conference provided the main policy thrusts relevant to national parks, all within the general Conservative philosophy of economic development. This resource-use orientation fitted particularly well with the feelings of members of the western caucus, especially its strong Alberta contingent, which provided an excellent forum for the powerful advocacy of commercial interests.

These interests resisted strongly the idea of increasing the importance of natural themes and correspondingly reducing the development of "artificial" recreation. This resistance, by Alberta Conservatives in particular, dates back to 1930, when R.B. Bennett (MP for Calgary West and later Conservative prime minister between 1930 and 1935) was the chief critic of the preservationist ideas in the National Parks Act (as noted in Chapter 2). Thus, although the Diefenbaker government had broad national representation, it was the Albertans who had the most direct experience with national parks and were most persuasive in government caucus and cabinet, and it was to these MPs that further expression and formalization of preservationist ideas in the draft policy statement were most unwelcome.

Thus, while the Parks Branch itself might have recognized the need to clarify the act and to redefine its own mandate, in the face of resistance from the Conservative caucus and cabinet and without any reliable organized interest group to support it, the branch was unable to proceed in formalizing the draft policy statement. Throughout the successive Diefenbaker mandates, despite some encouraging postures from the ministers responsible for national parks, the policy therefore remained in draft form.

In sharp contrast to the economic development approach of the Conservatives, the Liberals' general philosophy emphasized social policy objectives. During six years in opposition, the Liberals worked hard to devise a social program to attract Canadians, holding national conventions in Kingston in

1960 and in Ottawa in 1961. The approach that emerged, tilting the party slightly to the left, was based on growing Canadian nationalism and a positive liberalism that aimed at completing the system of social programs that had been started by previous Liberal governments. While this did not directly affect policies with respect to national parks, it did moderate the previous emphasis on economic development.

In addition, the Liberals showed an almost complete lack of interest in western Canada. For Lester B. Pearson himself, Canada was a triangle that comprised Montreal, Ottawa, and Toronto. In cabinet, only minor portfolios were given to western MPs, scant policy attention was given to western concerns, and in government caucus western MPs were often ignored. For example, when Jack Davis, an MP from Vancouver, suggested that the occasional cabinet meeting be held in western Canada to show the government's interest in the region, his ideas were treated with derision.[36] Walter Gordon, the minister of finance, was very blunt: "I'm an accountant in these things. The Toronto area has more seats than Saskatchewan, and we can win them."[37] For the Liberals, then, national parks, mostly located in western Canada, were a distant issue that did not command much cabinet attention.

Thus, it was more than a year before Arthur Laing, the Liberal minister responsible, who was personally supportive of national parks, was able to present the policy statement. After gaining approval in principle from cabinet, Laing formally announced the policy to the House of Commons on 18 September 1964. He gave a brief overview, emphasizing the government's intention to treat "national parks as sanctuaries of nature" that preclude "the exploitation of natural resources for the commercial value."[38] In addition to reviewing the new concepts of zoning and visitor service centres, the minister announced a new policy that would eventually exclude private residential occupation (except for people actually employed in the parks). At first, the response was positive and supportive, parliamentary discussion quickly focusing on questions about individual parks and local matters, but negative reaction was swift from outside Parliament, coming largely from commercial interests in western Canada. Just as swiftly, NPPAC and the Canadian Audubon Society countered by strongly supporting the policy.[39]

Negative reaction in Parliament came later, in the early months of 1966, and centred on the intention to limit residency, especially as it applied to the national parks in Alberta, where the idea faced stiff opposition from entrenched local interests. In fact, the limit was never implemented. In the ensuing debate, the MP for Jasper-Edson suggested that a special joint committee be established to investigate policy specifically pertaining to the mountain parks in Alberta and British Columbia, and later that year (in December) the Standing Committee on Northern Affairs and National Resources toured Banff, Jasper, and Edmonton to hear the concerns of park residents. In the long run, the parliamentary opposition was successful in that the debate over residency and townsites in the parks has continued to the present and has more recently been the focus of a special planning process in Banff National Park.[40]

In most respects, however, the Parks Branch was eventually successful in being able to implement the 1964 *National Parks Policy*. However, in order to succeed, it needed supportive interest groups and a government that was in favour of, or at least not opposed to, the protection of park lands.

The System Plan

Independent from the policy statement but part of the same thrust to define national parks policy, the System Plan was drafted in 1970 and is one of the critical documents in the parks policy corpus. Although the phrase "national parks system" had been used in the 1950s and even earlier, there was no unifying principle that distinguished Canada's national parks as a system rather than a mere collection. In other words, parks had heretofore been established according to several different sets of criteria, and only by accident did they share characteristics. As a system, parks would function together toward a unified objective and be selected according to a single set of criteria. Accordingly, in 1970 the Parks Branch devised a plan for a national parks system that would be based on the varying physiographic characteristics of the country. This plan initially divided the country into thirty-nine terrestrial regions with the objective of having each represented by at least one national park. Later, twenty-nine marine regions were added for a total of sixty-eight natural regions.

The purpose of the plan was to identify natural regions and natural history themes that were easily understood by casual observers as well as by trained scientists and would therefore give park visitors a sense of the difference and diversity of Canadian landscapes and show how individual parks represented those landscapes. Regions were to be distinguished using geological and geomorphological features and floral and faunal characteristics. For example, Region 1, the Pacific Coast Mountains, consists of high mountains, deep fjords, and dense rainforests along the British Columbia coast, whereas Region 2, Strait of Georgia Lowlands, includes the low-lying areas and shallow bays of the Fraser River estuary, the Gulf Islands, and southeast Vancouver Island. While both areas are part of the Pacific coast, there are obvious differences in topography, forest type, precipitation, and geological processes that distinguish the two and provide the basis for the designation of distinct natural regions.

As the *National Parks System Planning Manual* points out, the use of physiographic criteria for parks planning and selection facilitates a rationally based, nation-wide parks system by

1   helping to crystallize new policies and programs by focussing attention on deficient areas of representation (both Natural Regions and Natural History themes) and thereby emphasizing the need for an accelerated and streamlined program of expansion;
2   minimizing subjectivity in the process of new park selections;
3   making new park studies more specific and much more dependable and justifiable;
4   reducing the chance of adding undesirable elements to the National Parks System; and
5   helping to clarify the role of National Parks within the spectrum of parks and outdoor recreation areas in Canada.[41]

The significance of the System Plan is not only that it provided a set of unifying principles for national parks but also that it shifted their focus toward natural history, thereby strengthening an environmental perspective. In essence, parks were to be selected on the basis of natural or biophysical criteria rather than on potential recreational or scenic ones. It is also important to note that this attention to natural criteria injected an increased reliance on technical information and expertise into parks planning and diminished the role of local promotional interests, especially those of electoral or patronage politics.

Like the policy statement, the System Plan began modestly as a "management tool" for use within the Parks Branch, and several years passed before it received official recognition. Since then, however, the plan has become one of the pillars of national parks policy, forming the basis of planning and framing the discussion between federal and provincial governments about the further expansion of the national parks system. In addition, environmental interest groups have adopted it as one of the planks of their advocacy by urging the government to "complete the system."[42] Finally, the provinces, in some cases with encouragement from interest groups, have adopted it as a model for their own plans and planning procedures for provincial park systems. Completion of the system (by having at least one national park in each natural region of Canada) by some target date has therefore long been a popular goal within the overall parks policy community. In the 1990s, one such advocated objective was the year 2000.

Ideas and the System Plan
Ideas favouring a national park system had been discussed since the early 1950s, and indeed, as mentioned, the word *system* had been frequently used. However, since there was no definition of or consensus about the principle that should unify the various elements of that so-called system, parks officials searched intermittently through the 1950s and 1960s for a single unifying theme. Various concepts were considered. One early idea was to have

at least one national park in each province,[43] but this was not formally pursued, probably because it was regarded as insufficient. Another was to borrow the American system of many categories (including national parks, national monuments, national shorelines, and national recreational areas), but this approach was eventually rejected as too complex and confusing.[44] A third idea emerged from the need, as expressed by various commentators, to protect Canadian landscapes for future generations. The concept of parks as representative samples of Canada's natural beauty developed from these ideas and was already evident in documents as early as 1961.[45] By the mid-1960s, various documents referred to eight physiographic regions of Canada and commented that only four were then represented by national parks.[46]

Although the 1970 System Plan was essentially the first of its kind, the core idea, that of a national parks system based on biophysical regions, had in fact been emerging in several forums around the world through the 1960s. Since at least the early 1950s, academic biologists had been debating schemes for subdividing the natural world into realms and regions, subregions, and provinces based on geological, floral, or faunal characteristics. These ideas were strictly conceptual at first, but increasingly they were discussed as a potential framework for selecting natural areas for protection. Such discussions occurred within an international network of parks-related organizations, primary among which was the International Union for the Conservation of Nature and Natural Resources.

The IUCN had been formed in 1948 partly through independent initiative and partly with UNESCO's involvement.[47] Of several international conservation organizations, it was the one most directed toward nature conservation in general and national parks in particular. Throughout its existence, it has worked at monitoring and defining the criteria for protected areas around the world. In particular, it established in 1958, as part of its own committee structure, the International Commission on National Parks.

One of the first tasks of this commission was the compilation of a world list of areas actually protected at the time. This work led to more general discussions about those elements of the Earth's biological character that were currently protected and those that were not and finally (through the 1960s) about the concept of a global strategy for protecting representative samples of the world's various ecosystems. However, it was not until the mid-1970s that the IUCN and other international bodies concluded their discussions on ecosystem representation and began working toward a global network of protected areas based on this principle. Thus, these ideas had not yet coalesced into a technical-planning approach by 1970 when Canadian officials began work on defining their own System Plan.

Over the same period, the 1950s and 1960s, environmental and national parks policy participants in the United States initiated several studies for a future parks framework for that country. One of these studies was by the

Outdoor Recreation Resources Review Commission (ORRRC), which was established by Congress in June 1958 to determine the likely recreational needs of Americans through to the end of that century. While the ORRRC did not propose a system plan for the United States, it did present research into the nature, extent, and availability of wilderness areas in that country.

A little later the US National Parks Service (NPS) embarked on its own project and in early 1961 issued a handbook for the development of a US National Parks System Plan. The purpose of this project was to prepare a "well-rounded, complete and adequate system of nationally significant parks in appropriate classifications."[48] Under the scientific category, one of four in the proposal, "appropriate classifications" would include representative geological and biological features, "which depict all important earth processes and biomes."[49] The US System Plan was intended to incorporate the nine existing types of national parks (including historic parks, battlefields, and recreation areas) along with the "crown jewels" of the system, those major national parks, such as Yellowstone, that comprise large wilderness areas of noteworthy scenic value. Therefore, while the US proposal did not focus entirely on biophysical representation, it did, as Ronald Foresta has commented, shift the emphasis from a set of natural values emphasizing scenic wonders and visitor appeal to a set of ecological values based on the representation of biomes and physiographic regions.[50] The process of developing the US System Plan took the rest of the decade, and it was not until 1972 that the US plan became official.

Links between Canadian and American policy ideas are, in general, extensive and well documented, and the drafters of the Canadian System Plan, while relying heavily on ideas generated within their own government, benefited especially from the US approach to natural history themes. Some other related ideas would also have been drawn from the broader international discussion of the role of physiographic regions in parks planning. In the late 1960s, for example, only two to three years prior to writing their plan, Canadian parks and wildlife officials established formal links with the IUCN. Meanwhile in Canada, Saskatchewan had begun to apply some of the same principles, and at the Federal-Provincial Annual Parks Conference in 1963 the Saskatchewan representative presented a system plan, based on natural history, for that province's provincial parks.[51] Finally, the authors of the system plan drew on technical information collected and prepared by various Canadian agencies, such as the Geological Survey of Canada, and individuals to establish objective scientific criteria for the natural regions.[52]

Rationalism and the System Plan
In general, the System Plan benefited from the rise of rationalism in Canadian government. This analytical approach is often associated with Pierre

Trudeau and the period during which he was prime minister, partly because rationalism was his leitmotif but also because, during the sixteen years of his mandates, rationalism happened to be at its peak in Canadian government. Perhaps its most distinguishing feature in this period was Trudeau's organization of cabinet and central agencies, which Peter Aucoin has referred to as "rational management."[53] Besides the collegial debating style of cabinet to which Aucoin refers, rationalism permeated government in two other important ways. First, at the core of any rationalist approach is a reliance on facts and technical considerations. On this point, Trudeau's view of rational government was that the state "will need political instruments which are sharper, stronger, and more finely controlled than anything based on mere emotionalism: such tools will be made up of advanced technology and scientific investigation."[54] Second, rationalism depends on goal setting and planning. To avoid emotionalism and policy drift,[55] decision makers need specific objectives to work toward. Goal setting and planning were to take place at all levels of government, from the Privy Council and the Prime Minister's Office to the annual budget projections of each department and agency.

While Trudeau may have been the principal exemplar of rationalism, the ideas involved predate his time in government and were part of an earlier and broader context of change. In particular, goal setting and increased reliance on technocratic approaches to administrative and policy problems began at least as early as 1957, with planning for the Resources for Tomorrow Conference. As already described, that conference set out to establish a broad consensus on national goals that would direct future economic development, including those for national parks. Thus, while some of the goals themselves changed through the 1960s, the principle of setting them was already established in the late 1950s.

More or less concurrently, the Royal Commission on Government Organization made a larger contribution to goal setting by recommending radical changes to budgeting, personnel management, and other areas of government administration. Reporting in 1962, it recommended changes to the budgeting system that eventually became the Planning, Programming, and Budgeting System (PPBS), with the articulation, within each annual budget process, of five-year goals for all levels of the federal government. The PPBS was formalized by the first Trudeau government in 1969, but the rationalist approach to budgeting that it represented was implemented on a trial basis as early as 1960, while increasingly serious trials progressed throughout the decade. The PPBS thus affected the bureaucracy down to fairly junior levels and brought its rationalist message into the day-to-day operation of government, while for the Parks Branch the system plan (by setting out an orderly framework) evidently promised to be a helpful basis on which regular budget planning could be conducted.

The climate of rational management did not affect the definition of the national parks mandate directly, but it did form part of the context in which Parks Branch officials formulated their ideas. This was particularly true for the System Plan, which, by deliberately setting out rational criteria thereby constraining political influences on the decisions by senior officials and the minister, took much of the subjectivity (and some of the politics) out of park selection. In its introduction, the *National Parks System Planning Manual* says that, to be "acceptable to ... all agencies and individuals concerned," the plan's methodology "would have to be based on the natural sciences and would have to be relatively free of political and social influences."[56]

The Role of Bureaucracy

Development of the System Plan was an exclusively bureaucratic initiative. As the above outline suggests, the concepts of system planning were formulated in a broad international community of scientists and government officials in which early Canadian involvement was only marginal. However, as the ideas evolved, they came to this country mostly through the bureaucracy. Historically, the most important source of policy ideas about national parks for Canada has been the United States. National parks were initially an American idea, and by the 1960s there had been three-quarters of a century of exchange of ideas on that topic between the two countries. For system planning, it was no different. Canadian and American government officials held memberships in each other's professional organizations and frequently crossed the border to attend conferences and meetings. It is particularly important that, during the late 1950s and early 1960s, while the Americans were preparing to develop their System Plan, the two professional planners in the Planning Section of the Canadian Parks Branch had both studied for graduate degrees in planning at universities in Michigan, while the dean of forestry at the University of Michigan was also the chair of the ORRRC.[57] Through them, new ideas about natural history themes and other concepts of parks planning became part of the intellectual fabric of the Canadian Parks Branch.

At the same time, Canadian links with both American and international communities were strengthened with the First World Conference on National Parks in Seattle in 1962. Canada's connection with the international parks community further developed over the decade with a visit by an official from the Canadian Wildlife Service to the IUCN. Later, in November 1969, Canada sent a small delegation, led by officials from the Parks Branch and the Canadian Wildlife Service, to join that organization.[58]

While the scientific community in general, and the United States Parks Service in particular, were discussing the concepts of system planning, it was Canada that first wrote a National Parks System Plan. Considering its influence on Canada's national parks system and eventually on Canadian protected spaces in general, including those in the provinces, its origins were rather modest. While drawing on ideas from the United States, and more indirectly the international community, the System Plan was written entirely within Parks Canada by two officials[59] over a six-month period. There had been no ministerial request or any external pressure, by either provincial governments or interest groups, to produce such a plan. Nor was there a single political or administrative event that precipitated its drafting, although there were several background influences such as the need to define the potential fiscal requirements for national parks. Rather than being seen as political, the plan was regarded as purely technical; its aim was to help the Parks Branch identify new park sites,[60] and it was mainly for use by the Planning Section. Despite the relatively few people involved in writing the plan, its approach explicitly recognized the need to satisfy a wide range of interests in the policy arena: "There has long been a need to formulate a plan which would ensure a system of National Parks in Canada. Such a plan would have to be objectively laid out, using criteria which would be both acceptable to and understandable by all agencies and individuals concerned."[61]

As they had with the conceptual and drafting stages of the System Plan, the bureaucrats (this time including provincial parks officials) took the lead in promoting its adoption. To win initial support from a critical group of participants in the parks policy community, the plan was discussed with provincial agencies at the annual federal-provincial parks conferences. During the first few years of the 1970s, these conferences were attended only by federal and provincial parks bureaucrats, and the approval and informal adoption of the System Plan took place entirely within that limited forum. By 1975, a new assistant deputy minister described the System Plan as "just there" and used it to advise the minister on the probable direction of national parks development.[62]

Intergovernmental Relations

While rationalism was finding its way into the federal government, the intergovernmental context was also changing, and this change caused the Parks Branch to subtly reorient its philosophy about national parks. A confluence of two elements of the organization of government in the 1960s facilitated this shift in direction: namely, the "departmentalized" cabinet within the federal government and co-operative federalism between levels of government.

In his postulated three modes of cabinet operation, Dupré sees, with the rise of the modern administrative state, one mode that he calls the "departmentalized" cabinet where, as previously mentioned, government departments have significant technical responsibilities and are the locus of the necessary expertise to carry them out. To meet their responsibilities of policy formation and implementation, ministers must rely on the appointed officials who are the holders of the expertise. Simultaneously, in the departmentalized cabinet, the minister is the pinion who links the department to the cabinet in a setting where confidence among colleagues binds the group together. Each minister, bound to the cabinet by confidence and trust, therefore enjoys a relatively high degree of decision-making autonomy that then devolves, to some degree, to the appointed officials who provide technical expertise.

The development of co-operative federalism was contemporaneous with that of the departmentalized cabinet and like it an outcome of the rise of the administrative state. Following World War II, as the provinces began to assert themselves and to develop their own professional competence and programmatic interests, the federal government partially withdrew from many policy areas that it had previously occupied. This increased provincial administrative capacity led to a form of federal-provincial relations that addresses policy issues through, as Garth Stevenson puts it, "professional or programmatic goals that cut across, instead of reinforcing, the jurisdictional rivalries between the two levels."[63]

Dupré has enumerated several of the general conditions that apply for co-operative federalism,[64] and they interlock with features of a departmentalized cabinet to provide the framework inside which numerous public policies have been planned, negotiated, and implemented. Considerable attention has been given in the literature to the several social policy areas in Canada where intergovernmental co-operation has occurred in the 1950s and 1960s. Most of these conditions for co-operative federalism cited by Dupré also applied (and still do) to national parks, while the remainder are closely approximated. There were, for example, shared values and a common vocabulary among national and provincial parks planners, and there were strong intergovernmental trust relations that fostered future co-operation. Parks ministers, at both levels of government, are generally dependent on cabinet support, but departments had internalized that situation so that intergovernmental negotiators usually took care to incorporate intracabinet positions before bringing agreements to the cabinet table. In this way, departments, rather than cabinets, continue to reflect intergovernmental relations with respect to parks.

Although co-operative federalism is generally regarded as having ended in the late 1960s, co-operative relations often continued beyond that period and continued to influence the working levels of bureaucracies in many areas where policy subjects were not in serious dispute. This was the case for parks, where the forum of the Annual Federal-Provincial Parks Conference provided an opportunity for the two bureaucracies to work co-operatively together. In fact, federal and provincial parks managers and planners came together in the 1960s as they had not done previously.

Intergovernmental co-operation in this area began with the preparation for and the conclusions reached at the 1961 Resources for Tomorrow Conference. Prior to the conference, contact between parks officials in the federal and provincial governments had been intermittent, and there was no regular process for an open exchange of views. But as public demand for recreational space grew, parks officials from both orders of government increasingly needed to co-ordinate activities and policies. The necessity of a regular forum for intergovernmental parks discussions was therefore recognized at the Resources for Tomorrow Conference, and a resolution to establish such a forum was adopted. Following the conference, the federal Parks Branch took responsibility for convening annual conferences that would bring together parks officials from all governments to discuss both theoretical and practical problems in a professional and co-operative manner. Through the 1960s and beyond (they continue today), these annual conferences provided a regular forum for parks managers and policy makers to exchange views and define the roles (with respect to parks) of their respective governments.

Another outcome of the 1961 conference that provided a mechanism for co-operative federalism in the resources and parks arena was the creation of the Canadian Council of Resource Ministers (CCRM).[65] This council was established immediately after the conference and became a forum for discussion both within and between governments at the ministerial level as well as an important source of encouragement for discussion between the state and societal actors during the 1960s.[66] Co-operation between governments and the careful allocation of environmental responsibilities, an area not addressed in the British North America Act, was handled by the CCRM and its successor councils.

Genesis of the System Plan took place within this context of increasing provincial interest in the parks policy area, the forums of the Federal-Provincial Annual Parks Conferences, and the CCRM. Provincial governments' interest in their own parks had begun in conjunction with the promotion of tourism and the recognition of recreational potential within their boundaries (both provincial and park boundaries). Initially, this interest was in competition with federal ideas, which were also focused on the increasing demand for outdoor recreational space. For example, the federal government actively considered national parks sites for recreational and tourist purposes in terms of their proximity to urban centres. However, to avoid intergovernmental conflict, federal officials eventually sought a concept for parks that did not overlap with provincial ambitions. In the forums of the annual conferences and the CCRM, the provinces indicated their desire for the federal government to vacate the fields of outdoor recreation and tourism. The provinces were, in that period, less interested in ideas of wilderness protection or ecosystem representation (since parks were still viewed, in the 1950s and 1960s, as a use of resources), leaving the latter as an area for national attention. The provinces could argue that further federal withdrawal from this area was consistent with the transfer of resources to the western provinces in 1930. Eventually, the concept emerged that the federal government would, in general, vacate the outdoor recreation policy area but that the provinces would not object, in principle, to federal (or national) wilderness parks. This balancing of interests and mandates obviously favoured a shift toward a more wilderness-oriented view of national parks. Given the programmatic choices broadly available for parks, the interests of the two levels of government, and the pursuit of co-operative relations between federal and provincial officials, these intergovernmental relations resulted in the refocusing of national parks toward concepts of environmental representativeness and wilderness protection and away from recreation and economic development. The System Plan was partly responsible for this shift by raising for identification possible national park sites in areas very remote from most recreational potential. Equally important, such a plan was consistent with the mandate articulated in the 1964 *National Parks Policy* and therefore did not contradict established federal government policy.

The System Plan was able to satisfy another provincial concern: namely, that Parks Branch ambitions were finite. Once the system was complete, the federal government, theoretically, would not be requesting the provinces to give up more land and resources to the national parks system. The drafters of the System Plan recognized some of these provincial concerns and deliberately took them into account when establishing criteria that would be acceptable to all agencies and individuals concerned. Although increasing attention was being paid to interest groups, the "agencies and individuals" referred to here are almost certainly state (including provincial) agencies since the System Plan was viewed strictly as an internal management device and one that, in any case, societal interests were not aware of or involved in until after the relevant government agencies had adopted it.

Just as the provinces had influenced the orientation of the System Plan, so too did they influence its adoption. Here the annual federal-provincial parks conferences played a central role. During the conference following drafting of the plan in 1971, a Park System Planning Task Force of federal and provincial officials was struck and operated for the next three years, making annual recommendations to the subsequent conferences.[67] The System Plan was therefore able to satisfy two purposes: first, the rational planning concerns within the federal government and, second, the careful allocation of jurisdictional responsibilities that allowed both governments to be active in the parks policy field. In this spirit of intergovernmental co-operation and in the associated bureaucratic and ministerial forums, these decisions were made rather than on the open, often highly contested, stage of executive federalism that was emerging in the early 1970s.

Conclusion

The first period of parks policy development in the postwar era was dominated by the Parks Branch bureaucracy, and the initial steps toward articulating an environmental focus for protected lands can be largely and directly attributed to the actions of that bureau. However, this general conclusion masks several overlapping factors that reveal the motives, processes, and context of bureaucratic procedures and that provide a more nuanced explanation for this shift in policy. An understanding of both institutions and interest groups is critical for explaining the manner in which the bureaucracy was able to proceed in defining policy, but by far the most persuasive explanation for this process lies in the ideas that set the context of decision making.

Two sets of ideas in particular determined that context. The first set comprised relatively stable ideas as the background against which policy deliberation took place, and in this set a central belief was that it was correct and appropriate for bureaucracies to develop and propose policy. Although not all societal interests accepted their proposals (indeed some ideas were hotly contested), there was not yet a movement toward involving the public, or segments of it, in policy development (as there would be in later periods). Despite their privileged, initiative-taking position, Parks Branch bureaucrats were conservative rather than expansive in their proposals and stayed close to their existing mandate. Also in this set, and only slightly less important, were ideas about environmental protection that not only were foreshadowed by the 1930s legislation but also were emerging among the public in the postwar period. The existence of environmental ideas in the legislation established a path that bureaucrats could be expected to follow.[68]

The second set of ideas were those that had an application that was relatively fleeting but that nevertheless contributed to the context wherein policy discussion and bargaining took place. Most of these ideas have now either faded into the background or been transformed to fit a new context, but in the 1950s and 1960s they significantly affected the pattern of discussion. First among these constituents of the policy environment was co-operative federalism, which, despite its general demise in the late 1960s, continued to affect park policy processes until the early 1970s (at least). Another contextualizing idea in this period was rationalism. As with co-operative federalism, ideas of rational planning continue to be present in policy deliberations, but they are no longer championed by a prime minister and, to some extent, have been consciously supplanted by concepts of bargaining and local responsiveness. Finally, in the 1950s and 1960s especially, interest groups were regarded by key policy makers as adjunct to the organs of the state, to be called upon when required, but otherwise, for parks policy development at least, they were viewed as external to the process. As will be seen in subsequent chapters, groups increased in importance to become one of the major active and constant elements in the policy process, but in this early period ideas about their role placed them in a much more modest position. It is these ideas, both stable and fleeting, that, by allowing one to understand more fully the context in which policy development took place, finally explain the shift in policy that occurred during this period.

Following the framework outlined by these two sets of ideas, the 1964 policy statement can be explained by drawing on four of these factors. First, it is evident that the Parks Branch alone took the initiative to develop what became the 1964 policy statement and that its personnel, the interest groups already in existence, and various ministers all accepted that role for the bureaucracy. In this case, it was branch officials who recognized the need to achieve uniformity and consistency in national parks management across the country. Up to the mid-1950s, the act, as the branch acknowledged, had "been interpreted in many different ways over the years and these differences [had] caused conflict of purpose in the administration."[69] Despite this initiative, the policy was still seen, from a limited perspective, as simply a management tool, and "there was considerable hesitance about putting it in place, both at the administrative and political levels."[70] This ambivalence led the branch to draft the policy statement but to do so with relatively little deviation from existing practice.

Second, the branch's ability to restructure the policy environment, and the role of interest groups (itself a product of the restructured environment), must be taken into account since, even though the policy proposal was modest, it was evidently too dramatic for some societal interests. Therefore, to have it formalized, the bureaucracy had to address its own institutional position as a mere adviser about, rather than an advocate for, the policy. Here the bureaucracy was able to take another critical step in promoting the formation of the National and Provincial Parks Association of Canada to serve as environmental advocates. This association was also able to offset commercial interests (mostly in Alberta) coupled with the Conservative Party's general orientation and the regional approach of Alberta MPs who had a powerful constraining effect on the policy's implementation.

Third, to understand the details of the policy statement, it must be recognized that its content did not spring *sui generis* from the minds of government officials but was rather a modest adaptation of the ideas already inherent in the mandate of the Parks Branch. That is, officials were simply following a path already laid down by earlier decision makers. Moreover, the decisions contained in the 1964 document are limited and pragmatic in nature, attempting principally to establish a uniform and official policy in order to facilitate the smooth conduct of parks administration.

Fourth, this limited and pragmatic approach can be explained by the general conservatism of bureaucracy as posited by a number of scholars. For example, Charles Lindblom's incrementalist argument and Graham Allison's organizational process model both observe that agencies will continue along existing paths with only limited variation or innovation.[71] While this caution clearly characterizes the 1964 policy statement, something more is needed to explain the change that did occur or even the fact that the policy statement was worked on and kept alive for seven years. These facts can be explained by using Robert Montjoy and Laurence O'Toole's model of bureaucratic initiative taking. In one segment of their four-part model, they argue that agencies with vague mandates and new resources will show increased levels of discretion.[72] It has already been noted that the National Parks Act was vague, calling for both use and protection in its preamble, while in terms of resources the Parks Branch experienced a sizable increase in its budget allocation beginning in 1955.[73] How much this budget expansion might have offset the conservatism of the bureau is impossible to say, but it seems plausible that some balance between the two impulses led the branch to pursue policy clarification without proposing significant and dramatic changes to the mandate.

In much the same way that bureaucratic initiative explains the 1964 policy statement, it along with four subsidiary factors also explains the System Plan. Once again the Parks Branch developed the plan to meet its own management requirements, and understandably it did not involve public interest groups or the minister. However, the plan fit a larger context of policy change and acquired an importance perhaps not initially anticipated. First, there was increasing acceptance of the idea of wilderness parks. This concept was one in the set of background ideas and had been around since the nineteenth century, particularly within the American debates, but was relatively new to national parks in Canada, which were widely regarded as recreational spaces until well into the 1960s. Although the concept of wilderness parks had existed for many years, in the 1960s it was largely through the bureaucracy that the idea was adopted into management objectives and then, eventually, as policy. Second, there was a process of policy learning[74] in which members of the bureaucracy through their contacts with the academic scientific community, American counterparts, international environmental organizations, and Canadian government scientists were able to compile the criteria, and a framework, for a parks system based on wilderness principles. Third, this framework was both motivated by and eventually approved within the co-operative relationship between federal and provincial parks bureaucracies, a form of co-operation that conformed with broadly based criteria about provincial and federal objectives concerning economic development and parks establishment. Fourth, the System Plan fitted perfectly within the milieu of rational planning that permeated the federal government in the late 1960s and early 1970s. The plan allowed not only for objectives to be set for the parks but also for planners to fit their mandate well within the budgetary and legal framework that resulted from ideas such as management by objectives and the Planning, Programming, and Budgeting System.

As suggested, while not all of these factors have disappeared (perhaps none has completely), some, such as the unilateral role of the bureaucracy (at least for parks), co-operative federalism, and the centrality of rationalism, have diminished significantly over the succeeding decades. Yet in the 1950s and 1960s, these ideas, and the practices that flowed from them, helped to set the context in which the foundations of postwar national parks policy were established. At the beginning of the 1970s, the two pillars of that policy – the 1964 *National Parks Policy* itself and the System Plan, each with its own environmentalist ideas – joined with the institutional role of the bureaucracy to develop and advise on policy matters. This role was buttressed and constrained by the modestly increasing role of interest groups, by changing intergovernmental relations, and by the rationalist framework of government. Few of these ideas about the process of policy development survived into the 1970s, when a significantly different range of contextualizing ideas began to guide the policy development process.

4
National Parks and Public Participation, 1970-79

Public participation, which the Parks Branch had consciously sought in the late 1950s and early 1960s, was relatively modest during the late 1960s. Through this period, the branch continued to take the initiative in policy development and to manage parks according to its own perceptions of objectives and constraints, in full knowledge of the support that the NPPAC and other groups could lend it on the environmental side of policy debates. Public quiescence was to change dramatically in the 1970s, however, a decade in which a pattern of public participation in national parks issues grew, eventually becoming institutionalized in both legislation and policy. By 1979, the public was virtually an equal partner in rewriting the national parks policy statement.

To be precise, there were two publics. One consisted of the interested Canadian public in general, both those with particular and local interests in individual parks and those with general and national interests in the broader national parks system. The other grouping comprised Aboriginal Canadians. Their interests, initially at least, were not in national parks as such but in maintaining a legal claim to lands that the federal government wished to appropriate for national park purposes.

The changes in national parks policy in the 1970s resulted less from the conflict between ideas about development and the environment, as in the previous period, and more from discussions about how policy decisions on parks should be made and who should be involved. In short, there were changes in the process itself rather than in policy content. As this happened, however, there was a subtle shift in the meaning of national parks. Rather than parks belonging to or being the property of the federal state, the public took "ownership" of these national and environmental symbols. In the process, the Parks Branch lost its relative independence and its ability to solely determine the content of policy discussion to such a degree that public participation became, in effect, an element of policy.

This shift in approach from state initiative to institutionalized public participation was the result of two changes in state-society relations. One was the change in the general organization of societal interests in the national parks policy arena, which occurred in the 1960s, and the other was the involvement of Aboriginal peoples. The lifting of colonializing strictures that had been imposed on the latter for about 200 years, coupled with a historic, modified colonial position that enabled them to make claims against the Canadian state and its use of resources, made Aboriginal people integral to many national park decisions, especially those affecting lands north of the sixtieth parallel.

Three stages are evident in the development and institutionalization of public participation in this decade (really from 1968 to 1979). The first was a general development in public participation that arose directly from two controversial events in the early 1970s, a proposal to expand ski facilities in Banff National Park and the expropriation of property in order to create Kouchibouguac National Park. Both led to vigorous public protest and considerable embarrassment to the Parks Branch. The second stage came about with efforts to expand the national parks system into northern Canada. Seen as a challenge to Aboriginal claims to the land, these efforts resulted in a compromise that created a new category of park, the national park reserve, where land was held until Aboriginal land claims settlements were reached. The third stage, and in effect the institutionalization of public participation, came about with the rewriting of the national parks policy statement. Public action in the early 1970s made it clear that public participation was necessary in the future management of national parks, and when deliberations for a revised policy statement began in 1975, though they did so at the initiative of the Parks Branch, they included the interested public from their opening stages.

Public Participation

Public participation is a broad concept that can cover many forms of direct citizen involvement and whose meaning may depend on the circumstances in which involvement occurs.[1] For purposes of analysis, four broad categories among the mechanisms of participation may be defined. First, and most formal, individual citizens or organized groups have access to the courts. Important legal criteria determine who may take this route, such as the rules governing standing and access to information. Legal and political analysts have debated the degree to which the courts are available to the public in Canada, and on balance it appears that this has been a relatively little-used approach.[2] Second, there are various quasi-judicial boards such as regulatory and environmental-management agencies that operate under legislation that delegates rule-making authority to them. These boards often conduct themselves according to judicial rules of procedure and evidence so that their decisions will withstand judicial review if necessary. It is of critical importance that the board in each case determines the timing and nature of any public participation that may occur. Thus, the public usually joins the process after the essential elements of the decision have been formulated. Third, there are community-centred processes that may include informal "town hall" meetings with information brochures, questionnaires and suggestion forms, and friendly representatives from government agencies. These informal processes are meant to reach as wide a public as possible.[3] Finally, there are conflictual or protest approaches to public participation where the public demands a say in decision making regardless of the views of either quasi-judicial or administrative agencies. These approaches to public participation are qualitatively different from the other three approaches because they resemble mild (and sometimes not-so-mild) forms of civil disobedience. While they are not necessarily outside the law, there are, by definition, no specific written rules governing who may participate, the circumstances of participation, or which activities are included. This lack of specified order is in contrast to quasi-judicial and even community-centred models where participants and activities are well defined beforehand. The protest model nevertheless sits on a continuum of participation models because the protest can often be ameliorated and transformed into one of the other approaches if public authorities make one of the other forms of participation available.

Several authors have attempted to define the degree of public participation by outlining various typologies. Sherry Arnstein, who is most frequently quoted, has attempted to clarify the multiple understandings of public participation by proposing a typology of eight levels, as shown in Figure 4.1. The first two levels are non-participatory, according to Arnstein, since the public are merely recipients of decisions from state authorities. In stages three through five, the public are permitted a voice, although there is no means to ensure that these public voices will be heard or heeded, since the authorities retain the power to make the decisions. At level six, the public becomes part of the decision process, able to negotiate and to make trades with the power holders, and in levels seven and eight citizens have some real power in the decisions.[4]

Harold Eidsvik, working within the Parks Branch, adopted a model developed by the Canadian Council of Resource and Environment Ministers (CCREM, formerly the CCRM, now the Canadian Council of Ministers of the Environment, CCME) in the early 1970s using a similar, five-stage approach, as shown in Figure 4.2. This approach is less critical of the power of government agencies than is Arnstein's since it regards information and persuasion as aspects of participation. From this, Eidsvik suggests that public

Figure 4.1

Ladder of citizen participation

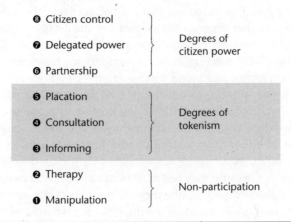

Source: Sherry R. Arnstein, "A Ladder of Citizen Participation," *Journal of the American Institute of Planners* 35 (1969): 217.

participation has always existed for national parks, though this claim, given the pro-participation mood of the time that it was published, puts the Parks Branch in a more favourable light than a more demanding definition would suggest.

Public involvement, as opposed to the mere dissemination of information, did not begin until the mid-1960s. It was, however, the consultation level (as defined by Eidsvik) that was used in the first public hearings of the 1970s.[5]

This level seems to correspond closely to level four, also called consultation, of Arnstein's ladder. Arnstein, however, in describing the methods of consultation, refers to attitude surveys, neighbourhood meetings, and public hearings. For her, people are viewed less as participants and more as "statistical abstractions," where the degree of participation is measured by how many people attended meetings or filled out questionnaires. In this stage of the ladder, public meetings are a vehicle for the power holders – officials organize and conduct meetings or other consultation processes, while the public simply comprise an audience.[6] In terms of the four broad categories of participatory mechanisms outlined at the beginning of this section, the practices of the 1970s fall mostly within the third category, the community-centred approach, which includes the consultation procedures described by Arnstein (her level four) and Eidsvik (his level three). Some additional attention must be given to the protest model, however, since conflict outside a framework of formalized, structured, and state-authorized rules and procedures was an important occurrence in the early part of the decade.

Figure 4.2

Citizen participation

			Area of citizen involvement in the decision-making process	
Information model	**Persuasion model**	**Consultation model**	**Partnership model**	**Citizen Control model**
An authority makes a decision and informs the public about it.	An authority makes a decision, then persuades the public to accept it.	An authority defines the problem, presents it to the public, invites comments and suggestions, then makes a decision.	An authority prescribes the limits and within these limits citizens share and may even assume the decision-making responsibility.	Citizens have the full right to participate in and assume the responsibility for decisions.

Area of authority to decide vested in political bureaus

Area of citizen involvement in the decision-making process

Source: Government of Canada, Man and Resources Conference, Toronto, 1972.

Throughout the 1960s, there were no regular mechanisms for public participation in national parks management or policy issues, and the National and Provincial Parks Association and other societal interests were mostly engaged in public education.[7] The first, but by no means the definitive, step in introducing public participation to the parks policy arena came in 1968. At the suggestion of the deputy minister, the minister responsible for national parks announced that management plans for individual parks would henceforth be open to public comment. Management plans themselves had been in existence since at least the late 1950s, but their preparation had been centralized in Ottawa, after which the completed plans were sent to the superintendent of each park for implementation. Later, in the 1960s, this process was decentralized somewhat as planners were placed in each of the four regional offices and plans were prepared there in consultation with park superintendents. After 1968, however, the management-planning process was decentralized even further to include the interested public. Despite the limited role given to public participation in official plans, public involvement expanded dramatically and, as the events of the decade would show, contained the potential for parks managers to lose command of the parks policy and management direction.

Ideas and Public Participation
The exact origins of public participation are not clear. Some would root the phenomenon in the very nature of liberal democracy,[8] particularly in the United States, where both the mythology and the practice of town hall meetings are strong. Wilson Head[9] and James Draper[10] have attempted to locate the origins of public participation more specifically in the propensity of Americans and Canadians to join voluntary organizations.[11] Reference to liberal democracy and voluntary organizations, however, obscures important differences in public participation practices found in Canada, the United States, and Britain. Such references also gloss over important temporal variations in the public's contribution to policy formation.

Public participation in the 1960s and 1970s, for example, was qualitatively different from the voluntary joining to which Head and Draper refer. Neither the hypothesis about liberal democracy nor that about voluntary organizations takes into account the importance of specific legal or administrative mechanisms that allow or provide for the judicial, quasi-judicial, or community-centred forms of public participation outlined above. A more useful approach is to see participation as not simply a spontaneous outgrowth of liberal democracy but also something that requires an enabling institutional framework.

Another aspect concerning the origins of public participation in Canada is that there appears to be a popular notion that the phenomenon developed in the United States and was then adopted in Canada. This view is consistent with the timing of the appearance of the practices in both countries, and it is intuitively appealing given the social, intellectual, and media links between the two countries. Nevertheless, this idea should be treated with some caution since the trail of influence from the United States to Canada has not been persuasively traced. At the same time, the experience with public participation in the United States is instructive because of what it helps to reveal about Canada and because, to the extent that the United States is often the source of Canadian ideas, it is important to see why US ideas about participation could be only partially adopted in Canada. An institutional context conducive to participation had existed in the United States for some decades, although it was reinforced more explicitly in the early 1960s. As Marcus Ethridge puts it, "the basic tools of participation were set in place long before public advocacy was widespread."[12] In 1946, the US Administrative Procedures Act (APA) standardized and brought up to date existing requirements for agencies to hold public hearings before making administrative rules. Judicial review of administrative agencies, which had been "established ... long before the APA," Ethridge argues,[13] was the most important contribution to citizen participation. Further opportunities for participation were instituted within specific American legislation in the early 1960s. Several writers have identified the 1960s Poverty Program as the origin of the American public participation movements of that and the following decade because the legislation empowering that program mandated that it have the "maximum feasible participation of the poor."[14] In addition, Marilyn Dubasak has pointed out that the US Wilderness Act (1964) and the US National Environmental Policy Act (1970) also made sweeping provision for public involvement in environmental issues.[15]

Canadians have similarly acknowledged the importance of institutional frameworks for public participation in this country, although mostly by noting their absence. Alastair Lucas observed in 1976 that "citizens' rights to participate in decisions by resource and environment-management agencies are not extensive" and that "agencies with discretion to permit opportunities for public participation are generally not doing so effectively or not doing so at all."[16] Dubasak, among others, has drawn attention to judicial arrangements such as legal standing and access to information, the absence of which (in the 1960s and 1970s) seriously undermined the ability of individual Canadians or interest groups to engage in effective intervention in policy processes.

The difference between the institutional arrangements of the United States and Canada may reflect a deeper set of institutional differences within these two polities. Ethridge has suggested that American opportunities for participation were shaped by forces aimed at governing the relationship between Congress and administrative agencies rather than necessarily providing for "grassroots" democracy. He offers three possible explanations for the expanded opportunities for citizen involvement in the United States, which reflect the particular macro-institutional arrangements of that country. First, legal conservatives saw the US Constitution as limiting rule making to Congress. When this view was not upheld by the Supreme Court, conservative legislators sought to constrain administrative discretion by expressly opening rule making to judicial or quasi-judicial review. Second, legislators, in pursuing their self-interest, will delegate authority to avoid the political costs of making a decision themselves. At the same time, elaborate procedural requirements will be put in place to restrict the independence of the agency with delegated rule-making capacity and keep it within the confines of the legislation. Finally, Ethridge argues, the agencies themselves may have sought provisions for public participation to establish their own power bases. He quotes Norton Long as saying that the American political system "does not generate enough power at any focal point of leadership" to enable administrative agencies to operate effectively.[17] Thus, by seeking public involvement, agencies can enhance their legitimacy in relation to Congress and with the public.

These arguments have certain parallels in Canada but are not fully persuasive because of the executive-centred nature of this country's Parliament. Since the role of the legislature is not part of the written Canadian Constitution,[18] there is no equivalent to the strict constructivist interpretation of the US Constitution with respect to the relations between the legislative and the administrative branches of government. The twofold position of the minister as the head of an administrative department and as a member of the legislature necessarily means that all departmental rules, at some stage, have ministerial approval. While Canadian politicians may be as likely as their American counterparts to calculate their self-interest, the nature of responsible government means that, even in those instances of administrative delegation, the minister and cabinet, rather than the judiciary, remain responsible for administrative decisions.[19] Procedural constraints on administration are less critical in Canada, therefore, since consequences of decisions redound to the politicians. Finally, unlike the American political system, the Canadian one does not lack a "focal point of leadership." Government agencies and ministers may still seek open public processes as a way of taking advantage of divisions within the public or, more subtly, within cabinet, as the example of the 1964 *National Parks Policy* shows. However, when the collective political will exists, a minister in the Canadian system does not need to seek public legitimacy, especially if it might stimulate opposition. In short, the executive-centred Parliament, responsible government, and ministerial responsibility constitute an institutional setting where the executive embodies, to some degree, both the will of the legislature and the discretion of the administration. Given the differences between the American and the Canadian political systems, the forces that Ethridge advances would be more compelling in the United States than in Canada, and the institutional prerequisites for public participation would therefore be more likely to appear in the former country.

These differences suggest that American approaches to public participation could only have provided a general example for Canada and that the historic pattern of citizen involvement in the two countries is quite different. Provisions for public participation appeared in many pieces of Canadian and provincial legislation early in the 1970s[20] as if in imitation of the US example, but the Canadian legislation was highly restrictive and gave complete discretion to state agencies whether to include the public in the deliberations. Despite some limited provisions in this legislation, the actual practice of public participation emerged in areas not actually covered by any laws. As it turned out, it is highly likely that public participation in Canada may have appeared in the parks policy arena even without a legislative framework for parks, where in the latter months of 1968 the Parks Branch hurriedly announced its intention to involve the public in developing management plans. Interestingly, the motive for this decision was the sense of competition felt by some federal officials toward their Ontario counterparts.

Participation in Canada began in Ontario in March 1968 when Abbott Conway, a citizen concerned about continued logging in Ontario's Algonquin Provincial Park, appeared before an Ontario legislative committee to express his concerns.[21] Faced with an unsympathetic response, Conway and several others formed the Algonquin Wildlands League a few months later and over the summer of 1968 proceeded to publicize aspects of the Ontario government's move to continue resource extraction in Algonquin. By the end of the summer, public interest had been aroused sufficiently that the provincial government promised to hold public hearings into the park's management plan, which was due to be presented that fall.[22] The principal forum for that announcement was the Annual Federal-Provincial Parks Conference held that year in Algonquin in late September. At this meeting, a level of interpersonal or intergovernmental competition between officials or agencies became apparent. When the Ontario official speaking for the provincial parks agency announced to his federal and provincial counterparts that Ontario would hold public hearings for the management plan, the federal deputy minister,[23] determined that his government should not be outdone, quickly arranged for the federal minister to announce that management plans for national parks would also be open to public hearings.[24] While the rivalry (often mooted rather than revealed) is interesting here, it is equally interesting to note that public participation was seen as a political good, one about which governments would endeavour to pre-empt one another. This competition indicates the degree to which the idea of public participation had become accepted by both state and society as an appropriate way of discussing certain kinds of policy matters.

Village Lake Louise

Although the program of public hearings for national parks management plans had been announced in 1968, the first hearings did not take place until April 1970. Over the spring and summer of that year, more such hearings were conducted for several national parks in the Atlantic provinces. This program of hearings continued the following year, and in April 1971 meetings were held for the Four Mountain Parks (the four contiguous Rocky Mountain National Parks of Banff, Jasper, Yoho, and Kootenay). These hearings, which were modest, conformed to what Sherry Arnstein and Harold Eidsvik have called "consultation." In other words, plans were drawn up by Parks Branch officials without public input and then widely distributed in preparation for public meetings, which were meant to gather the views of individuals and groups.[25]

At the same time as these plans were being prepared and arrangements were being made for public meetings, the Parks Branch was deep in negotiations with a consortium of companies intent upon the development of a new ski resort, Village Lake Louise, in Banff National Park. These negotiations were the result of three streams of activity coming together in the late 1960s.

The first of these activities was skiing, which had been permitted in the mountain parks in a small but increasing manner since earlier in the twentieth century. For Lake Louise, ski development began in 1930 with a simple request by a local ski club to build a small cabin for its members. This was followed in 1931 by another request, for more cabins and for a twenty-one-year lease in order to secure financing. The proposed lease was denied in Ottawa, although one five-year term was granted by the Banff office of the Parks Branch. Despite the policy that forbade private gain in national parks, this "ski club" began to look more and more like a commercial operation. In 1932, it was subleased to another operator; by 1933, there were forty paying guests at a time, and by 1935 shares were bought and sold for the Ski Club of the Canadian Rockies (SCCR). Thus emerged a pattern that Rodney Touche has called the "wedge": "In this five-year period were all the elements by which development typically took place in the Parks. The tiny cabin, the need to expand it to meet demand, the irregular transfer of ownership, the extension of use beyond the original intention, and a political end run to get Park funds used to help the commercial operation. All these themes were to continue recurring on an ever-enlarging scale."[26]

By 1946, the Parks Branch director, with the approval of the minister, assured the SCCR that the club would have "prior right to the construction of any ski-lifts in the area" and "whatever cooperation [the Parks Branch could] give to carry out a more substantial development."[27] In 1952, a simple ski tow was installed, but by then skiers were avoiding Lake Louise in favour of hills that had lifts. Therefore, after some delay, Lake Louise opened its first gondola lift in 1959, and in 1960 Lake Louise Lifts Ltd., a subsidiary of the SCCR, was formed.

The next stream of decisions leading to Village Lake Louise was the result of the Parks Branch's efforts to modernize visitor services generally in national parks. During the 1950s, while the 1964 *National Parks Policy* remained unofficial, the branch was planning to establish visitor service centres (VSCs), which would contain privately operated commercial services, in an attempt to strike a balance between the evident need to provide for the influx of tourists and the desire to control the spread of commercial developments. Although VSCs were part of the 1964 *National Parks Policy*, the branch had earlier identified Lake Louise for the first of these facilities and in 1961 presented a plan for such a centre to the Lake Louise Chamber of Commerce.[28] However, the plan remained unrealized throughout the decade, and, despite considerable promotional effort by the branch, relatively little accommodation was built. Thus, by the late 1960s, the facilities were unable to provide even basic services to the flow of tourist traffic.

As a result of limited response from private investors, the Parks Branch distributed in 1968 a detailed plan, the *Proposal for Development in Visitor Service Centre, Lake Louise*. Once again response was limited, but this time Lake Louise Lifts was able to join forces with Imperial Oil to form Village Lake Louise Ltd., a consortium with the specific purpose of responding to the Parks Branch proposal for the development of visitor facilities at Lake Louise.

The final stream leading to the Village Lake Louise proposal was the release of the Winter Recreation Policy in March 1965.[29] This document expressed the Parks Branch's desire to extend the use of national parks into the winter season, a period in which use had traditionally been low, and specified the terms of that expansion. The Winter Recreation Policy paralleled the 1964 *National Parks Policy* and was consistent with the "management tool" concept in recognizing the reality of skiing in national parks while endeavouring to define and control the location and extent of such developments. In brief, the policy stated that park managers should encourage the winter use of parks, including the development of a small number of well-designed ski areas. In addition, overnight accommodation and evening entertainment facilities consistent with holiday ski resorts would be permitted.[30] The number of sites was to be limited, however, and the definition of boundaries by the branch would also protect the prime environmental values of the parks.

Thus, the prior existence of commercial ski operations at Lake Louise, the government's failure to have developed a suitable visitor service centre there, and the Winter Recreation Policy all came together in the late 1960s and early 1970s. The new development company, Village Lake Louise Ltd., formed in January 1970, in March of that year signed a memorandum or letter of "intention" with the Parks Branch aimed at building "a year round centre encompassing a full range of visitors' services in an aesthetic mountain village atmosphere, including accommodation for 3000 visitors."[31] Over the next eighteen months, the company, working in close co-operation with the Parks Branch, planned a complex of hotels, restaurants, and other services; there was no involvement by the general public at this stage.

The first opportunity for the public to inquire about or comment upon the Village Lake Louise proposal was the public participation program for the Four Mountain Parks management plan, held in Calgary in April 1971. The public, particularly the National and Provincial Parks Association of Canada, which had already become aware of the planned Village Lake Louise and had already encouraged the branch to hold separate public hearings on it, made repeated calls for such hearings at the Four Mountain Parks planning meeting. These activists were increasingly mistrustful of Parks Branch officials because more information on the Lake Louise plan was not publicly available.[32] At several points throughout the April meeting, the assistant deputy minister (ADM) responsible for the Parks Branch responded by promising to hold public hearings in which the plans for Village Lake Louise would be "open to the full force of public debate, public dialogue, before decisions [were] taken."[33] According to Rodney Touche, this promise was a change in direction for the branch since the company had never been told that such public hearings were even a possibility. This change was in recognition of what the ADM saw as the "spectacular force" with which the public interest in the environment had grown in recent years.[34]

The promised special public hearings on Village Lake Louise were duly held in Calgary in March 1972, and prior to them both the company and environmental interests, especially NPPAC, diligently publicized their positions, which by this time were sharply drawn. The controversy raged over several months and featured strong participation on both sides, with the company distributing brochures to skiers urging them to write letters and support the proposal, while environmentalists and park supporters, for their part, submitted hundreds of letters and briefs to the public hearings. When the hearings were finally held, there was pandemonium: the proceedings were "intense ... punctuated with occasional booing, catcalling and one fist fight."[35]

Just over three months later, in July 1972, Jean Chrétien, the minister responsible for national parks, announced that the applications for the project had been rejected. The official reason was that the project was "too large,"[36] but Chrétien openly acknowledged that the reason he had cancelled the project was that the Alberta government was opposed to it.

Prior to making its decision, the federal government had in fact sought the views of the Alberta government. That province had long been dissatisfied with federal control of national parks in Alberta and was generally and historically in favour of more development within them. However, it was opposed to the specific proposal for Village Lake Louise, and, in exchange for support for the proposal, it may have tried to win more provincial control over national parks policy in the Rocky Mountains by suggesting that such support might be forthcoming if the federal government made certain concessions to Alberta.[37] However, the federal government was not willing to make the requested allowances and therefore had to decide about Village Lake Louise on its own. Since this was an election year for the federal Liberals, and the early signs were that the government had lost a substantial level of support among the public, it seems likely that Chrétien was not willing to take sole responsibility for approving Village Lake Louise in the face of strong opposition and lack of support from the Alberta government.

The direct effect of the public on Chrétien's decision is therefore not clear. Stephen Herrero has pointed out that the role the public and public hearings specifically had in the decision to cancel Village Lake Louise has never been revealed.[38] Rodney Touche, however, in examining federal documents released to the courts, has concluded that it was adverse publicity that convinced Chrétien to reject the project.[39] The situation was an acute embarrassment for the Parks Branch because it revealed a close working relationship with corporate development interests that was no longer acceptable to the wider public. It also caused problems in the relationship with corporate interests as they felt that the government had gone back on its word after its concerted attempt to attract private investors. Ultimately, Village Lake Louise Ltd. sued the federal government to recover the costs of developing its proposals.

Kouchibouguac National Park[40]

While Village Lake Louise was being planned and public sentiment was moving toward the confrontation of March 1972, on the other side of the country, in New Brunswick, another eruption of public feeling over a national park was brewing. This time, however, the issue was the initial establishment of Kouchibouguac National Park rather than development within an existing park. The conflict at Kouchibouguac was not about environmental matters but over the nature of state-society relations in the creation of a national park. The experience of this conflict dramatically changed the way in which the Parks Branch went about establishing national parks from that point on. The conflicts, or at least the level of energy in them, explicitly derived from the dramatic examples of citizen involvement in the civil rights and anti-war movements in the United States that had changed the public attitude toward what were seen as arbitrary government decisions. Despite broad social changes in New Brunswick, the organization of protest and the articulation of demands were greatly facilitated by a single organization, CRASE (Conseil régional d'aménagement du Sud-est), which was essentially created by one government and funded by another. While the manner in which Kouchibouguac Park was created almost certainly would have caused social, administrative, and probably political problems, the presence of CRASE clearly exacerbated and prolonged these issues. In doing so, it emphasized the need for planned public participation well in advance of park establishment, a process that the Parks Branch has followed ever since, including the development of national parks within the framework of Aboriginal land claims treaties in northern Canada, as discussed in the next chapter.

The idea of some kind of park at Kouchibouguac was initiated by the Province of New Brunswick in 1964-65. In 1969, after several years of discussion, the federal and New Brunswick governments agreed to establish a national park in Kent County on the northeast coast of the province. At that time, national parks agreements were essentially based on an exchange of value between the two levels of government. On the provincial side of the bargain, it was expected that the park would bring certain economic benefits to the region since there would be an injection of federal funds to develop the park as a tourist destination. For the federal government, Kouchibouguac satisfied the criteria of establishing parks to reflect outstanding natural features of the Canadian landscape, an idea that later became part of the System Plan.

The new park was part of the New Brunswick government's broader strategy of economic and tourism development, and the area planned for the park was one of the poorest in the province, indeed one of the poorest in Canada. In the early 1960s, 81 percent of families resident in the area designated for the park had annual incomes of less than $3,000 compared with 24 percent of Canadian families who had incomes below that figure. Even though New Brunswick was, in general, one of the lower-income areas of Canada, only 39 percent of New Brunswick residents fell below that income level. Most of the people in the designated park area lived on sporadic cash incomes supplemented by subsistence activities. In addition, since the area was not well provided with commercial or public services, the population tended to be relatively isolated both geographically and socially. At the same time, tourism, already expanding in nearby Prince Edward Island and other coastal areas of New Brunswick, seemed to be an obvious source of potential economic growth. However, aspects of the process for creating a park ran into fierce opposition from some local people. In fact, the model for public participation for Kouchibouguac does not, at first, conform to either the Arnstein or the Eidsvik (CCREM) level of "consultation" but was initially one of "informing" (level three), near the bottom of Arnstein's ladder (or the least-participation category of Eidsvik's list). Later, outside either of these frameworks, the relevant model is one of (often violent) protest.

Within national parks policy at the time, it was the provincial government's responsibility to acquire legal title to all the lands to be included in the proposed park and then to transfer them, unencumbered, to the federal government. In keeping with this approach, in 1968 New Brunswick began to assemble the land using the provincial Expropriation Act, which was straightforward and brutal in its simplicity. It enabled an order-in-council to simply declare the land in government title and then merely stipulated the registration of that fact in the provincial land office. No legal notice needed to be given to the previous property owner, and at Kouchibouguac none was (although other means were employed to inform them). The expropriations were carried out in two stages in July 1969 and September 1970.

The first stage of the expropriations went smoothly, perhaps because it was the first but also because the people affected were somewhat better off than those who followed, and the financial settlements they received were, correspondingly, more favourable. However, problems emerged with the second stage. Even between these two stages, numerous difficulties arose, some directly as a result of the way in which the expropriations were handled. Partly, these difficulties were the result of there having been no informed consent, which led to confusion, resentment, and eventual anger at the park and the public authorities in both governments involved. In addition, there were background conditions that complicated the issues. One was that a large proportion of the population affected by the expropriation were French-speaking Acadians who were experiencing a cultural renaissance parallel to and simultaneous with that occurring in Québec. For some, especially the unwilling "expropriates,"[41] the idea of being expelled from their land struck a deep historic resonance with the Acadian deportations in the 1750s. This removal was exacerbated by what Gerald V. La Forest and Muriel Kent Roy call "changing attitudes toward the state and its projects," observing that "in the 1960s society began reassessing the relationship of the citizen with those exercising authority and the bureaucratic entities that supported them."[42] Despite these and more detailed concerns, the response was not a spontaneous generation of public protest. That was to come only with the involvement of an extant organization, indeed one created as the result of federal legislation, borrowed ideas, and provincial government funding.

As the second stage got under way, rumours circulated that the amounts of compensation were less for the second group of evacuees than what the first wave had received. Equally troubling was the fact that, even if compensation realistically reflected the assessed value of the properties (and it did not in all cases), the actual amounts were still rather low, and the expropriates found that what they received would not enable them to re-establish themselves. In addition, they faced significant lifestyle changes and problems getting employment.

The inchoate grievances that arose from these concerns found expression after the expropriations in the early months of 1971 through the efforts of CRASE. This organization had been established under the framework of the Agricultural Rehabilitation and Development Act (ARDA), the federal legislation aimed at providing financial support to help people organize so that they could seek alternatives to the low-income agriculture that characterized some parts of rural Canada. ARDA was, in some senses, experimental in its search for solutions to rural poverty. One of many concepts within the ARDA universe, one that came largely from a Québec government initiative in the Gaspé region of that province, was the idea of "social animation." In an attempt to measure and understand rural poverty, a large project of *animation sociale* was being tested in the late 1960s in the belief that community organization and articulation of needs would lead to social and economic change.[43] CRASE was modelled on similar principles and had existed for some time prior to the conflict at Kouchibouguac. It was generally opposed to the park but as yet had no role in the process.

Faced with the evident social problems following the second phase of expropriations, the Interdepartmental Committee (of the New Brunswick government) approached the issue on two fronts. One was to revisit the process (including the determination of land values, resettlement of the population, compensation for lost income, and aid in the search for new employment), and the other was to provide funds to CRASE to assist the expropriates in organizing and articulating their concerns. From early 1971 until 1980, when funding was terminated, CRASE was an active and forceful (some have even suggested manipulative) exponent of the views of the former residents of the park.

Even though the province responded fairly quickly to local concerns, protests were carried on during the period between 1971 and 1974 under the influence of CRASE. As La Forest and Roy have expressed it, "much of the [provincial government's] response came in the face of protest. In this way, the expropriates, or at least some of them, learned the dangerous game of voicing dissatisfaction through organized protest, often with overtones of violence."[44]

It is impossible (and probably inappropriate to try) to separate what was protest against the province's actions from protest directed at the federal government. However, while the province was addressing concerns about relocation and compensation for land, the Parks Branch was negotiating fishing access, and compensation for loss of that access, in the waters of the park for the same people. At first, negotiations went smoothly, but in the middle of 1971, under the guidance of CRASE, the fishers began to express grievances about proposed fishery closures. CRASE and the commercial fishers presented their case to Ottawa in local meetings, in writing, and by travelling to the national capital to meet with the minister, Jean Chrétien. The New Brunswick government also intervened with Ottawa on behalf of the fishers. The Parks Branch responded by postponing closure of the fishery for a short time but was not willing to make further adjustments. This situation remained unsatisfactory to the fishers, and on 23 May 1972 they occupied the Kouchibouguac National Park administrative offices in protest. Other events of protest, barricading of roads, and (suspected) arson occurred until, by the summer of 1974, the situation had cooled and remained that way until 1979. In January of that year, Kouchibouguac was proclaimed a national park, and the National Park Fishing Regulations came into force. After warning the fishers, the Parks Branch seized some nets, which resulted in another occupation of parks offices. Subsequently, an order-in-council issued by the federal government restored the opportunity for those who had traditionally fished in these waters.

Aboriginal People and National Park Reserves
While local people who remain committed to a particular way of life may eventually be persuaded through coaxing and/or financial compensation to accommodate national parks, Aboriginal people have a deeper, indeed a constitutional, claim to the land. This status presented a new category of challenges as the Parks Branch began to consider establishing parks in northen Canada, where treaties with Aboriginal people had not yet been signed. In 1968, with the accession to office of the Trudeau Liberals, Jean Chrétien was appointed minister of Indian affairs and northern development and was thus responsible for both Aboriginal issues and national parks. Over the next six years, Chrétien contributed to the creation of ten new national parks. This was a dramatic change, considering that only four such parks had been established in the preceding forty years. Under rules laid down by the National Parks Act, new parks had to be individually proclaimed and their boundaries defined in a schedule appended to the legislation. The legal creation of the new parks that Chrétien had facilitated therefore required specific legislative action for their establishment.

To achieve this goal, in 1974 Parliament passed An Act to Amend the National Parks Act, a relatively simple piece of legislation to legally establish several of the national parks whose creation was presided over by Chrétien and to define their boundaries. However, the act was not intended to introduce new policy ideas. Nevertheless, through the intervention of Aboriginal people, a single but important change was made to the legislation and would affect the future national parks in more than half the natural regions yet to be developed under the System Plan. This change occurred because the act introduced a provision for the creation of "national park reserves," as legally distinct from national parks, so as not to prejudice Aboriginal land claims. While this provision had only modest practical effect at the time, it meant that Aboriginal people eventually became integral, perhaps even equal, partners in the process of developing the Canadian national park system.

These changes in 1974 followed two significant institutional changes in the 1950s and 1960s that made possible the kind of Aboriginal participation seen in 1974. First, beginning with changes to the Indian Act in 1951 and with the extension of the franchise to Inuit in 1950 and Indians living on reserves in 1960, there was a partial political emancipation, at least in terms of conventional political activity,[45] of Aboriginal people that enabled them to become engaged in land claims activity and thus affect the process of national park establishment in lands north of the sixtieth parallel and in British Columbia. Second, through the general activation of parliamentary committees and their greater institutionalization first under Prime Minister Diefenbaker and later, and more significantly, under Prime Minister Trudeau, Canadians had more access to their members of Parliament. Committees, therefore, became an important means to bring ideas and political pressure to bear on parliamentary deliberations.[46]

The nature of public participation for Aboriginal people nevertheless differs from the cases previously discussed in two important ways. First, Aboriginal people constitute a special public as a result of their cultural distinctiveness from the Canadian mainstream, their unique historical position in Canadian development and politics, and their separate legal status in the various relevant documents and conventions of the Canadian Constitution and particularly in the Indian Act. Second, the forum for public participation, which in this case involved only Aboriginal leaders, was Parliament itself, instead of a general forum arranged by appointed officials. It was before the Standing Committee on Indian Affairs and Northern Development, whose mandate covered both Aboriginal issues and national parks, that Aboriginal leaders were able to publicly make their arguments for special consideration when the bill to amend the National Parks Act was introduced in the House of Commons in late 1973.

Ideas and Aboriginal People

The ideas informing the modern legal status of Aboriginal land originate as early as the middle of the eighteenth century. Over much of the preceding century, the Iroquois had used diplomatic and military strategy to try to keep the French and English settlements out of their lands in the upper St. Lawrence valley and the area south and east of Lake Ontario. This approach was reasonably successful until 1753, when English settlement further encroached on Iroquois lands. To maintain peaceful relations, Britain and the Iroquois held a conference in 1754, and Britain adopted a policy aimed at protecting Indian lands. This policy was elaborated to become (part of) the Royal Proclamation of 1763 after victory in the Seven Years War left Britain the sole power in northeastern North America. The proclamation stipulated that all Indian lands west of the crest of the Appalachian Mountains could be sold only to the Crown, and, although the effect of the proclamation was short-lived in the United States, it continued to have a legal effect in Canada to the present.

In the United States, the proclamation's regulatory protection was carried on in the Supreme Court judgments of Chief Justice John Marshall, who accepted the political legitimacy of Aboriginal communities while acknowledging that their sovereignty was "necessarily diminished."[47] Writing in the 1830s in *Cherokee Nation v. Georgia,* Marshall argued that "Indian nations had always been considered as distinct independent political communities, retaining their original rights, as the undisputed possessors of the soil, from time immemorial."[48] In this and other judgments, Marshall established a theory of Indian sovereignty and Aboriginal title that continues to influence both American and Canadian jurisprudence.[49]

Despite the proclamation and the deliberations of John Marshall, Euro-North Americans, both in Canada and the United States, frequently ignored or minimized the declared rights of Aboriginal people. Public policy in Canada sought to suppress Aboriginal culture and, in 1927, through an amendment to the Indian Act expressly forbade Indian political action related to land claims.[50] Nevertheless, Aboriginal people quietly persisted, and after World War II both the public mood and public policies began slowly to acknowledge and respect Aboriginal claims.

Dramatic changes in the historic European-Indian relationship in Canada began with a 1959 joint Senate-Commons committee that made recommendations that, though modest, raised public interest in Aboriginal issues particularly among the press. Moreover, Aboriginal people themselves were working to change their own circumstances. Through the 1960s, the Indian-Eskimo Association organized a series of conferences and other political activities directed at government, including sponsoring the first academic study of Aboriginal rights in Canada.[51] In 1963, the Department of Indian Affairs initiated a survey of the current situation of Indians, and this study, the so-called Hawthorn Report,[52] became the foundation for further policy deliberations in the government and among academics. These efforts were only a small beginning, however, compared to the energy that erupted as a result of the Trudeau government's attempt to address Indian policy.

On 25 June 1969, that government issued its white paper[53] on Indian policy, in which it proposed to end the special position of Indians in Canadian law, a position that Alan Cairns (in the Hawthorn Report) has called "citizens plus."[54] The proposed policy would have seen the virtual elimination of the concept of "Indian" as a legal category within Canada. Indian status would have disappeared, along with the federal government's historic responsibility for Aboriginal people, thus making Indians ordinary citizens who would receive the same services from the federal and provincial governments as all other citizens. Existing Indian lands would have become privately held,[55] and presumably there would be no further claims to lands not covered by treaties.

The white paper proposals were a surprise to Indian leaders and created a firestorm of protest. Through the latter months of 1969 and the first half of 1970, Jean Chrétien, as minister of Indian affairs, and Prime Minister Trudeau repeatedly tried to persuade Aboriginal people and their supporters to accept the ideas in the white paper. By early 1970, the government's efforts to promote the policy had clearly failed, and in June of that year, in a meeting with the National Indian Brotherhood, Pierre Trudeau intimated that his government would not pursue the proposed policy. In March 1971, Chrétien stated formally that the government would not proceed with the terms of the white paper.[56] Notwithstanding its withdrawal, the white paper did have the lasting effect of politicizing Aboriginal people, who were now ready to pursue their claims as never before.

While the events surrounding the white paper and its withdrawal were playing themselves out in the political realm, a parallel process was unfolding in the judicial arena. Here, too, Aboriginal people pressed their claims for land and indigenous title. In 1969, the Nisga'a Tribal Council, in northwestern British Columbia, sought the court's recognition that the Nisga'a still held title to the land of the Nass River valley, despite the Province of British Columbia's insistence that such title, if it had ever existed, had been extinguished. After the BC courts held for the province, the case went to the Supreme Court of Canada, which, ruling in 1973, also failed to support the Nisga'a case. However, the reasons given in the decision had the effect of supporting the existence of Aboriginal title and consequently changed the progress of Indian land claims discussions for all of Canada.[57]

National Park Reserves: An Amendment to the National Parks Act
Despite this newly charged political and legal atmosphere for Aboriginal issues, the task of legally establishing and defining new national parks was seen as a relatively simple one. Thus, Bill S-4, for this purpose, was introduced and passed in the Senate[58] with brief discussion, and no significant changes, in the early months of 1973. The bill then went on in December 1973 to the House of Commons and to the Standing Committee on Indian Affairs and Northern Development, where it received more detailed discussion.

In this committee, particularly from some of the witnesses who appeared before it, Bill S-4 ran into stiff opposition. One of the objectives of this legislation was to allow the government to set aside land in Yukon and the Northwest Territories for the establishment of three new parks. While travelling to Whitehorse prior to formal deliberation of the bill, the committee heard the concerns of local Aboriginal people about one of the parks and how it affected their lives and their future land claims. Representatives of several individual bands spoke about the loss of livelihood caused by the creation of the Kluane Game Sanctuary (the precursor to the national park in question). These concerns related to the lack of employment opportunities for Aboriginal people in protected lands and unfulfilled promises from government over the years. Chief Ray Jackson of the Champagne-Aishihik Band, in a highly prescient proposal, suggested that consideration be given to the granting of full control of the maintenance and administration of Kluane National Park to local Aboriginal people. He also spoke eloquently about the loss of self-respect and the incremental loss of land that Yukon Aboriginal nations had experienced. Chief Elijah Smith was more specific about land claims, saying that "our land claim negotiations with the federal government are not finished"[59] and that, with a reference to the Nisga'a Tribal Council's land claim case, as a last resort Yukon indigenous people would also go to court.[60] The presentations made by these Aboriginal leaders reinforced opinions that had already been mooted by some members of the standing committee.

These ideas were strengthened when the committee met again in Ottawa and heard a presentation from the Inuit Tapirisat of Canada (ITC), with law professor Peter Cumming[61] as their spokesperson. Cumming argued that the proposed legislation would serve to expropriate Inuit lands but without following the proper expropriation process. If the government recognized Aboriginal title, Cumming argued, then it should purchase or expropriate the land as required by the National Parks Act, and if there was uncertainty about title then Parliament could pass appropriate legislation to clarify the legal position of the government's actions. On the other hand, if the government did not recognize Aboriginal title, Cumming suggested, then it should be willing to have the matter taken to court.

Against the backdrop of the reasoning of the Supreme Court justices with respect to the Nisga'a land claim, the withdrawal of the 1969 white paper, and the growing public sentiment in favour of fairer treatment of Aboriginal people, these presentations before the standing committee constituted considerable pressure for a change in the wording of the proposed legislation. The committee debated the issue at length, and in the end the wording of the bill was changed: "to set aside for a national park" became "to set aside as a reserve for a National Park of Canada, pending a settlement in respect of any right, title, or interest of people of native origin therein."[62] In effect, therefore, the act established a new form of national park, the national park reserve. This change affected the progress of park establishment not only for Kluane National Park in Yukon and Auyuittuq on Baffin Island (the latter a concern to the Inuit) but also for all the other parks on lands for which treaties had not been signed, including those in British Columbia, Québec, and Labrador. Of more importance, it meant that Aboriginal people now became central players in discussions about the nature and character of those parks, since national parks had become an integral part of land claims negotiations.

The 1979 National Parks Policy Statement

As has been shown, the early years of the 1970s were a very active and sometimes turbulent period for the Parks Branch. Many new parks had been added to the system, creating new demands on the branch. The system itself had been redefined so that the activity of developing national parks had changed. Perhaps most critical, however, policy and management processes had changed with the introduction of active public participation, which at Village Lake Louise and Kouchibouguac had been highly confrontational. In other places, for several new parks, including some south of the sixtieth parallel, Aboriginal people as a special public were now deeply involved. Finally, although public participation in management plans announced in 1968 progressed without serious objection in most cases, this process also placed heavy demands on both Parks Branch and public participants and had to be re-evaluated within a few years of its implementation. These experiences demonstrated that the existing policy framework was not adequate for the branch to carry out its mandate and that the rewriting of it was necessary. It was evident that new approaches needed to be taken to bring the public into a discussion of national parks issues.

Accordingly, a new policy, which was both a more specific and a more elaborate statement than its predecessor in 1964,[63] was completed and received cabinet approval in March 1979. It reiterated the state's commitment "to protect for all time representative natural areas of Canadian significance in a system of national parks and to encourage public understanding, appreciation and enjoyment of this natural heritage so as to leave it unimpaired for future generations."[64] The document also set out policy for establishing new parks and included a commitment that "Parks Canada in conjunction with the provincial or territorial government will consult with local communities and the interested public prior to the establishment of a new national park."[65] In addition, it reaffirmed that "where national parks are established in conjunction with the settlement of land claims of native people an agreement will be negotiated between Parks Canada and representatives of local native communities prior to formal establishment of the national park."[66] Finally, the policy statement committed the Parks Branch to have public involvement in the management-planning process for each park from the earliest stages.

Ideas and the Policy Statement

Awareness of the weakness of the 1964 policy statement surfaced as early as December 1966, when the Standing Committee on Northern Affairs and National Resources held meetings in Banff and Jasper National Parks. Subsequent to those meetings, and in response to the public interventions at them, the Parks Branch prepared a "Statement on the National Parks of Canada" for the committee. Most of the discussion centred on the townsites of Banff and Jasper and the legal status of those communities,[67] which, along with other comments, indicated a general uneasiness with the 1964 policy statement.[68] This was, of course, a beginning to the pressure for policy renewal that would come later with the tumultuous events of the early 1970s.

The ideas that went into the 1979 policy had been present throughout the 1960s and 1970s. The environmental ideas incorporated into the document were restatements of the ideas in the 1964 policy, while the System Plan, which was already published, was simply incorporated in the 1979 policy document. Ideas about public participation, as they had been refined during the 1970s, were also included in the policy. In effect, therefore, the 1979 policy collected, recognized, and formalized the ideas of the preceding decade.

Development of the 1979 Policy

Following discussions in the standing committee in 1966-67, there were several attempts to reconsider the national parks policy, including a proposal in 1972 to take the matter to public hearings. However, the minister did not support this idea, and it was therefore not until 1975 that a major initiative was undertaken to revise the policy. Early in that year, the responsible assistant deputy minister directed the Parks Branch to begin drafting a revision, but unlike development of the 1964 policy statement this new policy quickly included external views, first those of the provincial and territorial parks officials and later those of the interested public.

The first step in this revision process consisted of discussions within the Parks Branch, although it also took provincial views into account at the early stages by considering, in a paper by the chief of the Planning Section, the perceptions of the senior administrators of provincial and territorial parks. After the internal deliberations, provincial and territorial officials were formally involved when copies of the draft policy were distributed to them. More or less simultaneously, Parks Branch officials held a seminar with a selected group of non-government parks experts. This seminar was followed by more internal discussions, including those with regional officials of the branch.

Not until late 1977, however, when the process was nearly three years old and had been through several consultations, was a copy of the draft sent to the minister (J. Hugh Faulkner), who had held this portfolio for less than three months. After receipt of his comments in the spring of 1978, a new draft was sent to federal departments, provincial and territorial parks officials, and approximately 300 societal groups and individuals across Canada. In October 1978, a conference[69] sponsored by the University of Waterloo, the National and Provincial Parks Association, and the Parks Branch was held in Banff. There were strong calls for more public involvement and, in particular, for public hearings with respect to the policy process (as distinct from the management process), a measure for which the Parks Branch had previously made no formal provision.[70] In response to this suggestion, the branch quickly organized a series of cross-country workshops before the December 31 deadline for comments. The final preparation of the policy document took place in December and early January within the branch itself and incorporated these comments. One of the requests made during the workshops was that the branch make public its reasoning for accepting and rejecting specific ideas by publishing a summary of the comments and the changes that they prompted. The resulting document, *The Response to Public Comments on the Parks Canada Policy,* reveals some of the influences that the public process had on the overall policy.[71] Included in it is a list of the participants that shows the views of those organizations that occupy the opposite ends of the preservation-development spectrum and that there was a preponderance of groups from the preservationist end. The document also states that it was toward these views that the policy was ultimately directed. It notes that "there was a general concern that protection was downplayed in the objective statement for the program and for certain of its activities."[72] In redrafting, the branch made it clear that environmental protection within the parks was its primary objective. Other changes support this theme, such as the addition of a program for environmental review. In addition, in response to public concern, the commitment to public participation was affirmed and expanded.

Despite the tendency to emphasize protection,[73] the official drafters of the policy continued to strike the balance between use and protection initiated in the National Parks Act (1930). For example, there were numerous suggestions to include the word *preserve* in the clauses and sections of the policy statement in order to strengthen the environmental preservation approach toward the parks, but these suggestions were rejected as too restrictive for a national park that would, according to the policy, include various built services and recreational facilities. On the other hand, suggestions for increased private-sector development were accepted only when subject to the limitations of the environmental protection concepts of the policy.

The final session of the cross-country workshops was held at the end of November 1978. As this was nearing the end of the third Trudeau mandate, the Parks Branch scribes worked feverishly to complete the draft policy in preparation for cabinet approval in March 1979, just as the government's attention was turning to the election that it was to lose to the Progressive Conservatives led by Joe Clark just over two months later. Although the outgoing Liberal government had given official approval to the policy, the new Conservative minister, John Fraser, also gave it his sanction in September 1979.[74]

As can be seen, the process for developing the 1979 policy was dramatically different from that of its 1964 predecessor. Notably, it involved external participants from the beginning, first through discussion with provincial counterparts and then with parks and wilderness experts outside government. Once again, however, the minister was involved only in formalizing policy. Chrétien's reluctance to hold hearings on the policy issues did not prevail (though Chrétien was not in the portfolio by then) in the face of the willingness of the appointed officials to include the public and in the face of citizen pressure for such a role. It should be emphasized that the Banff conference itself and the following round of regional workshops powerfully reinforced the public's role in defining the content and process of the new national parks policy.

Conclusion

The second period of parks policy development in the postwar era was dominated by the public or at least by various segments of the public. During this time, the significant development for national parks was not so much a strengthening of environmental protection as a change in the social meaning of national parks in such a way that parks were no longer solely instruments of government policy, whether for economic development or environmental protection. Changing the social meaning resulted in altering both the public's and the government's attitude toward the "ownership" of parks so that it became difficult, indeed almost impossible, for parks officials to make effective decisions without the approval of some element of the public. This transformation was in the spirit of the democratic ideas about parks expressed by American thinkers in the nineteenth century. By the 1970s, however, rather than elites or the state granting democratic opportunities, the people had seized them. Thus, parks became more than places of recreation; in addition, they became expressions, both locally and nationally, of the people's relationship to the land. By the end of the decade, this meaning was accepted by both state and societal actors despite the conflicts between the two throughout the 1970s. Both interest groups and institutions are key ingredients to understanding how this shift in meaning took place, but the most convincing explanation for this transformation derives from ideas that set the context in which popular demands were met.

In terms of environmental protection, there was modest strengthening and entrenching of provisions in the policy, but this was achieved mainly by limiting, through an official commitment to public participation in the 1979 policy statement, the potential for unilateral executive decisions. (It is ironic, however, that some public involvement, especially with respect to Kouchibouguac National Park, was to resist protective measures.)

There were two sets of ideas, those that were relatively enduring and those that were more short-lived, that influenced policy development in the 1970s. The first set included well-established ideas about environmental protection and Aboriginal rights. There were also policy ideas specific to parks that, by this time, were deeply embedded in the national parks system and resulted from the National Parks Act (1930), the 1964 *National Parks Policy*, and prevailing practices. In other words, the basic framework of policy did not change significantly in this period, and the 1979 policy statement adhered closely to previously expressed ideas except that some were elaborated. The most important additions were provisions for public participation and recognition of Aboriginal interests.

Ideas about public participation, about who should be involved in decision making and how that involvement should take place, comprise the second, more transitory, set. Although these ideas were included in the formal policy and continue to be recognized today, the open, flexible, and responsive pattern of bureaucratic accommodation of public participation in the 1970s has since become limited to a more formalized, structured, and planned approach to including the public. The highly public pattern of participation experienced in this decade had virtually disappeared by the 1980s as government sought to reassert control over such processes. Despite a strong public voice and the readiness of the Parks Branch to adopt public participation, it was not entirely willing to include the public in all its decision-making processes. Even as the 1979 policy statement was being developed, it took renewed pressure to make the branch incorporate public views.

Public participation, in general, continues to be recognized by the federal government both in formal policy and in practice. For example, the Canadian Environmental Assessment Act (1992) (CEAA) makes provision for it in two places, although critics argue that the vagueness of and the loopholes in the rules make the act unreliable as a guarantor of public participation in environmental review proceedings. The ministerial and bureaucratic discretion that is retained by this act, and which the critics lament, appears to be the result of a view that public participation is seen as a prerogative of the state, not the public. In 1988, when the Federal Environmental Assessment Review Office (FEARO) articulated what appeared to be official policy toward public participation, it declared that "a public hearing is not a privilege granted to the public, but in fact a service requested of the public by the government to help it make an informed decision."[75] The perspectives contained in the CEAA and expressed by FEARO reflect the reality that public-initiated participation had declined. Citizen activity did not go away, but it did become more organized, more bureaucratic, and less "participatory" than in the 1970s.

This framework of two sets of ideas with the contributing influences of interest groups and institutions provides an explanation for the events relating to Village Lake Louise and Kouchibouguac and an explanation of the change in meaning and the adoption of public participation in official policy. In much the same way in which most participants in the 1950s and 1960s thought that it was right and proper for bureaucrats to take the policy initiative, in the 1970s this view had lost currency, and it was widely thought that it was right and proper for the public to determine, or to participate in the determination of, the content and application of policy. For both government officials, who solicited it, and the public, who demanded it, public participation was seen as a political good. To satisfy this demand, a wide variety of forums was established, from commissions of inquiry to town hall meetings, in attempts to capture the essence of the public's will.

For Village Lake Louise and Kouchibouguac National Park, for example, public participation as a public good resulted from a series of small events arising out of intergovernmental competition. At the time, the public, with respect to both provincial and national parks, was demanding participation in decision making through organized interest groups. While the federal government provided forums for discussion concerning national parks, there was considerable uncertainty among government officials, and lack of definition in general, about what was to be achieved in these forums. The background ideas about parks, however, were essentially unchanged.

Ironically, organized groups were relatively weak in this period. The NPPAC, so active with respect to Village Lake Louise, was in a financially tenuous position throughout the decade and nearly folded toward the end of the 1970s because there simply was not enough money or, in other words, broad public support for it to carry on its activities.[76] Similarly, CRASE was a government-created and -funded organization that turned out to be short-lived when government money was withdrawn.

Since the government was unclear about what it wanted, and groups were weak, ideas about public participation remain the effective explanation for the part that the Village Lake Louise and Kouchibouguac controversies played in changing the meaning of parks.

Parallel to more populist ideas about citizen participation, Aboriginal involvement in parks decisions resulted from a new, or renewed, set of ideas about these people's right to be consulted on the uses of land to which they had a claim. In this instance, participation in parks issues may have been new, but it was based on much older ideas about Aboriginal rights. These ideas were in fact institutionalized in the Royal Proclamation of 1763, in the British North America Act (section 91[24]), in pre-Confederation treaties signed by colonial governments, in numbered treaties signed by the

Canadian federal government after 1867, and through recent judicial decisions, all of which recognized Aboriginal rights and rendered them, in effect, constitutional in nature (until 1982, when they were constitutional in reality) in that governments could not unilaterally abrogate those rights. Unlike more populist views of public participation, these institutionalized ideas gave Aboriginal people a right of access to a forum in the courts and a differential claim to access to Parliament. Despite the presence of these ideas in constitutional documents and treaties, the practice of governments for nearly half a century was to ignore the claims made by Aboriginal people. Even in the late nineteenth and early twentieth centuries, they had been given only limited recognition in that treaties were signed with Indian tribes but were seldom fulfilled. Opportunity for Aboriginal involvement in national park discussions was therefore, for practical purposes, a new one, and the ideas behind it that contextualized discussion were also, essentially, new.

While Aboriginal organizations may have been in a stronger constitutional position than general public interest groups, even they were not populist groups. Some, such as the Inuit Tapirisat of Canada, were leadership driven and responded to national parks expansion with the help of outside expertise.

Drafting of the 1979 policy statement partially institutionalized ideas about public involvement by broadening the process and including a wider spectrum of participants since policy processes would now involve the federal cabinet, Aboriginal people, organized groups, and national parks officials. As with the preceding subjects, this result can be partly explained by understanding the interaction of institutions, interest groups, and ideas. Given that some of the ideas were themselves institutionalized, the relationship among these three is especially intricate. Unlike preceding policy documents, the 1979 statement was initiated by the bureaucracy but immediately involved select members of the public. Although this was seen in terms of providing appropriate advice to the minister (in this case publicly sensitive advice), it also opened a new relationship between the institutions of the state and the public.

The public's contribution to the draft policy statement did not stop with solicited advice, however. At later stages of the drafting process, members of the interested public, both well and loosely organized, became central in determining the final content of the document. This interaction between government institutions and environmental interest groups (along with extant ideas about national parks) in drafting the policy statement explains much of the direction of the 1979 paper. However, this interaction would not have taken place, or at least not in the way that it did, without these contextualizing ideas about the legitimacy and importance of public participation.

Thus, ideas about public participation provided the context in which background ideas, weakly organized interest groups, and state institutions interacted to change the meaning of national parks. It is public participation, as the contextualizing idea, that is the central explanation for each of the three principal policy developments of the period.

5
National Parks and the Initiatives of Organized Interests, 1984-93

By the 1980s, highly visible grassroots public participation had diminished and was replaced by a more professional and technocratic relationship between government and the public, now represented mostly by well-established interest groups. More important, however, it had moved beyond the beginnings represented by the consultative approaches of the 1970s to a stage where environmental interest groups were beginning to take independent initiative in influencing the national parks agenda. To put this another way, the relationship between state and society had advanced from a situation wherein state agencies sought the support of organized interests to one in which organized interests were able, on occasion, to seize and direct the national parks agenda. Moreover, because of these new forms of group involvement, the tension embodied in national parks policy between the concepts of use and preservation underwent a subtle but distinct shift toward enhanced preservation. All the implications of the events that caused this shift, such as new access to the courts and increased Aboriginal involvement, have not yet, in the early years of the twenty-first century, been fully realized.

The ability of organized environmental interests to influence the national parks agenda directly was a result of the increasing capabilities of these groups and the creation of opportunities for access by key decision makers within the institutions of government. In terms of sophistication, since the 1950s, environmental interest groups had become increasingly institutionalized, developing complex organizational skills, enhanced technical knowledge, broad networks of support with individuals and with potential coalition partners, and greater awareness of government processes. Fortuitously, access to the minister and his executive influence during the 1980s was facilitated briefly but critically by Tom McMillan, the minister himself, who in two important instances made his ministerial offices available to organized environmental interests, thereby giving them increased influence over the decisions that were made.

Since policy processes do not fit neatly into chronological packages, the period under analysis in this chapter does not really begin in 1980 (following the authorization of the 1979 national parks policy), nor does it end in 1989. Rather, the span of formative policy processes for this period is from 1984 to 1993, essentially paralleling the Mulroney years in government; the years 1979-84 were quiet ones for the Parks Branch (in that major issues were not salient). During this period, roughly the 1980s, four major events or developments concerning national parks arose, the unfolding of which both illustrated the altered nature of the policy context and effected important changes in the policy itself.

The first was the agreement for a national park reserve on South Moresby Island. While other national parks were established in this period, none shows as clearly the manner in which organized interests could, in favourable circumstances, circumvent the bureaucratic process. In particular, the South Moresby experience illustrates features that are important in the state-society relationship, even though they did not directly affect institutionalized policy structures.

By contrast, the second policy event, a set of major amendments to the National Parks Act, including adoption of an explicit environmental protection ethic, did change central policy structures. While the act was put on the agenda by the bureaucracy, the Canadian Parks and Wilderness Society used the legislative committee hearings, with the support of the minister, as a means to introduce its ideas into the proceedings.

The third major change was also contextual as the courts altered the rules governing public interest standing. This change allowed environmental groups new access to the judiciary and enabled them to use the courts to force the government to act within the limits of the law. Interest groups were thus able to operate outside the standard operating procedures of the Parks Branch and to discipline the branch with respect to the National Parks Act.

The fourth development of this period was establishment of new national parks, which, in sharp contrast to the past, included provisions for the formal involvement of Aboriginal people in parks management. In addition, and significantly, there was a change in parks policy permitting Aboriginal people to use renewable natural resources inside national parks.

The Campaign to Protect South Moresby

In 1987, after nearly a decade and a half of effort by environmentalists, the southern part of Moresby Island, one of the two principal islands of the Queen Charlotte group off the northern coast of British Columbia, was set aside as a national park reserve. The process by which this was accomplished diverged sharply from the previous bureaucratically managed process of park identification and establishment in that environmental interest groups were able to take the initiative and the power to choose the park site away from the Parks Branch.

The public nature of the South Moresby experience was not unique in the politics of parks and protected areas (at both federal and provincial levels) during the 1980s and 1990s. For example, in Nova Scotia, public opposition prevented a national park from being established at Ship Harbour, and in Saskatchewan local concerns had a strong influence on the timing and the boundaries of Grasslands National Park.[1] In a similar but more comprehensive initiative, the World Wildlife Fund (WWF) launched a campaign called Endangered Spaces in 1989, forming and leading a coalition of environmental groups that extended organizational and scientific assistance to some provinces, funded projects jointly with the federal government, and provided leadership by identifying possible park sites.[2]

While South Moresby was therefore only one of several instances in which public involvement significantly determined the outcomes of parks' decisions, it is one of the earlier cases and serves as a clear example of how organized environmental interests can initiate and define national and provincial parks policy decisions. The history of the creation of the South Moresby national park reserve therefore illustrates how the sophistication of organized groups can exert a continuing pressure on the Parks Branch and the minister to accommodate and incorporate group interests.

There were two distinct stages in the campaign to protect South Moresby. The first, from 1974 to 1984, focused attention on the BC government, particularly in relation to its forest management policies. At this stage, the BC government was essentially able to "contain" the initiative taken by environmental interests.[3] One of the effects of this containment, however, was that over this period the proponents for a protected South Moresby wilderness gained critically important experience in the techniques of policy advocacy and broadened their coalition to include influential partners across Canada and in the international community. By 1984, the campaign had moved beyond the borders of British Columbia and had become an issue of national interest. At this stage, the provincial government ceased to be able to contain the issue, and the federal government, including the prime minister, became directly involved. South Moresby then became a matter of summit federalism and attained a level of symbolic importance for Canadians. What is significant from a national parks policy perspective is that, throughout all thirteen years of the campaign, the Islands Protection Committee (IPC[4]) and other environmental interest groups drove the agenda. While these groups found many sympathetic and supportive partners within state structures, the key ideas and the initiatives remained those of the groups themselves.

Ideas and South Moresby Island

The campaign to protect South Moresby was an alliance between two different but compatible, even mutually reinforcing, streams of ideas and political action. First, Aboriginal land claims were the motivating force behind the involvement of the resident Aboriginal population, the Haida, who had maintained their claim over the entire archipelago of the Queen Charlotte Islands since the arrival of Europeans in the late eighteenth century.[5] The concepts of Aboriginal claims to the land reach back over two centuries, and these concepts provide the framework in which Haida expressions of land ownership are articulated. However, the politics of Aboriginal land claims in British Columbia are fraught with the lack of legal definition since, with the exception of two relatively small parts of the province, land there had not, until recently, been surrendered by Aboriginal people in treaties. On the other hand, the provincial government had consistently argued (in the past) that Aboriginal title was extinguished during the nineteenth century, a position that Aboriginal people have not accepted. In 1991, shortly after their election to office, a new New Democratic Party (NDP) government reversed this century-old claim and recognized Aboriginal title to the land. Among other things, this reversal has led to the signing of a treaty with the Nisga'a First Nation in northwestern British Columbia.

From 1924 to 1951, Aboriginal people were prohibited by law from legally or politically pursuing land claims, making their efforts since 1951 look like recent issues.[6] Moreover, until 1960, status Indians, including the Haida, did not have either federal or provincial franchise and were thus unable to pursue the usual routes of political appeal that individuals in a democratic society might take. It is also likely that until the 1950s the Haida lacked the capacity to take up the land issue since they were still recovering from a catastrophic collapse of their population a century earlier.[7] For the Haida (as for other Aboriginal people), assertion of ownership of their ancestral land, which they see as more than simply an economic resource, was an integral part of the re-establishment of cultural identity.[8] Indeed, the land and its characteristics, such as vegetation and wildlife, define the Haida. Protecting South Moresby from resource extraction, mainly logging, was therefore an important part of the process of Haida cultural renewal. Significantly, Haida land claim efforts were both contemporaneous and loosely integrated with province-wide activities among all Aboriginal people.[9] The pre-eminent event of the period was the neighbouring Nisga'a Tribal Council's land claim case that went to the Supreme Court and that added political impetus to the efforts of the Haida.

The second stream of ideas was the postwar environmental movement, which had been gaining momentum since the 1960s and which arrived on the islands in the early 1970s, when efforts to protect South Moresby began. The concepts of environmentalism that exploded onto the political agenda in the 1960s and 1970s had developed dramatically in the United States in response to increasing concerns in that country about the dangers of radioactivity from atomic testing and threats of chemical pollution.[10] Developing along with these more dramatic concerns was the preservationist side of environmentalism, with its origins in the late nineteenth century.

Using the term "ecologism," Anna Bramwell describes the concepts inherent in preservationist thought, which has long included ideas about an earthbound identity and a sense of lost folk heritage. According to her, these ideas were initially associated with what she calls the "soft right," but after their consequent association with national socialism and other extreme right-wing movements in the 1920s and 1930s they re-emerged after World War II as part of the "soft left."[11] In the latter guise, they were picked up as part of the American counterculture of alienation in the 1960s. While Bramwell devotes most of her analysis to Britain and Germany, she does argue that American ecologism similarly identifies with ruralism and the concept of an earthbound identity. The "back to the land" movement associated with 1960s counterculture is consistent with this view.

For Canadians, ecologism and environmentalism, to use Bramwell's terms, were almost certainly intensified from ideas emanating from the United States in the 1960s. Canada's own earlier proponents of naturalism, such as writers Ernest Thompson Seton and Archibald Belaney (Grey Owl) and the painters of the Group of Seven, probably helped to prepare receptive conditions for environmentalism. Later, the role of scientists and professional resource managers (as shown by the deliberations in and outcomes from the Resources for Tomorrow Conference) revealed a strong domestic foundation for environmental ideas. However, the main ideas and the timing suggest that the active components of the Canadian ecology movement in the 1960s borrowed heavily from south of the border. In the South Moresby case, for example, two of the principal activists moved to Canada, as adults, from the United States.

Bramwell's equation of ecologism with folk heritage ideas and an earthbound identity readily explains the compatibility between the Haida and many modern environmentalists. If nothing else, both seek to preserve a (nearly) lost past. A more direct connection may be seen, however. Bramwell argues that ecologists have sought to discover "what went wrong" for modern humans and to find the "original state of virtue."[12] That state, for some, remains extant in non-westernized tribes who still live in a golden age. In these terms, perceiving an identity between environmental and Aboriginal values, resulting in opposition to industrial forestry, was natural.

The Efforts of Organized Interests to Create a Park[13]

The campaign to protect the South Moresby wilderness began modestly. In 1974 near Tlell, on the Queen Charlotte Islands, Guujaaw, a Haida, and Thom Henley, an American draft dodger, drew up a proposal for a protected wilderness area and an agreement for an organization called the Islands

Protection Committee (IPC). This plan was in response to a proposal by the forest industry to begin logging on Burnaby Island, one of the smaller islands in the South Moresby area. The fledgling IPC first won the support of the Skidegate Band Council, which then facilitated a discussion between the IPC and logging company representatives. More meetings followed between the logging company and the band council and with officials from the provincial Ministry of Forests and the federal Department of Fisheries. Then BC Premier Dave Barrett visited the islands, and as a result the provincial government announced a five-year moratorium on logging on Burnaby Island. The logging company dropped its initial application but immediately applied for and received permission to log Lyell Island, also a part of the area proposed by the IPC for protection. The committee then appealed to the province for protection of the whole of their proposed wilderness area, and the government responded by offering to conduct a study of the whole region. A pattern thus began that featured the continuation of logging while governments carried out additional studies and conducted various types of public consultations, a pattern that was to continue for more than a decade.

After this setback in their appeal, the wilderness advocates pursued many venues of political participation. A rapid change of approach in response to their initial lack of success was possible because, as Jeremy Wilson has noted, their very diversity was one of their more important political assets and one that "manifests itself in a wide repertoire of political approaches."[14] South Moresby supporters thus went on to attend public meetings and to take part in other participatory mechanisms. They also used the news media and other devices of mass communication to raise public awareness and to gather public support. Finally, they formed alliances across a broad scope of organizations, including those in the international community. For more direct contact with the state, they approached nationally elected officials, seeking their support in Parliament, and thus moved the issue beyond provincial politics and onto the national agenda. Here it became a key issue in intergovernmental relations, including becoming a point of discussion at the level of first ministers.

This sequence of public participation events began for the IPC in 1974 with the appointment of the (British Columbia) Royal Commission on Timber Rights and Forest Policy. Although the committee did not actually appear before the commission,[15] it took the opportunity thus afforded to examine technical information on forestry, fisheries, ecology, and economics and to consider the process of public deliberation. Another high-profile public decision-making process in the region at about the same time, and one in which the IPC was directly involved, was the West Coast Oil Ports Inquiry, an investigation into whether the federal government should allow Alaskan crude oil to be transferred from tankers to a pipeline at Kitimat.

The ocean passage of the tankers would have bordered the Queen Charlotte Islands on two sides, putting the coastal areas of the South Moresby wilderness at risk of an oil spill. Finally, in 1977, the BC Forest Service established the Queen Charlotte Islands Public Advisory Committee to get local input for its policies. Members of the IPC were especially active participants on this committee.

None of these procedures had any immediate effect on official decisions to continue logging in the proposed wilderness area but, by affording the public a chance to participate, these mechanisms provided wilderness advocates with an opportunity to develop organizations and skills that they used in many later forums not only in British Columbia but increasingly across the country. To some extent, the ability of the public to participate in various meetings raised the profile of the South Moresby wilderness proposal and shifted it from the provincial to the national stage.

One of the most important public forums to touch on this debate was the Canadian Assembly on National Parks and Protected Areas held in Banff in 1985. Sponsored by the federal government, this conference of government agencies and environmental organizations was to mark the centenary of the Canadian national parks system. Not only was the assembly thus symbolically important, but it was also the debut for the newly appointed minister, Tom McMillan, one of whose responsibilities was to mend relations between the government and the environmental community after these relations had been badly damaged by McMillan's hapless predecessor, Suzanne Blais-Grenier.

While the conference had been carefully organized in advance, groups from British Columbia found ways to supplement the official agenda with a powerful campaign to bring South Moresby to national attention and especially to the attention of the new minister. According to Elizabeth May, the efforts of the BC groups coupled with those of national environmental organizations such as the Canadian Nature Federation and the Canadian Parks and Wilderness Society (CPAWS) (the renamed and reconstituted NPPAC) were so effective that the conference concluded with a unanimous resolution in favour of protecting South Moresby.[16] When the new minister rose to speak, he declared to the meeting that the terms of the resolution would be a top priority for him. While this conference was particularly effective in broadening the scope of the debate, other public forums in Toronto and Ottawa also kept the issue high on the public agenda.

Meanwhile, the second set of tactics being used by South Moresby advocates focused on mass communication. Significant attention by the news media first came in 1979 when two individual Haida and the Islands Protection Committee, now the Islands Protection Society (IPS), took the provincial minister of forests to court. While the courts later became an important element in the policy process for wilderness protection, this court challenge had no legal effect on the outcome of the South Moresby proposal. It did, however, generate important press coverage that brought South Moresby to the attention of the general BC population, thus broadening it from a local to a provincial issue.

The South Moresby advocates appreciated the importance of broad public support and actively sought to cultivate it rather than to leave to the news media the task of disseminating information. One of their approaches was to appeal to the naturalist affinities that they saw as inherent in the BC population with a beautifully presented book on the scenic and environmental features of the South Moresby wilderness.[17] These approaches, initially aimed at the BC public, became national (anticipating the later shift in focus to the federal government) with a broadcast in 1982 on the CBC Television program *The Nature of Things,* hosted by David Suzuki. As May has put it, Suzuki's "presence on television was both familiar and authoritative ... If [he] told Canadians about South Moresby, Canadians would listen."[18] Suzuki's involvement in the South Moresby campaign led to more television shows, the third of which prompted hundreds of Canadians to write to the federal minister of the environment. Television also dramatized the issue when Haida elders appeared in court and blockaded logging roads. RCMP officers, arresting elderly Haida women in colourful traditional regalia, provided ideal conflict-laden news, thus helping to popularize the issues and galvanize the public.

Third, over the thirteen years of the South Moresby campaign, new groups joined an ever-widening coalition of organized interests, including some with international connections. Together these interests provided to the wilderness protection community even more of the diversity that (as observed above) is one of its chief assets as well as ever increasing publicity and prestige. For example, when the Valhalla Wilderness Society gave its full support to the South Moresby proposal in the early 1980s, it had successfully persuaded the provincial government to protect a mountain wilderness in the Kootenay region of the province, and its key organizer, Colleen McCrory, had received the Governor General's Conservation Award for the efforts. At the national level, conservation groups such as the Canadian Nature Federation, the Canadian Parks and Wilderness Society, and the World Wildlife Fund Canada joined the campaign. As various participants identified aspects of special interest, or became frustrated with the status quo and changed their tactics, new organizations were continually being formed. One of them, the Western Canada Wilderness Committee (formed in 1979), is now one of British Columbia's largest environmental organizations and a skilled "symbol monger."[19]

As the groups coalesced and multiplied, international attention also began to be directed to the Queen Charlotte Islands. In 1979, UNESCO nominated Ninstints on the far southern part of the Moresby wilderness as a world heritage site, while the Pacific Seabird Group, representing biologists from thirty-nine countries, also urged that the area be protected. In 1985, some US conservation groups nominated South Moresby to the IUCN list of the world's most threatened natural areas. The National Parks Conservation Association, the Audubon Society, and the Sierra Club (all of the United States) addressed Canada's ambassador to Washington on the need to protect South Moresby. International attention became an even more crucial issue as British Columbia prepared to host Expo '86, which local and national groups sought to use as an opportunity to present the South Moresby issue to a wide international audience. As a result, in the spring of 1986, the UN-sponsored World Commission on Environment and Development (the so-called Brundtland Commission) held public meetings in Vancouver, and the South Moresby issue reverberated through its hearings.[20]

Finally, the South Moresby campaign won the support of many high-profile Canadians who were not in political office, such as (in addition to David Suzuki) artist Robert Bateman, business leader Maurice Strong, and Haida artist Bill Reid.[21] In terms of symbolism, Reid's support was perhaps the most effective. As an artist of considerable Canadian renown, he had been commissioned to provide a monumental sculpture, the *Spirit Canoe*, for the new Canadian embassy building in Washington, DC. In early 1987, however, Reid stopped work on the project, saying that he could not use "Haida symbols to advertise a government" that would not co-operate with the Haida in their legitimate requests.[22]

These three general strategies, moving the issue from the provincial to the national stage, developing widespread public support, and fostering a broad network of coalition partners domestically and internationally, effectively moved the South Moresby issue high on the national agenda, well beyond the technocratic decision and advice framework of the Parks Branch. In the final four or five years of the process, government officials at both provincial and federal levels were responding to initiatives taken by societal actors rather than developing and proposing ideas within state institutions. The private initiative pre-empted the carefully devised System Plan diverting both budgets and personnel away from the routine agenda.

Response of Governments: British Columbia
Despite a sympathetic hearing from the NDP premier in late 1974, the BC government response (particularly after the return to power of the Social Credit Party in 1975) was to find ways to limit the effect of the preservationist campaign. Jeremy Wilson has described the Social Credit approach toward wilderness advocacy as one where the government attempted, often successfully, to limit meaningful involvement in forest policy decisions by organized environmental interests. Some involvement by environmental groups in such decisions may have been necessary partly to co-opt these

groups and to moderate their highly visible strategies, but, says Wilson, "key state actors [treated] the forest environment movement as a phenomenon that had to be contained. The movement was offered a mixture of symbolic and substantive concessions ... designed to limit the damage to capital."[23] Elizabeth May describes the response more ironically as a "study industry," in which successive information-gathering processes flourish while the status quo continues.[24] From 1975 to 1986, four major (and several minor) public participation processes and government studies drew the energies of the wilderness movement into inconclusive forums and partly pacified the general public's concerns about South Moresby.

The first of these was a report prepared by the Environment and Land Use Committee Secretariat (ELUCS),[25] a report promised by Dave Barrett and finally delivered four years later (in 1979). It proposed "multiple use" of South Moresby, which meant that logging would continue in most areas where there was marketable timber. Meanwhile, the previously mentioned Public Advisory Committee on the Islands (established in 1977), made up of a cross-section of the island residents, became a forum for airing opposing opinions on logging and forest protection but achieved little in terms of useful decision making, so much so that in the fall of 1979 (taking a hint from the provincial government) the committee disbanded itself. At about the same time, the government established the South Moresby Resource Planning Team, a group of representative officials of provincial and federal resource management agencies who, like the ELUCS people before them, took more than four years to issue their report. It presented four options ranging from widespread logging and mining to protection for much of the proposed areas. However, logging on Lyell Island, by now a point of considerable tension between the two sides, continued. Briefly in 1985, the BC environment portfolio was occupied by a minister sympathetic to wilderness protection. Despite his appointment, another study group, this time the Wilderness Advisory Committee (WAC), was set up to look at the South Moresby and other proposals for wilderness preservation in the short period of four months. Echoing the most preservationist option of the South Moresby Resource Planning Team, the WAC proposed protection for 90 percent of the South Moresby wilderness area but not for the high-profile and highly contentious areas where logging continued.

While there was an overall trend in these reports toward recommending greater degrees of protection, probably as a result (by 1985-86) of greater public interest in the issue, such recommendations were generally not adopted by the provincial government.[26]

Response of Governments: Canada
Tensions between the Government of Canada and that of British Columbia had existed almost from the beginning of the South Moresby wilderness

proposal. Since the federal government's jurisdiction over fish habitat meant that the Department of Fisheries[27] took an active interest in logging practices, it had clashed in 1973 with the provincial government over damage to fish habitat on Lyell Island. The National Parks Branch meanwhile had been alerted to the possibility of national park potential on South Moresby and, while expressing interest in the natural values of the area, deliberately declined any further interest.

Speaking to the South Moresby Resource Planning Team in January 1980, John Carruthers, chief planner with the Parks Branch, said that, within the national parks System Plan, Pacific Rim National Park (on Vancouver Island) already satisfied the need for representation of the West Coast mountains and that the financial and personnel constraints meant that the Parks Branch would be devoting its efforts toward regions not yet represented in the national parks system. Thus, "from a strategic planning point-of-view," Carruthers concluded, "we are not going to actively pursue the goal of a terrestrial National Park on the Queen Charlotte Islands."[28] While he did suggest some other policy mechanisms for protecting South Moresby, his ideas really amounted to leaving the issue within provincial jurisdiction.

Meanwhile, the South Moresby proposal was garnering increased attention in partisan political circles in Ottawa. Political support in Parliament began in 1979 when Jim Fulton was elected NDP member of Parliament for Skeena, the federal riding in which the Queen Charlotte Islands are located. Fulton had been a probation officer prior to entering federal politics and had worked with the Haida to help reintegrate their youth into traditional culture. As an opposition member, his influence was limited, but he established a strong rapport with Conservatives such as Tom McMillan and John Fraser, both of whom would later become central participants in the federal efforts to make South Moresby a national park. In addition, Fulton provided an important base in Ottawa for South Moresby campaigners. The potential importance of Parliament was also understood by the wilderness proponents, and, although the issue remained predominantly provincial in the late 1970s and early 1980s, the Western Canada Wilderness Committee surveyed members of Parliament to gauge support in Ottawa for South Moresby protection. Among the sympathizers at this relatively early stage were former Prime Minister Joe Clark and Vancouver MP (later Speaker of the House) John Fraser.[29]

The decisive contact with Ottawa, and the action that effectively moved South Moresby onto the national agenda, came in 1984. Colleen McCrory, fresh from receiving the Governor General's Conservation Award, took time in Ottawa to promote the South Moresby cause. There she met with Charles Caccia, the federal minister of environment for the Trudeau Liberals, who was immediately supportive. Caccia took up the idea of making South

Moresby a national park and wrote to his BC counterpart formally suggesting this solution. Caccia and the Liberals were soon out of power, however, and the South Moresby idea received little federal support or attention during the brief tenure of his Conservative successor, Suzanne Blais-Grenier. In less than a year, however, Blais-Grenier succeeded in alienating the environmental community, the personnel within the department, and eventually the prime minister and was replaced in August 1985 by Tom McMillan, one of whose challenges was to rebuild the relationship between the department and environmental interest groups.

Establishment of Formal Intergovernmental Relations with Respect to South Moresby

As the new minister, McMillan made a trip in October 1985 to South Moresby, where his statements in support of a national park, or some other form of protection for the island, and his attempts to seek a solution to the dramatic Haida blockade of logging roads in November of that year prompted several key BC politicians to suggest that he keep his federal nose out of British Columbia's business. The province's intransigence was further expressed when the prime minister spoke with BC Premier William Bennett at the First Ministers' Conference in late November 1985.

When William Vander Zalm replaced Bennett as premier of British Columbia in July 1986, the official government position became more flexible. In September of that year, before a provincial election, McMillan and BC Minister of the Environment Austin Pelton met and cleared up a long-standing impediment to possible intergovernmental negotiations about South Moresby: namely, the concluding details of the establishment of Pacific Rim National Park.[30]

Although the September meeting led to an agreement to begin negotiating for a national park on South Moresby, Pelton was not included in the new Social Credit government after the October 1986 election, and the new cabinet quickly expanded the logging option on Lyell Island. McMillan met with his new provincial counterpart, Stephen Rogers, in February 1987, but Rogers was more sympathetic to logging than was Pelton, and the meeting ended in an impasse, with McMillan threatening to cancel any plans for a national park. At this point, the negotiations moved to the summit level of intergovernmental relations. At the first ministers' meeting in March 1987, Prime Minister Brian Mulroney raised the South Moresby issue with BC Premier Vander Zalm, and the two of them evidently reached some form of agreement, as the throne speech, read shortly after, promised provincial action for a national park for South Moresby.

The rapport did not end intergovernmental wrangling over this issue, however. For the next four months, there was continuing argument and counterargument as the provincial government alternately threatened to withdraw from negotiations and demanded more money or other concessions from the federal government. In the end, a park that had been estimated to cost the federal treasury $20 million in 1984 was finally agreed to in 1987 for $106 million.

The National Parks Act (1988)[31]

Effective organization and political strategy were equally important in influencing changes to the National Parks Act in the same time period. By the early 1980s, there had been no significant amendments to the act since its inception in 1930, with the exception of the 1974 provision for national park reserves to allow for negotiation of Aboriginal land claims.[32] Since then, human population expansion, new technologies, and provincial policies had dramatically changed the overall environment in which national parks operated. Thus, the act was no longer fully capable of providing for the adequate administration and enforcement of national park policies. Some consideration had been given to the need to revise the act in the late 1970s, but this process was pursued quietly within the Parks Branch.[33] After the appointment of Tom McMillan to the environment portfolio in July 1985, however, the branch moved quickly to assemble a series of proposed amendments that were introduced to Parliament in December 1986. After a seventeen-month delay, the bill went to the legislative committee for detailed discussion in June 1988, and it was rushed through third reading to become law in August.

When it was introduced, the bill's content was mostly administrative in nature, bringing into the act, for example, certain de facto policies that were established in practice but not in law. While several of the provisions had the effect of strengthening environmental protection in national parks, there was no revision in the act's general philosophy. This did change at the legislative committee stage, where a new provision was adopted that significantly altered the direction of the act. The original 1930 preamble remained, with its ambivalence between use and preservation, but a new clause mandating "ecological integrity" as the first priority in park management was added. This clause now guides national parks administration. It and its wording came almost directly from the submission to the committee by the Canadian Parks and Wilderness Society. Since substantive changes to bills in committee are uncommon, this development illustrates the unusual coincidence of political influences that occurred during its passage.

Ideas and the National Parks Act

The proposed amendments to the act grew out of the environmental ideas of the 1970s and the technical and political circumstances of the 1980s and came from three loci within the parks policy community. First, the Parks

Branch, which had been the repository of ideas about and experience with national parks for over a century, continued to be a prime source of ideas for the 1988 amendments. Several of the ideas arose from modern administrative problems experienced by the branch, such as a much-needed amendment to the penalties for poaching in national parks.

Second, the Task Force on Park Establishment, a group of citizen experts, suggested a wide variety of more visionary ideas, although only one of the group's ideas, that of a citizens' heritage fund, was actually included in the proposed amendment.[34] The task force report nevertheless gave support to the broader concept of environmental protection, arguing that "parks and protected areas are our lifeline to an ecologically stable future"; rather than parks being a "repudiation of economic development, ... they balance it."[35]

Third, environmental interest groups, of which CPAWS was the most important, contributed key ideas to the legislative discussion, the most important of which was the idea of managing parks according to principles of "ecological integrity." This concept, while presented articulately by CPAWS, had been initially expressed in the 1979 policy statement. Therein the government[36] set out as its basic policy that "ecological ... integrity [is] Parks Canada's first consideration and must be regarded as prerequisite ... to use."[37] Therefore, the concept had its origins in the public discussions that contributed to that policy in the late 1970s. In fact, the policy scribes changed the wording of the penultimate draft (in 1978) in direct response to public comments "so that protection is clearly the aim"[38] of the Parks Branch. Nevertheless, it was CPAWS, not the Parks Branch, that recommended that these ideas and this phrasing be entrenched in the 1988 legislation.

A second set of ideas implicit in the CPAWS submission to the legislative committee was to vest a stronger power of oversight in Parliament and therefore to limit the discretion of the minister in national parks management. Along with other references to Parliament, CPAWS recommended that management plans for individual parks be tabled in Parliament every five years and that the minister report to Parliament on the state of the parks every two years. These recommendations contributed to the somewhat long history of ideas about trying to limit the minister's discretionary power over parks management. In the 1960s, for example, the Glassco Commission had recommended that an independent commission be created to administer national parks.[39] Later, the System Plan explicitly sought a method of parks selection that would be free of political factors. Similarly, the 1979 policy, while not explicitly attempting to limit political considerations, nevertheless did constrain the minister's discretion by the process of public legitimation and publication of the policy statement itself. The CPAWS recommendations did not refer to these earlier ideas but, by seeking to bring major parks decisions into the open in Parliament, would have the same effect of limiting the scope of the minister's discretion.

Role of the Bureaucracy

Standard operating procedures characterized the bureaucracy's small but crucial role in the amendment to the act. As the government's repository of experience, Parks Branch officials were able to identify the need to amend the act in the new minister's briefing material. Moreover, the bureaucracy responded to the request to draft proposed amendments in a distinctly conservative vein reminiscent of the proposals of two decades earlier. The proposed amendments that were prepared in 1985 reflected those administrative problems that the branch needed to resolve in order to carry out its mandate, but no new vision or revitalized general philosophy emanated from the branch itself.

For example, among the changes included in the branch's proposed amendments were provisions for increased fines for poaching in parks. Unchanged for fifty years, the $500 maximum fines were little more than a "licence fee" since wealthy hunters would pay $50,000 for a prized trophy animal. When provincial penalties for illegal hunting on adjacent lands were, on average, nearer $2,000, it was virtually impossible for national park managers to use federal rules to keep poachers out of national parks and to protect park wildlife. Similar modern management issues, such as regulation of the use of all-terrain vehicles, a relatively recent innovation, also needed attention in legislation.

Role of the Minister

When McMillan became minister of the environment, the department was in disarray following the brief fractious tenure of Suzanne Blais-Grenier, and the portfolio had become a political liability for the newly governing Mulroney Conservatives. Having taken the Conservative cost-cutting rhetoric seriously, Blais-Grenier had eliminated more than 20 percent of the Canadian Wildlife Service positions, including those of many experienced field scientists with internationally acclaimed reputations. The scientific and environmental communities were outraged and repeatedly called for her resignation. Moreover, Blais-Grenier's decision was taken against the advice of the deputy minister, from whom she increasingly isolated herself. Her lack of popularity was complicated by allegations that she had used government funds for personal travel, and these allegations contributed to her image as an embarrassment for the government.

Prime Minister Mulroney was anxious to restore the Conservative government's credibility on environmental issues, and in a cabinet shuffle in 1985 appointed McMillan with instructions to repair the government's relationship with the environmental community. Since politicians in general, and newly appointed cabinet ministers in particular, tend to be ambitious, this would have fitted well with McMillan's own (probable) goals. By making some noteworthy contributions to the environmental portfolio, he would increase his chances to enhance his political career just as Jean Chrétien had done in a similar position almost two decades earlier. A discrete, well-defined task that he could accomplish during his tenure would be attractive in the circumstance and the need to amend and update the National Parks Act presented itself as just such a task.

In addition to selecting the act for special attention, McMillan sought constructive assistance in two other ways. First, he established the Task Force on Park Establishment to provide new ideas for the future of national parks and wilderness protection.[40] The task force met through 1986 and had a close working relationship with both the minister and the drafters of the amendments. Second, McMillan appointed Elizabeth May to his ministerial staff as a special adviser and liaison person with organized environmental interests. May had earlier distinguished herself in a spirited, though unsuccessful, court challenge to stop aerial chemical spraying of forests on Cape Breton Island. Her role, as seen by McMillan, was that of an "environmental ambassador" in the minister's office.

Taken together, the minister's initiatives were essential for the introduction and passage of the amendments in Parliament. However, his contributions were in initiating and facilitating this process. The actual content of the amendments, and therefore the nature of the policy, came partly from the bureaucracy, with a crucial addition from CPAWS.

Role of Parliament

Parliamentary arguments over the National Parks Act in the 1980s mirrored debate about the same act more than fifty years earlier. On the one side were proponents of greater access to commercial development in national parks and a more robust promotion of tourism, most of them Alberta Progressive Conservative MPs who represented, and worked in tandem with, commercial interests in the Alberta national parks. These MPs also worked in close co-operation with the Alberta provincial government, which had long disliked the exclusive federal control over Banff and Jasper, two of the prime tourism locations in the province.[41] This lobbying effort, including a list of proposed amendments drafted by the Alberta MPs, was largely conducted within government caucus and therefore mostly out of the public view. The long delay between the first and second reading was the result, at least partly, of this caucus debate.

On the other side of the debate were proponents of increased wilderness preservation for parks. This time, however, their view was advanced, not by the general public, but almost exclusively by organized environmental interest groups that were active prior to the committee stage of the legislative process. The close working relationship between the minister and environmental groups during the South Moresby campaign had impressed on the minister the general philosophy of wilderness protection, even if their discussions did not include specific references to pending amendments. Equally important, several groups, such as CPAWS and the Canadian Nature Federation, maintained close contact with departmental officials responsible for drafting the legislation and with the minister himself. Finally, several members of the Task Force on Park Establishment had close communication with members of key interest groups and were, therefore, part of a network of interests promoting greater environmental protection for parks.

Despite the importance of these contacts, the most significant opportunity for the participation of proponents of nature preservation was their appearance before the legislative committee. Their success at introducing substantive amendments to the bill was highly unusual, as parliamentary committees have not generally been a means to effect significant change in legislation.[42]

Role of Groups

The witnesses who appeared before the legislative committee for Bill C-30 can be roughly divided into four categories: environmentalists, Aboriginal representatives, commercial skiing advocates, and spokespersons for the townsite of Jasper. Broadly speaking, these categories conformed to the dichotomy between preservation (environmentalists and Aboriginal representatives[43]) and use (commercial skiing advocates and spokespersons for Jasper townsite).[44] Despite clear differences between these two broad sets of interests, they were not in direct, overt opposition. The commercial and townsite spokespersons had local concerns about Banff and Jasper National Parks, in that they wanted to ensure that changes to the act did not (in their terms) adversely affect those areas, but they had little or no interest in a national policy for national parks. On the other hand, the environmentalists had broader, system-wide interests and, while vitally interested in the outcomes for Banff and Jasper, saw the potential for important gains in the legislation without engaging in a zero-sum conflict over those two parks in particular. In the end, both groups achieved their objectives. The local and commercial interests were able to maintain the status quo, while the national environmental interests were able to effect important changes to the legislation.

While both outcomes are important, the environmental additions represent another step toward a stronger preservationist policy for national parks. Whereas the basis for environmental protection in the preamble to the act in 1930 was vague, the amended act (1988) was much more specific and instructive: "Maintenance of ecological integrity through the protection of natural resources shall be the first priority when considering park zoning and visitor use in a management plan."[45]

This wording came almost verbatim from the CPAWS submission to the legislative committee. Although other environmental organizations appeared before the committee, CPAWS had the most comprehensive submission and received the most time to speak. Its first recommendation was for a statement to recognize ecological integrity for national parks: "The Minister shall ensure that the maintenance of ecological integrity and protection of natural resources is of primary consideration in the administration and management of national parks and is a prerequisite to use."[46] As the committee debated changes to the proposed amendments, opposition MP Charles Caccia moved a motion to include a clause that contained the CPAWS recommendation. On 14 June 1988, at the penultimate meeting of the committee, this motion was rejected by Parliamentary Secretary for Environment Pauline Browes, who argued that, because the preamble to the National Parks Act (1930) already provided for the ecological protection of national parks, further change was unnecessary. As a result of her direction on the matter, the motion was defeated by the government members on the committee.

The establishment of CPAWS had been premised on the idea of environmental protection for national parks, and members had devoted considerable thought to its submission and crafted its recommendations to suit the minister. The organization's executive director, Kevin McNamee, had a good working relationship with the minister (derived, at least partly, from their joint participation in the effort to make South Moresby a national park), as did several members of the committee. In particular, McNamee (who presented the written brief) attended all the sessions of the committee and met with committee members, other MPs, bureaucrats, and the minister's staff between sessions. This attentiveness yielded results for McNamee and CPAWS. After the session during which Browes rejected the proposed ecological integrity amendment, McNamee discussed the matter with the press, who were also in attendance,[47] and with government officials. McNamee was able to point out that, because the words *ecological integrity* were already present in the 1979 policy, inserting them into the act would simply serve to elevate the existing concept into legislation and would not, on the face of it, "change" policy.

Within hours, the minister and his officials drafted a new "ecological integrity" clause for resubmission to the committee the following day. Thus, on 15 June 1988, at the last meeting of the committee before reporting to the House of Commons, Charles Caccia, for the second time, proposed an amendment for a clause inserting the principle of ecological integrity into the act, and this time government members supported the amendments, which subsequently passed, giving the National Parks Act more explicit expression of the preservationist ideal.

Like the creation of Gwaii Haanas National Park Reserve, as the South Moresby area is now officially named, the 1988 amendments were unusual because of the particular coincidence of an initiating and supportive minister and an astute and experienced interest group able to present balanced, largely acceptable ideas. While the minister and the forum provided by the legislative committee were essential for interest groups (spearheaded by CPAWS) to insert further protectionist clauses in the legislation, CPAWS also learned to use other state institutions to advance the cause of national parks environmental protection.

National Parks and the Courts

In addition to concerns, by some, about levels of commercial recreation, resource extraction continued to be a lingering issue for parks management but mostly to the extent that the Parks Branch endeavoured to buy back outdated logging and mineral claims in some of the older parks. This was not so in Wood Buffalo National Park, however, where logging continued seemingly with full approval of the branch.

In 1956, the minister responsible for national parks had given permission to the Denney[48] Logging Company to log 226 square miles of timber in Wood Buffalo over the next twenty-one years despite the National Parks Act's requirement that all parks be maintained unimpaired for future generations. Inexplicably, this and subsequent local permits were granted while resource extraction (including logging and mineral activity) and livestock grazing were generally in decline in national parks.[49] Indeed, in several instances, the government had purchased companies' logging rights in order to bring an end to timber harvesting while still respecting outstanding commercial claims. Yet for Wood Buffalo, the permit to log was transferred from one company to another and in 1965 extended for an additional four years. In 1981, when the first agreement expired, a completely new logging permit was issued, for another twenty-one years, for another large section of the park.

In January 1992, following several changes to judicial rules in the previous decade, CPAWS took the minister to court, charging that he had acted illegally in granting logging permits and contravened the authority of the National Parks Act, first in 1956 and then with each subsequent permit. The suit was successful, effectively stopping logging in Wood Buffalo. Critically, this decision also established an important precedent concerning the meaning of the National Parks Act and inaugurated the ability of organized interests to ensure, through the courts, that the terms of the act will be upheld. Central to the ability of groups to go to the courts were changes in the rules of standing and the articulation of public interest.

Ideas, the Environment, and the Courts

Ideas in public policy may be about process or about substance (or both). While substantive ideas about wilderness preservation and the value of ecological integrity in national parks were already well established in the policy arena, the new ideas that gave CPAWS access to the courts in the Wood Buffalo case were almost entirely about process. The crucial ideas that gave rise to modified rules concerning public interest standing were about expanding the rights of citizens to use the courts to hold governments to account and to pursue public policy objectives outside bureaucratic and/or executive processes.

Standing (the right, as granted by the court, to bring an issue before that court for adjudication) has been traditionally granted only to those plaintiffs who have suffered some immediate and individual injury as the result of someone else's action. If a loss, unique and specific to the individual, cannot be identified, then the courts may refuse to hear the claim, saying that the issue is one of public interest and therefore can be brought before the court only by the attorney general. An example, frequently quoted in the legal literature, of someone failing to get standing in an environmental issue is the case of Mr. Hickey, a Newfoundland fisher, whose livelihood was destroyed when toxic effluent from the Electric Reduction Company poisoned the waters of Placentia Bay. When Hickey endeavoured to sue, the court ruled that, while his loss was greater than that of other people, it was not unique to him because it was the public right to fish and not his individual income that was at issue, and all actual and potential fishers were similarly deprived of that right. Since the injury was not unique to him, Hickey did not have the right of access to the courts.[50]

Canadian courts began to loosen the rules of standing in 1975 when Joseph Thorsen challenged the Official Languages Act. Here the Supreme Court ruled that an exception to the uniqueness standard could be made if the individual could demonstrate that he or she had a "genuine" interest in the matter, if no single individual was uniquely affected and therefore likely to pursue legal action, and if the issue was within the competence of the courts. Not long afterward, Mr. McNeil challenged the Nova Scotia film censorship legislation and, although not himself directly affected by the legislation, was granted standing as the courts recognized that there was "no other way, practically speaking, to subject the challenged Act to judicial review."[51] Then, in 1981, Joseph Borowski challenged the therapeutic abortion provisions of the Criminal Code of Canada, and although he too was not directly affected by the legislation the court expanded the idea that his challenge was the only effective means of bringing the issue before the courts.

Each of these cases had essentially challenged the validity of the legislation in question. In *Finlay v. Canada (Minister of Finance)* (1986), however, the court gave standing to a plaintiff seeking to force the government to carry out its own legislation rather than to question the legislation itself. Mr. Finlay, a welfare recipient, had been required by the Manitoba government to repay a previous overpayment in his social assistance. He responded by arguing before the Federal Court of Appeal that this reduced his income below his "level of need" and that, because the Canada Assistance Plan stipulated that eligible recipients should receive assistance according to need, Manitoba's action was in violation of the plan. The favourable decision of the court forced both levels of government to administer assistance in accordance with the legislation. The Supreme Court of Canada upheld the view of the Federal Court of Appeal that "what is at stake is the right of the citizens of Canada to have the Consolidated Revenue Fund of Canada applied in accordance with the law."[52] That the courts should allow citizens public interest standing in cases that might require governments to act in accordance with the law was an important step in allowing environmental interest groups to ensure the application of environmental legislation.

Evolution of the rules of standing did not confer an automatic right to be heard, however. On issues of public interest, the courts reserve the prerogative to grant or deny standing. For the guidance of the judiciary, the Supreme Court identified three tests to determine who might be granted standing. First, the person bringing the claim must have a genuine interest in the matter. Second, the court must be satisfied that there are no other reasonable means to bring the matter before the courts. Third, if the issue is justifiable, then the courts should not decline to hear it on the ground that it is a policy issue within the realm of the other branches of government.[53]

For environmental interest groups, the new rules of standing created an opportunity for greater use of the courts, although they first had to persuade the judiciary that groups had a genuine interest in environmental matters and were not bringing frivolous issues before the bench, that they were not, in the court's words, "mere busybodies." This use happened quickly, especially in British Columbia, where in several cases groups were accepted as representing the public interest. In *Western Canada Wilderness Committee v. B.C.*, for example, in 1988, the judge ruled that "the 1500 members of the Western Canada Wilderness Committee ... are not mere busybodies. They must be regarded as concerned citizens interested in ensuring that lawful process is followed."[54] This and subsequent cases demonstrated that the courts were willing to grant public interest standing to environmental groups, although groups had to apply in each case.

Arising as if to meet this opportunity, a new non-profit group, the Sierra Legal Defence Fund (SLDF),[55] was established in 1990 in Vancouver to act on behalf of the Western Canada Wilderness Committee, CPAWS, and other groups seeking access to the courts. The SLDF not only sought to be environmental legal specialists but also sought, in the absence of specific and relevant legislation, to establish a series of cumulative legal precedents in environmental law that would compensate for the lack of environmental protection in legislation.

Since its formation, the SLDF has, together with CPAWS, taken advantage of the new rules of public interest standing to use the courts rather than public opinion, rational argument (i.e., outside the courts), or parliamentary debate to ensure that the minister and the government honour the provisions of the National Parks Act (although the SLDF also uses non-judicial avenues to advance an environmental agenda). The first case of the alliance between the SLDF and CPAWS was over logging in Wood Buffalo National Park.

Wood Buffalo National Park

Wood Buffalo National Park was established in 1922 to protect and preserve the last remaining herd of wild, free-roaming, North American bison. Since preservation was not otherwise a feature of national parks until the 1970s, this park was almost half a century ahead of its time.[56] Wildlife protection had nevertheless become a concern of bureaucrats and politicians alike in the late nineteenth century as the once enormous herds of plains bison and other wild animals were virtually eliminated across North America. In the early years of the twentieth century, the superintendent of Banff National Park had noted the public's interest in captive wildlife displays and recommended their expansion.[57] As a result, the federal government took several steps to protect what it saw as the wildlife heritage of (western) Canada. One of these steps was to purchase 700 plains bison from a private source in Montana and to create a national park to accommodate them, although this park turned out to be relatively short-lived.

At the same time, another effort for wildlife conservation was focused on the remote Athabasca country of northern Alberta, where wood bison populations had also been declining in the first decades of that century. After nearly ten years of internal discussion, the federal government established Wood Buffalo National Park for the principal purpose of protecting the wood bison population. It was recognized that this park would not be a tourist destination like Banff and Jasper National Parks; indeed, the park was not even administered by Parks Branch authorities but by the Northwest Territories and Yukon Branch (later the Northern Administration Branch), which was also within the Department of the Interior.[58] The wildlife conservation objective rested less comfortably in this branch, which had more of an economic development mandate than did the Parks Branch. Rather than treat Wood Buffalo strictly as a national park, the Northern Administration Branch thought that the National Parks Act had been used merely for legislative convenience to protect the bison and was never meant to have a broader purpose. The minister responsible for parks in the mid-1930s, T.A. Crerar, hinted as much when, in 1937, he spoke approvingly about Canada's national parks without mentioning Wood Buffalo, not even including its area in the statistics to which he referred.[59] Because the park seemingly was not intended to function like other national parks, the Department of the Interior gradually allowed increasing amounts of resource extraction to occur there. Initially, this was limited to traditional Aboriginal activities such as trapping and to small-scale mining for local purposes.

Following World War II, however, resource use accelerated largely on the justification that it provided jobs for local Aboriginal people. In addition, after the war, Canada expanded its uranium mines on Lake Athabasca (to the east of Wood Buffalo) and used the timber resources of the park to provide building material for these mines. By allowing logging in the park, the government violated the National Parks Act. At first, Eldorado Mining and Refining, the government-owned uranium mining company, operated the only logging claim, but forestry operations later expanded to four companies spread over 287 square miles of the park.[60] By 1956, Swanson Lumber Company had one sawmill in the park and was planning a second, while Denney Logging Company was planning its first. The Northern Administration Branch recognized that this situation violated the National Parks Act, but, rather than curtail logging, its solution was to transfer responsibility of the park to the Parks Branch. However, this transfer took until 1969 to complete.

In the meantime, the minister responsible for both Northern Administration and National Parks Branches continued to permit logging in the park. The original twenty-one-year agreement (1956-77) was transferred on several occasions to different companies and in 1965 extended to a new termination date in 1981. Logging continued after 1981, however, and in 1983 the minister of the environment authorized a twenty-one-year agreement effective from 1981 to 2002. This agreement specified that Canadian Forest Products (the logging company) would file a management plan every five years and an operating plan annually. In 1991, shortly after the formation of the SLDF, the company filed its annual plan, and in January 1992 the SLDF, acting on behalf of CPAWS, took the superintendent of Wood Buffalo, the director of Parks Canada (the Parks Branch) for the Prairie and Northern Region, and the minister of the environment to the Federal Court of Canada.

Two issues in this case fit the SLDF's strategic objectives. First, to request standing in the public interest so as to proceed against the minister, the SLDF established that CPAWS has a genuine interest in the administration of the park and that there was no other way to bring the matter before the court. After identifying CPAWS and its membership, the "Statement of Claim" presented the group's interest in this public matter thus: "Among the purposes of the Canadian Parks and Wilderness Society are the promotion of public awareness and understanding of ecological principles and the inherent values of wilderness, the protection of Canada's wild ecosystems in parks, wilderness and natural areas, and preserving full diversity of species and their habitats. Since its formation, the Canadian Parks and Wilderness Society has involved itself extensively in issues concerning the management of national parks of Canada."[61] Second, the SLDF lawyers wanted to establish a public trust precedent. They thought that the preamble to the National Parks Act (1930) established a statutory trust for the government to see that national parks are "maintained unimpaired for future generations" and that bureaucrats are responsible to the public for ensuring that this trust is upheld. CPAWS (and the SLDF) also argued that the minister and the Parks Branch had lacked the statutory authority to grant, in 1981, the renewed twenty-one-year logging permit. In the "Statement of Claim," they assert that "by entering into the 1983 Agreement the minister breached a trust and/or fiduciary duty owed to the Plaintiff and the people of Canada, and acted contrary to the provisions of the National Parks Act then in effect. Further, the 1983 Agreement was illegal and invalid in that the said minister was without statutory or any other lawful authority to enter into the agreement under the statutory regime then in effect, and exceeded his jurisdiction by so doing."[62]

What followed was remarkably undramatic. After CPAWS was granted standing and an initial statement of defence in court, the Parks Branch quickly capitulated and came to an agreement with CPAWS. Both organizations then made a joint application to the court requesting a ruling on the logging permit. The court complied, ruling that, indeed, the branch and the minister did not have the authority to grant a renewed logging permit (they had not had the authority in the 1950s either). This ruling thus gave judicial sanction to the agreement reached by the branch and CPAWS and bolstered the SLDF position that bureaucrats and ministers may not administratively exceed the authority granted to them in legislation. Not only did logging come to an end in Wood Buffalo National Park, but also the environmental protection aspects of the National Parks Act were strengthened by this limitation on administrative discretion.

Skiing in Banff National Park and Environmental Protection[63]
While the challenge against logging in Wood Buffalo ended relatively easily with basic agreement between the Parks Branch and CPAWS, later attempts to establish legally appropriate environmental review procedures for national parks were more difficult. Skiing had been practised in Banff National Park since the 1930s. In the 1980s, one of the commercial establishments in the park was Sunshine Village Corporation, which operated facilities dating from that early period.

In 1978, the corporate predecessor to Sunshine received permission from the Parks Branch, including the minister, to expand its ski area and ancillary services. Although some of this took place over the next few years, the entire expansion was not completed. In 1986, Sunshine, as new owners of the operation, reconfirmed this permission for expansion with the branch, and, although the company's plan needed some modification as a result of environmental concerns raised by the branch, officials worked with the corporation's planners and otherwise facilitated the pursuit of the expansion plans. Finally, in August 1992, the plans were approved. Public information sessions were to be initiated by the company, but it was decided that a full public consultation process was unnecessary. Although a press release in September 1992 said that each element of Sunshine's expansion would be subject to environmental review, in December CPAWS was unable to get assurances that an official review would actually take place. Meanwhile, the expansion proceeded as planned.

After several months without clear official answers to its questions, CPAWS commenced court action in October 1993 by applying for an injunction against Sunshine's permit to clear trees from the area of the expanded ski run. The application was denied, but it began a complex, three-year series of court battles in which CPAWS sought, at first, four objectives:

1 an order declaring invalid the September 17, 1993, construction agreement between Sunshine and the Parks Branch;
2 an order declaring invalid the October 7, 1993, timber cutting permit;
3 a declaration that the approval in the 1992 letter from Minister Charest was without effect;
4 and an order that a full public involvement assessment and review be conducted.[64]

The pursuit of these objectives was complicated in any event but was made more so by the change in government in November 1993 and by the new government's adoption of a different approach to these issues. As the case (or, rather, multiple linked cases) progressed, it was not always immediately clear why CPAWS continued to be involved in the proceedings. The issue of standing was paramount. Since CPAWS did not have property or related interests in the matter, it did not have "standing as of right,"[65] and there was considerable discussion as to whether it should be granted public interest standing.

Even as the cases progressed, the objectives of CPAWS seemed to disappear. The first two of its four objectives became moot because, as the legal proceedings took place, the construction and tree clearing were completed. Then, with the change of government, the new minister undertook, in March 1995, to appoint a full environmental review under the Canadian Environmental Assessment Act (1992).[66] Once the government had stated its intention in this regard, Sunshine argued that CPAWS could "no longer claim that there [was] no reasonable or effective way to bring the issue before the court."[67] However, the court reasoned that, although the government appeared to be acting in the public interest, as defined and argued by CPAWS, it was "far from convinced ... that the interests of CPAWS and those of the Attorney General, which did not always coincide in the past, will necessarily do so in the future."[68] Therefore, although the CPAWS objectives had either become moot or were essentially satisfied, the court granted it standing, permitting it to stay in the proceedings and to press for a full environmental review. This was important since Sunshine was simultaneously arguing that the new minister could not order (essentially retroactively) the environmental review that had been appointed in March 1995.

In August 1996, the court ruled on several aspects of the Sunshine ski hill expansion plans and concluded that the (new) minister was able to order a full public environmental review and that such a review was required by law, as CPAWS had argued. In addition, the Federal Court of Appeal upheld the public interest standing for CPAWS through the many twists in the case (though lower courts had not always done so), even declaring that standing should be granted although the government was doing (at that point) what the group wanted.[69]

While there were no immediate and direct changes to policy resulting from this case, it did reconfirm the public interest position of CPAWS with respect to environmental issues in national parks and drove home that, as was recognized by the court, the public interest may need defenders in addition to (or despite) the attorney general. The insistence on having development issues in national parks assessed in front of an open public review process would necessarily bring greater scrutiny to decisions that in the past were routinely made by branch officials, or the minister, in close conjunction with private interests and away from public view. Thus, the National Parks Act, with its environmental protection provisions strengthened in 1988, will be implemented and enforced with a greater role for the public (likely through environmental interest groups) and less discretion by the government.

National Parks and Aboriginal People

As with other aspects of national parks policy, Canada has been somewhat in the forefront of a worldwide shift in emphasis in favour of including Aboriginal or indigenous people in policy development and even accommodating their presence within the parks themselves. At one level, this seems to be at odds with the increasing thrust for environmental protection. However, there has been an important change in understanding what constitutes "ecology" and therefore what is involved in environmental protection. In the past, ecological protection would have meant keeping an area pristine, or free from human intervention, whereas by the 1980s and 1990s it was recognized that no part of the Earth, save Antarctica, has been unaffected by human activities in the pre-industrial era. Acknowledging and allowing for human presence have therefore been important developments in the definition of the concept of natural ecosystems. Where humans fit into this concept and how they may affect so-called natural ecosystems are matters of significant debate. Anthropologists and biologists continue to study the precise nature of the influence of human predation on and competition with other animals. For example, drawing on some of the literature on these topics, Raymond Chipeniuk has argued that in Canada 10,000 years (since the retreat of the last ice age) is sufficient time for the co-evolution of plants and animals. He points to evidence that prehistoric patterns of barren grounds caribou grazing and migration were influenced by the presence of human hunters.[70] Based on this and similar evidence, Chipeniuk expresses the view that "the absence of native hunter-gatherers from northern national parks is a departure from the natural ecosystems of pre-Contact times."[71]

These ideas, part of a broader scientific debate about the definition of nature, were formally addressed by the IUCN Commission on National Parks in 1984 and again at the Fourth World Congress on National Parks and Protected Areas in Venezuela in 1992. At the 1992 congress, the World Wildlife Fund sponsored a week-long workshop to discuss the relationship between local peoples and protected areas. Here, the so-called Yellowstone model of national parks was criticized as being "based on ignorance of the historical relationship between people and their habitat and the role people play in maintaining biodiversity in forests and savannahs."[72] Interestingly, an Aboriginal Canadian, Chief Bill Erasmus of the Dené Nation, chaired this workshop.[73]

Ideas and Indigenous Peoples
As suggested in the earlier discussion of Aboriginal people and Canada's national parks, there has been a general trend toward greater inclusiveness and a sense of expanded rights for indigenous peoples in all aspects of society in the post-World War II period.[74] In Canada, this was partly manifested in changes in the 1974 amendments to the National Parks Act that allowed for the establishment of national park reserves. Another important step in this direction was the Mackenzie Valley Pipeline Inquiry (also known as the Berger Inquiry). In 1974, Thomas Berger, then a justice on the Supreme Court of British Columbia, was invited by the federal government to conduct an inquiry into the proposal to build a natural gas pipeline from the oil and gas fields of the arctic coast of Alaska, across the northern coast of Yukon, and up the Mackenzie River valley to southern Canada and thence to the United States. This undertaking would have been one of the largest

private-sector construction projects in Canadian history and would have had significant effects on the lives, communities, and local economies of the indigenous peoples all across these northern areas. Reporting to the federal government, Berger recommended that no pipeline be built across northern Yukon and that the area be protected as a wilderness park in which, he further recommended, provision be made for Aboriginal people to continue to carry on their traditional hunting, fishing, and other activities. On the subject of a wilderness park and the place of Aboriginal people in it, nowhere is the argument made more clearly than by Berger himself: "The park that I propose for the Northern Yukon should be set up under the National Parks system, but it would be a new kind of park – a wilderness park. It would afford absolute protection to wilderness and the environment by excluding all industrial activity within it. Of course there would have to be guarantees permitting the native people to continue to live and to carry on their traditional activities within the park without interference."[75] On the practical role of Aboriginal people with respect to the park, he said that

> Preservation of the wilderness and of the caribou herd is plainly in keeping with the desires of the native people. But, there are essential conditions that would have to be observed; the native people must be guaranteed at the outset their right to live, hunt, trap and fish within the park, and to take caribou within its boundaries; and the people of Old Crow must play an important part in the management of the park, and in particular, of the caribou herd. It is my judgement that the establishment of the park and of a management plan in cooperation with the native people, building both upon their knowledge and experience and that of the scientists who have studied the caribou and the Northern Yukon biota, can be consistent with and complementary to the principles.[76]

Finally, on the significance of the park to Aboriginal people and to other Canadians, Berger highlighted its importancce to their identity:

> It may be said that no one will visit the park because it is too remote. Only the wealthy, it may be argued, will have the opportunity to see the caribou and to enjoy the solitude and the scenery. But Canadians of ordinary means and less are there now, enjoying these wonders of nature. I speak, of course, of the native people. Is that not enough? Canadians from the provinces do not have to visit the wilderness or see the herd of caribou to confirm its existence or justify its retention. The point I am making here is that the preservation of the wilderness and its wildlife can be justified on the grounds of its importance to the native people.[77]

Despite his eloquence, Berger's plea might have been dismissed (as the recommendations of many such commissions of inquiry are). Since Berger, as the lawyer who acted on behalf of the Nisga'a Tribal Council and took the *Calder* case to the Supreme Court of Canada in 1969-71, was already well known to be sympathetic to Aboriginal claims, it might have been possible for a government determined to go ahead with the pipeline project to ignore him. However, the government did accept the central recommendation of his report: that there be a ten-year moratorium on pipeline construction to allow time to negotiate Aboriginal land claims. In the end, the recommendation for a northern Yukon wilderness park was accepted also (in all but name), and it was established through negotiation with Aboriginal people.

Berger's idea for a wilderness park was supported by two other elements in the overall context of ideas and institutions. One was the general worldwide increase in awareness by governments of the presence and rights of indigenous people. The other was the necessity, resulting from court decisions (especially the *Calder* case), for the Canadian state to negotiate land claims agreements with Aboriginal people.

The rise in awareness of the presence and rights of indigenous people with respect to national parks appears to have been a diverse and widespread but uncoordinated accumulation of instances that began in the 1970s (although it was not addressed coherently until well into the 1980s). Since the model of national parks adopted by the IUCN was one based on ideas about parks that emerged in the United States in the nineteenth century, there existed a central criterion to establish parks free from human habitation. The United States (along with Canada, New Zealand, and Australia), rare among the world's countries, was sparsely populated as Europeans spread across the land. The American model of national parks, therefore, was developed in somewhat unusual circumstances. As parks began to be promoted around the world as part of an environmental conservation strategy, the principle of a park free from human occupancy was difficult to implement in countries with long-established rural populations. At conferences of parks officials in the 1970s and 1980s, some officials focused on how to "get rid of people." At the same time, however, others began challenging the model of parks without resident people and advanced the idea of Aboriginal and related rights, cultural preservation, and rural development.[78]

Such ideas reflected a growing number of "anomalies" in the prevailing model, in which two themes were present. One related to the establishment of national parks in areas where rural people had lived for centuries but without distinct legal or constitutional claim to the land. The second (of importance to Canada) involved the creation of national parks where Aboriginal people held some form of unresolved constitutional claim.

The former case was common in Asia and Africa, where national parks planners were confronted with resident people of long standing. In Nepal in the 1970s, for example, the government sought to establish Sagarmatha National Park to encompass Mount Everest and the surrounding area. However, the Sherpa people, who had lived in the area for centuries, were not in favour of a park, especially if it meant that they would have to move, which in this already well-occupied country would have been a difficult matter for both Sherpa and government alike. In addition, the Sherpa did not like the expected limitations that a national park would place on their resource use and other activities. It was partly through the persuasive powers of Sir Edmund Hillary, who was highly respected among the Sherpa, that resistance to the park turned to tentative acceptance so that, when the park was created in 1976, the government allowed the 2,500 Sherpa to remain living within park boundaries and to continue their farming and other resource-use activities. Indeed, one of the priorities of the park was to endeavour to preserve the culture of the Sherpa people, with the requirement that management include recognition of their rights.[79]

In a somewhat different relationship with national parks, the Phoka people of northern Malawi were removed from Nyika National Park in the 1970s, but after suffering from disease and economic hardship in their new location they were selectively allowed back into the park to pursue their traditional beekeeping and honey production. As a result, the economic circumstances of the people improved, and violations of the park actually diminished.[80]

In the "new" countries of Australia, the United States, and Canada, the impetus to accommodate the claims of indigenous peoples with national parks came as part of a process of formal Aboriginal claims that have been occurring in each country since the mid-1970s. In Australia, for example, two national parks, Kakadu and Coburg, were established in 1979 and 1981, respectively. Both allowed Aboriginal people the right to continue to live, hunt, and gather food within the parks. Interestingly, Kakadu National Park was established as a result of a recommendation from a commission of inquiry that took place from 1975 to 1977 into uranium mining in the region,[81] just as the Berger Inquiry, in the same period, was influential in the establishment of parks in northern Yukon.[82] The legislation enabling this accommodation of Aboriginal residence and traditions with national parks was passed in the late 1970s. Nancy Weeks suggests that the desire to make Kakadu a national park motivated the change in legislation and that the park is therefore an "archetype of this new approach to national parks and native peoples in Australia."[83]

Kakadu National Park established two important departures from previous management practices in parks in Australia and elsewhere,[84] practices that were quickly followed in Coburg National Park. First, Aboriginal people were involved in park management in advisory roles, as wardens, and by providing cultural information and traditional knowledge about the park's biota. Second, Aboriginal people continued to pursue many of their traditional activities, such as hunting and food gathering (although these activities were now somewhat bureaucratized as Aboriginal knowledge became incorporated into the management practices of the park).[85]

In the same period, the United States was in the process of resolving land ownership issues in Alaska (which had received statehood only in 1959). This involved a staged process in which national parks (and other protected lands) were allocated from a declining base of federal lands after the state and Aboriginal people had received their portions. In 1980, the Alaska National Interest Lands Conservation Act, essentially a "national parks act" for Alaska, became law. In legislating for national parks, this act made express provision for rural residents, both Aboriginal and non-Aboriginal, to use for subsistence wildlife and other resources in the parks. While there was some consideration given to the needs of Aboriginal people in the preparation of this legislation, there is in the end no specific recognition of a distinct Aboriginal claim to use the resources for subsistence, since non-Aboriginal people have equivalent rights. Nevertheless, American legislators did recognize the importance of "the opportunity for rural residents engaged in a subsistence way of life to continue to do so."[86]

It is likely impossible to determine the full extent to which examples such as these have affected recommendations or policy decisions in Canada. Canada's approach to these issues was contemporaneous with those in other countries, but no single decision or country's practice is clearly antecedent to the rest. Nevertheless, by the 1970s, there were many bilateral links and multilateral forums on parks and indigenous people where these ideas might have been exchanged. For example, Sally Weaver notes that papers on the subject, though few and generally unsatisfactory (in her opinion),[87] were present at the Second World Conference on National Parks in Indonesia in 1983. It seems probable that Canada's actions were part of a worldwide response to the end of the imperial and colonial period that saw the recognition and emancipation of minority, especially non-European, peoples in many countries.

Land Claims Negotiations
While ideas about the rights of Aboriginal and other resident peoples in national parks were influential, it was the institutional, or quasi-constitutional, position of Aboriginal people in Canada that led first to comprehensive land claims negotiations and then to direct Aboriginal involvement in parks and parks management. The inability of the federal government to proceed with the white paper on Indian policy in 1969 and the reasoning of the

Supreme Court with respect to the Nisga'a land claims case in 1973,[88] as well as a growing political and legal sophistication among Aboriginal people in Canada, made it imperative that governments, both federal and provincial, negotiate to resolve their land and other claims. At the same time, capital-intensive industries, particularly petroleum and mining businesses, wanted the legal status of northern land clarified so that they could proceed with resource exploration and development without the possible future upheaval of legal challenges.[89]

In 1974, following the white paper and the Nisga'a claims decision, the federal government established the Office of Native Claims (ONC) to begin the process of negotiation. The work of the ONC was complicated by a variety of different processes all requiring prompt attention, such as cut-off lands (which government officials had earlier taken illegally from established Indian reserve land), treaty land entitlements (which resulted from incomplete land allocations at the time that the numbered treaties were signed in the nineteenth century), and comprehensive claims. North of the sixtieth parallel the situation was no less complex, although for different reasons. In the North, there were four principal areas over which Aboriginal people had laid claim: the eastern Arctic, the western Arctic, Yukon, and the Mackenzie River valley. In the eastern and western Arctic, the claims were by single entities, the Inuit and the Inuvialuit respectively, but in Yukon there were fourteen separate First Nations within the Council of Yukon First Nations (formerly the Council of Yukon Indians), each with its own claim. In the Mackenzie valley, there were spatial and cultural differences between the Dené and Métis people. The negotiations for each of these areas were drawn-out affairs taking seven to ten years to reach agreement.

While there were Aboriginal claims throughout Canada, the comprehensive claims of Yukon and the Northwest Territories were the ones that had the greatest effect on national parks since it was in northern Canada that parks were explicitly held in abeyance until land claims were settled. As the name suggests, the comprehensive claims led to complex discussions involving land, revenue sharing, financial compensation, surrender of Aboriginal title, self-government, and many other matters, including national parks. In addition, the negotiations were fraught with differences in cultural approach between Aboriginal people and government negotiators, in decision-making style, and in fundamental objectives. Aboriginal people wanted to retain Aboriginal title to the land, whereas the federal government wanted to extinguish Aboriginal title.[90] Another significant difference between the two sides was the nature of joint or co-management arrangements of natural resources, including parks. While co-management presumably is premised on some form of consultation, for the Vuntut Gwitchin the standard government methods of notification and discussion were insufficient. They wanted the power to give and withhold consent.[91] Similarly, some Inuit believed that they should have a veto over the decisions of the Parks Branch in national parks, but that proposal was rejected[92] because, recognizing the minister's responsibility to Parliament, government negotiators would not agree to sharing or delegating final decisions. The various joint management committees that were eventually established would, in the government's view, simply provide advice, with the final decision continuing to rest with the minister. These and similar issues, both in general and specifically with respect to national parks, caused the negotiations to proceed slowly and occasionally to come to a halt.

Given this complexity, the federal government in all likelihood could have established parks in the North on its own land after the conclusions of negotiations. However, it suited both sides to include parks in the division of land during negotiations. This approach was, no doubt, less costly in terms of land choices for the federal government, but it meant accepting and adopting ideas about Aboriginal use of the renewable natural resources in parks and Aboriginal partnership in parks management.

One of the first orders of business in the negotiations was, therefore, the allocation of land. The offer made by the federal government to Aboriginal people was for them to select certain quantities of land from within their traditional territories that they would hold in fee simple, while the remainder would become Crown land under the jurisdiction of the federal government. Some Aboriginal land would hold subsurface rights, while traditional uses such as hunting, fishing, and trapping were to be granted widely on Crown land. As part of this land allocation process, parks were integral to the negotiations in part because some lands had already been set aside as national park reserves.

While the federal government insisted that it hold title to the land in national parks, Aboriginal people, at first suspicious, eventually saw advantages for themselves in the parks' existence since the government was willing to negotiate hunting and fishing rights throughout most of the areas under discussion. Accordingly, Aboriginal people came to see parks as "friendly" land use designations that, if managed jointly, could meet Aboriginal objectives for economic development, hunting and fishing opportunities, and wildlife conservation. Thus, by helping to meet some Aboriginal goals, parks allowed limited Aboriginal land selections to be made elsewhere. For its part, the federal government wished to discuss national parks early in the process since it wanted to settle their location before other decisions were made.[93] National parks, therefore, served the purposes of both Aboriginal people and the government in the negotiations. In turn, the negotiations provided Aboriginal people with a lever by means of which to involve themselves in national parks. Both sides benefited: the government has been able to establish these parks and to hold title to the land, while Aboriginal people have been able to retain their traditional practices and to share in the management of these new land uses.

New Park Administrative Practices

The recognition of Aboriginal presence and even Aboriginal rights within national parks is in one sense not new. In 1922, when Wood Buffalo National Park was established, Aboriginal people were permitted to continue their traditional resource-harvesting practices there.[94] These activities have continued into the present but were modified in the 1970s by the issuance of permits and by the creation of the Wood Buffalo Park Hunters and Trappers Association to advise on wildlife management issues. With the signing of the Cree Band Settlement in 1984, these arrangements became the subject of a formal agreement, essentially an updated treaty, part of which was the establishment of a Wildlife Advisory Board on which Cree Band members formed a majority.[95] While the history of Cree use of renewable resources in Wood Buffalo National Park significantly predated the events of the 1970s and 1980s, it is worth noting that this arrangement did not serve as an example, model, or stimulus to further the presence of Aboriginal people in national parks activities and management in the 1920s or later.[96] It was not until a new set of political ideas and forces arrived in the 1970s that a broadly based relationship between national parks and Aboriginal peoples developed.

As a result of modern Aboriginal claims and negotiated settlements, national park practices in the North came to differ in two ways from previous procedures, just as they had for Aboriginal people in Australia's Kakadu and Coburg National Parks: first, hunting and other subsistence resource uses are not only permitted but also seen as integral to the parks; second, Aboriginal people now participate in the management of northern national parks. Thus, contrary to the trend to remove human presence and resource extraction from parks, the new northern parks agreements expressly include Aboriginal presence and resource use.

While the precise arrangements vary from agreement to agreement, the nature of the Aboriginal role can be illustrated by one of the more explicit treaties. The *Vuntut Gwitchin First Nation Final Agreement,* signed in May 1993, for the people and the region of northern Yukon around Old Crow, along the Porcupine River, stipulates that Vuntut National Park will "recognize and protect the traditional and current use of the Park by Vuntut Gwitchin in the development and management of the Park."[97] While this clause is rather general in "recognizing the traditional and current use," the agreement is specific with respect to hunting and fishing, saying that "Vuntut Gwitchin shall have exclusive right to Harvest for Subsistence within the

Park, all species of Fish and Wildlife for themselves and their families in all seasons of the year and in any numbers, subject only to limitations prescribed pursuant to this schedule."[98] Similar provisions are made for the harvest of edible plants and for the trapping of fur-bearing animals, the pelts of which may be sold commercially. Throughout these provisions, reference is made to the right to use both traditional and current methods of harvesting wildlife and plants. In addition, Vuntut Gwitchin may maintain or build such cabins or camps within the park as are necessary for them to pursue their subsistence activities and trapping.[99] While these rights seek to interfere as little as possible with access to and use of the park's resources, the agreement also allows for the exchange of wildlife and plant foods among Vuntut Gwitchin and with neighbouring First Nations people in order to maintain the exchange relations that are part of these local societies: "Vuntut Gwitchin shall have the right to give, trade, barter, or sell among themselves, other Yukon Indian People and beneficiaries of adjacent Transboundary Agreements all Edible Fish and Wildlife Products and edible Plant products harvested by them for Subsistence ... in order to maintain traditional sharing among Vuntut Gwitchin and other Yukon Indian People ... for domestic but not for commercial purposes."[100] All of these harvesting rights are subject to the conservation of plant and wildlife species, and some are subject to the terms of international agreements such as the Migratory Birds Convention Act and the 1987 Canada-USA Agreement on the Conservation of the Porcupine Caribou Herd. Moreover, the Vuntut Gwitchin have the authority to manage or otherwise regulate hunting, fishing, and harvesting activities, although they are expected to keep records of the harvests. Decisions about conservation and protection of species will be made jointly between the Vuntut Gwitchin and the government. Similar provisions as those set out in the *Vuntut Gwitchin First Nation Final Agreement* are found in other land claims agreements in Yukon and Northwest Territories.

While these territorial lands are still under federal jurisdiction (although territorial governments participated in the negotiations), and the federal government had authority to negotiate concerning the land base, in British Columbia the federal government had no such jurisdiction. Nevertheless, it has reached an agreement with the Council of the Haida Nation that allows the Haida the continued use of renewable resources in the Gwaii Haanas National Park Reserve (the South Moresby area). In the *Gwaii Haanas Agreement,* one of the objectives is "to sustain the continuity of Haida culture and ... to continue to the attainment of this objective in the Archipelago by providing for the continuation of cultural activities and traditional renewable resource harvesting activities."[101] These activities include hunting, fishing, trapping, and gathering plants for both food and medicinal purposes. In addition, trees may be cut for ceremonial or artistic purposes and for shelters or buildings constructed for various cultural activities.

The *Gwaii Haanas Agreement* is the most explicit recognition of Aboriginal rights in national parks in British Columbia. However, most of the area of that province has not been treated away from Aboriginal people, and claims remain outstanding on it. As Aboriginal people have registered their claims with both federal and provincial governments, the land of national parks, both existing and proposed, has been involved. The provisions of the *Gwaii Haanas Agreement* and those of the northern agreements will undoubtedly set precedents for future discussion. Concurrently, a similar situation prevails on the Atlantic coast, where Aboriginal people are pressing land claims in Labrador while consideration is simultaneously being given to national park proposals (and mining interests are anxious for clarification so that they can proceed with mineral development).

The variously named joint management or co-management arrangements are the second change to the conception and administration of national parks that arose from the negotiation of Aboriginal land claims agreements. At the time of writing, the organizational structures and formal rules have been agreed upon, but the precise nature of joint management has not been worked out. At the level of structures, the land claims agreements have established committees or management boards across northern Canada, with equal membership from the federal government and from the relevant Aboriginal nation.

For Vuntut National Park, for example, access to and management of renewable natural resources are administered by a Renewable Resource Council responsible for management issues both inside and outside the park. It comprises six members, three nominated by the federal government and three by the Vuntut Gwitchin First Nation. The council is given various powers to ensure its relative autonomy, such as the ability to select its own chairperson and a requirement to have its members reside within the traditional territory of the Vuntut Gwitchin. Councils are integrated into a formal decision-making network that includes the minister of Indian affairs and northern development (who is not directly responsible for national parks), the First Nation, and the Fish and Wildlife Management Board. This board is responsible for management issues for the whole of Yukon, which includes fourteen separate First Nations, and co-ordinates the recommendations of the fourteen individual Renewable Resource Councils. The board, like the councils, is made up of members nominated equally by the minister and by the Council of Yukon First Nations.[102] The Renewable Resource Council for Vuntut National Park, as with other such councils (where relevant), may make recommendations on most issues of the park's management.[103] Again, there are some variations in councils throughout northern Canada, but the basic features of equal government and First Nation's appointment, local residence of council members, and a certain degree of autonomy are common throughout.

Farther south, the *Gwaii Haanas Agreement* establishes the Archipelago Management Board (AMB), which consists of four members, two each from the Government of Canada and the Council of the Haida Nation. The chair is shared concurrently by a member from each authority. For Gwaii Haanas National Park, the AMB is actively involved in detailed, day-to-day park management rather than simply advising the minister. Virtually all aspects of park planning and administration come within the AMB's purview.[104]

The nature of the *Gwaii Haanas Agreement* and the Archipelago Management Board give the Haida a more authoritative role, in some respects, than their counterparts in the North. However, while the federal government endeavoured to protect the minister's discretion in the northern agreements, court decisions may give more force to the co-management councils than the federal negotiators had intended. In July 1997, the Federal Court ruled that "consultation and consideration must mean more than simply hearing." At issue was advice given to the minister of fisheries and oceans by the Nunavut Wildlife Management Board, one of the agencies created by the Nunavut final agreement, that the minister then disregarded.[105]

Conclusion

Three main developments in national parks policy between 1984 and 1993 need explaining. First, it is necessary to explain, on the one hand, the influences behind the strengthening of the formal provisions for environmental protection within the National Parks Act and, on the other hand, what gave rise to the protection of South Moresby and its consequent enhancement of environmental symbolism for national parks. Second, an understanding is required of the causes of the court-mandated increase in discipline in applying the environmental protection measures of the act. Third, the new relationship between Aboriginal people and national parks must be defined and explicated.

Each of these policy developments was dominated by organized groups[106] that were able to use various ideas and institutions to persuade, in some cases to force, central decision makers to adopt the various groups' objectives and demands. Societal organizations were successful because they were able to mobilize and to operate with great sophistication within a framework of institutions that enabled them to find alternative avenues toward realizing their goals when some routes were foreclosed. In short, it was not the raw power of groups in terms of electoral influence or ownership of capital that explains their success but a subtle interaction of groups, ideas, and institutions. To fully explain the policy developments of the period, however, it is also necessary to explain the interaction of these three factors, which was different in this period than in others. To this end, the most persuasive explanation for policy change was the set of ideas that established the context for the interaction of factors and for successful group intervention in decision making.

As in the two previous periods, two sets of ideas determined the context. First, there were relatively stable background ideas such as those relating to the role of bureaucracy in policy development that have been part of the policy context throughout the postwar period (and earlier). In addition, general ideas about environmental protection, which had been present especially since the 1960s, but also before, continued to be the central subject of policy debate. By the 1980s and early 1990s, ideas about public participation in policy deliberation, although not defined precisely, had been incorporated into legislation and other policy documents and thus had begun to form another of the stable background ideas. Among them, in contrast to the situation in the 1950s and 1960s, was the belief that it is right and proper for the public to play a key role in initiating and developing the details of public policy. The protest modes of public participation that had been common in the 1970s had, however, been replaced by more structured and expert involvement in the 1980s and 1990s.

The second set of ideas was new to the 1984-93 period. Within the general idea about the legitimacy of public involvement, there were specific manifestations favouring organized groups. Although not unique to this period, provisions by parliamentary committees for appearances by the public tend to focus on and favour groups. In addition, when the courts took the monopoly over public interest standing away from attorneys general and extended it to court-sanctioned individuals and groups, it was groups that were most able to take advantage of the new rules. Finally, there were new ideas about the relationship between Aboriginal people and the land and between these people and the institutions and procedures of Canadian government.

By the mid-1990s, several of these ideas about groups working within the framework of state institutions appear to have been firmly established and therefore differ from some of the more fleeting ideas of the 1960s. Nevertheless, the application of these new ideas may not predominate in the future, and therefore their contextualizing role will be correspondingly diminished even if the practice remains. That, of course, will be determined only with the passage of time. Despite the uncertainty about the future of these ideas, for the present analysis they clearly set the context in which the interaction of background ideas, interest groups, and institutions takes place and thereby provide the critical explanation for the policy changes in the third period of postwar national parks policy development.

The events surrounding the establishment of Gwaii Haanas National Park Reserve (and, more broadly, the role of groups in selecting and establishing national park sites) and the inclusion of interest group phrasing in the amended National Parks Act both show that, to some degree, groups were capable of capturing the initiative and setting the agenda on national parks issues. Indeed, with respect to both the South Moresby campaign and the amendments to the act, group action was able to override the original agenda put forward by the bureaucracy. In what was almost a reversal of the situation in 1964, when the Parks Branch needed societal support to promote the policy statement, in the 1980s the bureaucracy and the minister's office facilitated ideas and proposals put forward by interest groups. Whereas the Parks Branch had been able to restructure the policy environment in order to pursue its own objectives in the early 1960s, in the 1980s it was groups that were busy restructuring the policy environment. Moreover, not only were groups effective in action, but they were also widely accepted in this role by other actors (despite some strong disagreement on specific issues), including the forest industry, the BC government, the Parks Branch, and the federal cabinet.

Groups were able to do this because, in the long years since the 1960s and especially through the public participation activities of the 1970s, they had developed a high degree of sophistication in mobilizing ideas, both symbolic and scientific, and in understanding the workings of government institutions and political forces. In doing these things, interest groups had themselves become institutionalized, in Paul Pross's terms, by having organizational cohesion, extensive knowledge of government, and stable memberships, among other characteristics. They were also institutionalized in Stephen Krasner's terms by developing breadth wherein they became densely linked to other organizations and activities upon which they had a widespread impact.[107] Because of this institutionalization of groups, it became more difficult for government decision makers to ignore them and act autonomously or semi-autonomously.

Despite their evident capability and their centrality in the debate over the issues, interest groups and related ideas about public involvement did not exist in a vacuum. The institutions of federalism and parliamentary government were essential elements in these policy development processes. The preservation of South Moresby was successful largely because groups were able to move the issue from the provincial to the national sphere. For the amended National Parks Act, the existence of a parliamentary committee that provided the opportunity for groups to present their views directly to legislators was essential to the effectiveness of groups and the flow of ideas. Perhaps even more important was the position of the minister, who was able, in a sense, to over-rule the majority of the committee members and accept the CPAWS proposal on wording for the new legislation.

Another essential institution in this process was the existing policy (i.e., the National Parks Act [1930] itself and the 1979 policy statement). As with earlier changes to policy, the 1988 amendments, despite the significant contribution from CPAWS, were dependent on an already established path in that they followed directly from existing policy. While the Parks Branch may have been too conservative in its drafting of proposed amendments, CPAWS avoided being too radical. In fact, McNamee was at pains to show that the wording he was proposing was drawn directly from existing, cabinet-authorized policy documents. The existing policy, therefore, established a path for all participants in the process, not only for those in government.

The organization and activities of groups, the federal nature of the country, and the essential deliberative role of legislators and Parliament all contributed to the effectiveness of groups. What ultimately gave them the place and opportunity to be heard, however, was the idea that it was acceptable and appropriate for them to participate. The BC government in its multiple advisory committee processes, the federal minister responsible for national parks, the Mulroney cabinet, and the institutions of Parliament through its committees all legitimized the role of public interest groups. This idea, which has not always been accepted by Canadian government authorities or is not accepted in all policy fields, contributed decisively to the context for the making of choices about Gwaii Haanas National Park Reserve and the 1988 amendments to the act.

While Parliament, the minister, the bureaucracy, and interest groups were concerned with the content of legislation (and other formal statements), the courts concerned themselves with how the law was applied in practice. One definition of policy, offered by Mark Sproule-Jones, suggests that it exists "only at the interface of relationships between goods and individual citizens" and that parliamentary debates and official policy reports are of limited relevance in understanding how governments actually work.[108] In this sense, court decisions have contributed to a shift in policy emphasis toward greater environmental protection in national parks by ensuring that the administration of parks will be carried out with greater adherence to the law. As with the protection of South Moresby and the revised wording of the act, this shift can be directly attributed to interest group initiatives. In the examples of the legal challenges reviewed above, CPAWS and the SLDF have appealed to the courts to force an otherwise indifferent government to apply the terms of the National Parks Act. Once again, however, groups operated within the framework of existing institutions, the judiciary and its rules on the one hand and the existing legislation on the other. More important, the change in the court's rules regarding public interest standing was crucial to group initiative and success. Although public interest standing constituted a change in the rules, and therefore in the institution of the courts, the new rules were the result of the idea that the public should have the opportunity for this access to the judiciary, if none other existed, in order to ensure that governments act according to the law. Therefore, the enhanced faithfulness with which the act will be applied (in future) and the consequent strengthening of actual environmental policies are the results of background ideas about environmental protection, activist group politics, and the institutions of courts and the law. Significantly, the catalyst for this particular interaction was the contextualizing idea about the right of citizens to make their governments behave.

In much the same way, the change in policy to accommodate Aboriginal people and their continued use of parks' resources can be explained by understanding the interaction of background ideas, active Aboriginal organizations, and constitutional and governing institutions. Once again, the particular interaction of contributing factors took place in a context that was determined to a large extent by new ideas about the place of human beings in natural ecosystems and by renewed ideas about Aboriginal rights.

As with the other major parks issues in this period, it was Aboriginal organizations that took the lead in this change by negotiating the terms of land claims agreements and the character of new national parks. However, these organizations, like others, functioned within an existing framework of institutions, although the effects of these institutions often occurred before the beginning of the period under consideration here. Among these institutions were the courts that progressively articulated Aboriginal rights and legal claims to untreated land. They provided the authoritative institution that, as the application of the terms of the National Parks Act shows, could force indifferent or reluctant governments to act. The rights that the courts articulated were themselves institutionalized, however, in the quasi-constitutional status that Aboriginal people possessed before their formal constitutional recognition in 1982.

In addition to the revival of institutionalized ideas about Aboriginal rights, this special status of Aboriginal peoples was given particular meaning with respect to national parks in the late 1970s as another institution, the Mackenzie Valley Pipeline Inquiry, initiated and participated in the development of ideas about the appropriateness of permitting indigenous people to continue to live in and use the resources of national parks. As these ideas gained popularity within the national and international parks policy community, it became feasible for new parks to be established with rules quite different from those for parks created earlier. Although this particular inquiry may be unique in the annals of such commissions in Canada, because of the particular commissioner directing it, it was paralleled by a similar one in Australia with similar outcomes and illustrates just how such commissions can be effective. There can be little doubt that the outcomes for park developments in (what were formerly) Aboriginal lands in northern Canada were strongly affected by this commission.

Inasmuch as national parks are themselves institutions, the situation in northern Canada allowed for a change in the rules because the institutionalized path of parks was not well established there. By comparison, with the exception of Gwaii Haanas, national parks in southern Canada continue to strive to be free of resident people, although that situation, too, may be subject to change as other Aboriginal people work to reassert their revitalized rights.

Thus, the modern relationship between Aboriginal people and national parks, especially in northern Canada, was the result of the interaction of active, recently emancipated, Aboriginal organizations, constitutional provisions both ancient and modern, the institutions of the courts, and ideas about Aboriginal rights. The interaction of these elements can be further explained by the emergence, since the 1970s, of ideas about the rights of Aboriginal or other indigenous people to be involved in the decisions that affect their communities. This Aboriginal position in relation to parks included the modern idea about the role of humans, especially hunting and gathering people, in natural ecosystems and the concept of allowing these people to continue to live in parks and to use park resources. This liberalization with respect to Aboriginal people is part of a broader social recognition, including that by Parliament and the courts, that citizens have a right to be actively and intricately involved in the development of public policies.

6

Repossession by the State: National Parks and "Reinvented" Government

Despite the debates of the past, the 1990s was possibly the most turbulent decade for parks in the past half century since several of the ideas of the period, as well as decisions taken early in it, represented some of the greatest threats to the integrity of parks since the 1960s. Most of the discord, however, occurred within the government itself. While many groups, environmental and others, were aware of the conflict and offered their contributions, the principal issues, the main participants, and the central action were all within the federal government. The key elements of this debate revolved around the question of the best and most appropriate organizational framework for parks administration. While there was no expressed and overt effort to diminish the environmental protection characteristics of parks policy, there was great anxiety among many, both inside and outside government, that one of the consequences of changing the organizational structure and the governing principles was that parks would lose their safeguards and be subject to increasing commercial pressures.

In the 1990s, new ideas about cost recovery and market discipline presented a different, even a conflicting, conceptual basis to the environmentalist ones then established in national parks management. Moreover, in contrast to the processes through the 1970s to the 1990s, where environmental interest groups and Aboriginal organizations had asserted formative influence over large components of the parks agenda, the new ideas of the 1990s came solely from government. The application of these ideas amounted to a reassertion of state-directed decision making such as had been seen prior to the 1970s. In a sense, the state repossessed national parks as instruments of state management.

Market-oriented ideas and the changes that they engender represent a new era in parks policy and, with a recharged state initiative, a new phase in the meaning of parks. Despite these seemingly contrasting processes, the outcome of these new methods of administration was to strengthen rather than weaken the now well-established protectionist policies. For analytical purposes, this period begins in 1993, although ideas about government restructuring and about business-like methods have their origins in the 1980s. After the Liberal return to office in 1993, these ideas were applied to the administration of parks and reflected the changed context of decision making from earlier periods. By the end of the decade, two major pieces of legislation had consolidated the preservationist mandate, while some of the earlier decisions that threatened parks had been reversed. More than consolidation had taken place, however. The meaning of parks had changed subtly, and the administrative framework was altered dramatically. As a result, Canada's national parks are now more strongly protected than at any time in the past, but they are also, oddly, less about the environment. In order to understand the current situation, four contributing developments need to be considered. Two of them largely reflect the continuation of existing components of the policy context, while the other two are new.

First, interest groups, active since the early 1960s, took an even more innovative and comprehensive role, particularly under the leadership of the World Wildlife Fund. Although its initiatives were not uniformly successful, the WWF did, with its Endangered Spaces Campaign, provide a vision for parks and protected areas that surpasses the one offered by governments (both federal and provincial, in this case). However, the modest effect of the campaign on federal government plans (it seemingly had greater effect on some provinces' policies) is a testament to the repossession of the parks agenda by the federal state.

Second, in 1993 the Parks Branch was transferred from the Department of the Environment to the newly created Department of Canadian Heritage during a major reorganization of government structure. This shift was decided in the very centre of government, in the Machinery of Government Secretariat within the Privy Council Office and by the prime minister. Reportedly, it came as a "complete shock"[1] to many people in the branch, although the thinking that underlay the decision had been circulating for many years. Since both national parks and national historic sites as well as other "heritage" responsibilities reside in the branch, the move to the heritage department served to unify two purposes that had previously coexisted awkwardly. Now parks, along with historic sites, canals, and battlefields, were grouped clearly under a "heritage" rubric and were, presumably, less about environment and more about public memory.[2]

Third, Banff National Park or, more specifically, Banff townsite and the consequences of decisions taken over a century ago constituted an intractable policy problem. After thirty years without resolution and after numerous scientific studies chronicling the ecological problems of the park, in 1994 the minister of Canadian heritage launched a broadly based public inquiry, the Banff-Bow Valley Study (BBVS), into the environmental health and the future possibilities for Banff park and town. The conclusions of this study strongly reinforced the protectionist ethic and helped to solidify an ecological standard for all national parks. The experience of this process led the government to commission the Panel on Ecological Integrity, which, in turn, led to a new national parks act in 2000 that afforded the strongest protection yet. While the BBVS was a very open process of public participation with extensive representation from diverse interests, including environmental ones, the primary motivation for the study was the administrative need to bring stability to the continuing management decisions for Banff. Municipal, commercial, and property-related issues plagued senior management in Ottawa, who had to devote considerable time and effort to addressing a surfeit of appeals and delegations.

Fourth, dominating the policy agenda of the 1990s, government deficits and accumulated debt challenged policy makers to search for new ways to conduct public business. Expanded revenue-generation measures and the development of special operating agencies are among the responses by government to these problems. These new approaches are relevant to national parks since the Parks Branch was transformed into a special operating agency, called the Parks Canada Agency, and will, in its new incarnation, be responsible for raising some of its own financial resources. Important in its own right, the agency, as a different kind of organization from the branch that preceded it, may contribute differently to changes in policy substance as future decisions are made within a structure where the agency is one of the main pillars, although it is not designed to be a policy agency. After only six years, it is too early to tell how the agency will influence policy.

The importance of the events described in this chapter is that they illustrate the shift in the locus of decision making away from public involvement and group initiative and in favour of internal government resolution in which business-oriented concepts of administration serve as the contextualizing ideas. The central thesis of this analysis is that changes in contextualizing ideas, such as the ones presented here, condition the application of substantive ideas, including those already institutionalized in formal policy. This interaction may result in new and unanticipated outcomes. Indeed, the events outlined in this chapter constitute three stages in a stepwise process of reaffirming park purposes. The first step is the appearance of a new set of contextualizing ideas. These ideas, for the 1990s, are clearly about fiscal efficiency and market orientation. The second stage concerns the alterations made in the decision-making framework, which in this case is the creation of the Parks Canada Agency. The third is a consolidation of environmental protectionism for national parks. This last stage might not have been expected given the private-sector origins of these new contextualizing ideas; however, policy makers within the government have adapted these ideas and merged them with institutionalized ones about park protection to support rather than undermine ecological integrity objectives.

Both heritage-oriented and market-focused ideas have subtly changed the meaning of national parks by re-emphasizing their economic position within government and by shifting decision criteria toward consumer-focused concepts of utility. However, this renewed economic orientaiton has been combined with stronger ecological integrity requirements that enhance protection of parks themselves while at the same time reducing their "environmentalist" focus in the broader network of wilderness protection.

The World Wildlife Fund and the Group of Eight

As this analysis has shown, interest groups have been deeply involved in parks policy development since the 1960s and by the 1990s were well established members of the policy community. One of these groups, the World Wildlife Fund, has been present in Canada since 1967 but was not a prominent participant in the national parks community until, in the 1980s, it adopted a central position in two separate but related events. First, it developed the Endangered Spaces Campaign aimed at expanding the amount of protected area in Canada, and it did so by enhancing the use of science in land protection decisions. Second, the WWF took a leadership role in relation to other groups and initiated the formation of an eight-member coalition of national environmental groups with the intention of taking a stronger policy development stance.

While the WWF initiatives were important in their own right for future parks policy and administrative development, it should be noted that they also fit in with the continuing presence and increasing sophistication of other groups – such as CPAWS, the SLDF, and the Canadian Nature Federation – as they concurrently participated in policy discussions or took issues before the courts.

Ideas and Environmental Interest Groups

The two initiatives undertaken by the World Wildlife Fund partially redefined extant ideas rather than added new ones. The most important of these two overtures was the Endangered Spaces Campaign, a ten-year program aimed at prodding federal and provincial governments to expand their efforts at protecting representative wilderness areas. To promote wilderness protection, the WWF both undertook its own scientific program and cooperated with governments to define and map the ecological zones for each province and territory. Similar in principle to the process by which the Parks Branch determined its thirty-nine regions for the System Plan in 1971, although much more elaborate in design, the WWF began its campaign with an estimate of 350 ecological zones. After detailed data gathering and mapping, however, it measured 486 zones.

As a result of the WWF plan, ecological protection in national parks became both more and less important in the 1990s. It became more important as parks were identified as an example of enhanced protection relative to other federal agencies' policies. In its 1995-96 report, for example, the WWF stated that, "apart from the national parks system plan, the federal government lacks a clear protected areas strategy."[3] This statement recognizes that the concept of "protected spaces" is broader than that of parks and proposes that different kinds of custody may need to be applied to different places. In such a scheme, national parks provide a high level of protection compared to other devices, and, under the influence of the further strengthening of environmental measures overall, parks protection would be further secured. At the same time, parks themselves became less the centre of environmental concern as advocates and planners diverted their attention toward other vehicles for wilderness and wildlife preservation, such as provincial parks, wildlife sanctuaries, and ecological reserves.

Therefore, in addition to an advocacy campaign, the WWF's efforts included a sophisticated and rational foundation for the advancement of public policy. As a national project, this surpassed anything done by governments individually or on a co-operative basis. Indeed, at the start of the program, six of Canada's then thirteen jurisdictions had an insufficient knowledge base to enable them to decide rationally about protected areas.

The second WWF proposal, for a national coalition of wilderness conservation groups, expanded upon existing ideas about public participation to suggest a more-or-less equal partnership with government in which individual groups and the coalition itself would have distinct roles in protecting wild lands and would take an active role alongside government in pursuit of these activities. This conception of groups was already implied in the court challenges brought forward by CPAWS and the SLDF, but the WWF initiative took the idea into a wider realm of state-society relations. While the foundation of these ideas had been worked out in the preceding decades, this new manifestation revealed a coherence and institutionalization of those concepts that reinforced interest group stature within the policy community. This repositioning of groups had the potential to strengthen their position and to serve as a counterpoint to the market-oriented ideas inherent in cost recovery and special operating agencies.

The Endangered Spaces Campaign

The Endangered Spaces Campaign was launched by the World Wildlife Fund in 1989 and was aimed at encouraging governments to set aside, for protection, lands that would represent all of Canada's natural regions. Parallel to the scientific basis of the national parks System Plan, the WWF campaign nevertheless took a more detailed approach and divided the country into 486 regions, seeking protection of some representative space within each. The initiative consisted of several steps. First, the WWF assembled and, where they did not exist, developed maps of different ecological regions in Canada.

In the first annual report, the organization declared that mapping was completed for eight of the twelve subnational jurisdictions. Moreover, only six of these jurisdictions, plus the federal government, had established criteria for ecological representation. Second, the WWF identified regions that did not currently have protected representative spaces. Third, it worked closely with relevant governments, especially provincial ones, and promoted the protection of areas within regions unrepresented in a new network of protected areas. From the outset, annual reports commented on specific decisions taken by provincial premiers and cabinets expressly in response to the campaign. As a score-keeping and promotional device, the WWF presented annual report card grades from "A" to "F," which ranked the performance of governments.[4]

The campaign was the largest environmental advocacy effort in Canadian history, according to WWF data. At its end, all fourteen jurisdictions (with the creation of Nunavut in 1999), numerous First Nations, over 250 organized groups, many corporations (some of which surrendered resource claims in order to facilitate the establishment of protected areas), and over 600,000 individual Canadians participated. Yet this massive, well-funded, scientifically based campaign yielded only modest results. The number of square kilometres of protected park more than doubled during the campaign; however, just under 7 percent of the country was covered, which was lower than the 12 percent campaign goal. Moreover, only 132 of the 486 ecological zones were deemed by the WWF to be "adequately or moderately represented" as the program closed.[5] While most of the data are presented on the basis of the provinces, the federal government achieved a modest one-third (37 percent) increase in its protected area. It is uncertain whether this represents the influence of the campaign, however, because the Parks Branch had been moving ahead with these plans in any event. As a measure of federal government achievement, its annual report card grades rarely rose above a "C," and often its achievement was in the planning-and-good-intentions category.

While there were a number of significant contributions to the protected areas policy arena by the Endangered Spaces Campaign, it appears that it had little appreciable effect on the establishment of terrestrial national parks. Given the size, scope, credibility, and popular support for the WWF project, this outcome is surprising and seems to represent a level of government autonomy in sharp contrast to that of earlier periods.

The Group of Eight

The campaign led directly to another WWF initiative aimed at enhancing co-ordination among interest groups. While intergroup co-operation had existed at least since the formation of the National and Provincial Parks Association of Canada in 1963, one of the most ambitious coalitions was brought together by the World Wildlife Fund in November 1987 and continued into the 1990s. Dubbed the Group of Eight, this coalition consisted of the eight largest national wilderness and wildlife conservation groups in Canada.[6] The purpose of this alliance, in the view of the organizers, was to create a partnership with governments, both federal and provincial, in order to establish a co-ordinated national program that would fulfill the principles articulated in the Endangered Spaces Campaign.

Underpinning the Group of Eight was the realization that these groups, particularly when taken together, were able to bring important resources to a parks partnership. The coalition members possessed, or could obtain, impressive scientific and resource management expertise, stable organizations with large memberships, substantial funds, and the ability to broker decisions among different groups. The policy capacity of this coalition had considerable potential in view of declining budgets in government agencies at the time. Moreover, with fewer such resources, agencies had less leverage over groups and thus were less able to broker co-operative arrangements among them (or, perhaps, even between agencies within government).

Despite these resources and regardless of the benefits that this intended partnership could provide to the minister, the coalition had limited success. Neither the minister nor senior officials showed much enthusiasm for meeting with the group; most of the initiative came from the coalition. Moreover, Parks Branch officials continued to meet with individual interest groups despite the potential advantage of co-ordination within and by the coalition. In the late 1990s, the government further distanced itself from the idea of an environmentalist coalition when the Parks Canada Agency Act was passed. This legislation calls for a biannual meeting of the minister, agency officials, and representatives from a wide spectrum of interests, including, appropriately, those from the cultural and historic sites side of the mandate. Attendance at these meetings is by invitation only. While one is assured that all relevant interests are present at these meetings, it is clear that, through this means, the state has taken control of the process.

Implications of the New Strategies of Groups
The WWF initiatives and the ideas behind them have two important implications for the role of interest groups and their future within parks policy debates or, for that matter, protected areas in general. First, the Endangered Spaces Campaign and the expansion of concepts about environmental protection further institutionalize national parks by, to put it in Stephen Krasner's terms, deepening and broadening their position in a network of protected areas. Maintaining ecological integrity is no longer, for environmental groups, limited to the matter of official national parks policy but has acquired greater depth by being defined more explicitly in scientific terms and by being applied in a more comprehensive system across the

country. The ecological integrity idea is further deepened by emphasizing its place in parks policy and management decisions and, in turn, reinforcing the manner in which the System Plan (1970) and the amended National Parks Act (1988) remove parks decision making from the political realm. In turn, by concentrating on the provinces and expanding interest group involvement in ecological issues, the WWF initiative broadened the protectionist context in which national parks are an integral part of the national whole rather than simply a single policy concern for the federal government.

Indeed, this expansion of the concept has been reinforced by two proposals to link together a series of protected areas on a vast multijurisdictional basis. The Yellowstone-to-Yukon initiative in western North America and the Algonquin-to-Adirondacks concept in the east seek to combine protected lands regardless of their official status into extensive networks of wilderness, migration corridors, and reserves. National parks would, in such a system, be essential elements but would also blend into the requirements of the larger systems. Both these proposals remain visions with only modest increments toward their ambitious objectives.

While the undertakings of the WWF have helped to institutionalize ideas about ecology and parks, they were also part of a broader institutionalization of interest groups themselves, as was made evident by the importance of groups in establishing the legitimacy of the Banff-Bow Valley Study and the development of the Parks Canada Agency, as discussed below. Finally, it is important to observe that this broadening has been largely directed by groups themselves and reveals a set of well-developed political skills and an autonomous capacity to pursue political objectives. Despite this process, however, the newly increasing ability of the state to manage the national parks agenda has internalized environmental interests and created what is, in effect, a state-directed policy network.

The Department of Canadian Heritage

In 1993, Brian Mulroney stepped down as prime minister, and on 25 June Kim Campbell assumed the office after having been elected by the Progressive Conservative Party as its leader. Within days, Campbell announced an extensive reorganization of federal government departments and a reduction in their number from thirty-two to twenty-three. Among these changes, the new Department of Canadian Heritage was created out of various offices, branches, and other administrative components that were transferred to it from dismantled or altered departments elsewhere in the government. Bilingualism policy, multiculturalism, broadcast regulations, the Canadian Broadcasting Corporation, amateur sport, and citizenship, together with Parks Canada and its mandate for national parks and national historic sites, were brought together under one minister.

The transfer of parks out of the Department of the Environment and into the Department of Canadian Heritage raised new issues. One was a subtle shift in focus as the defining mandate became "heritage," a concept distinct from environmental protection. While the protection of heritage blends (nearly) perfectly with the protection of ecological integrity in parks, the objective is to protect parks to memorialize the past, even a mythic past, rather than to foster activist protection and an engagement in managing a wider environmental future. Even though protectionist policy was strengthened later in the decade, the move to the heritage department represents a subtle but important realignment for national parks. Another issue was that the new administrative home was not yet established or defined. As a result, parks, along with the myriad other components of the new department, were about to face a complete restructuring of their organizational form.

Although some reasoning can be imputed after the fact, there is no publicly available rationale for this transfer. Changes to the machinery of government are decisions taken by the prime minister, usually on advice from the Privy Council Office, and as such are covered by the requirements of cabinet confidentiality. Therefore, the reasoning behind them is unknown outside of a few officials at the very centre of government. However, some details are known about the context of these changes, and these details help to present a plausible argument about why this transfer took place.

Background

Beginning with Margaret Thatcher's election as prime minister of the United Kingdom in 1979, the dominant agenda for many governments in western democracies was to reduce the size and reach of government. The election of Brian Mulroney and his Progressive Conservative government in 1984 emphasized a similar program in this country. Thus, through the late 1980s and early 1990s, the Mulroney team also struggled, with only modest success, to gain control of the federal government's finances by, among other things, reducing the size and scope of government.

At this time, the Machinery of Government Secretariat, a small group inside the Privy Council Office that reports through the clerk of the PCO to the prime minister, had been examining whether the organization of government, as an issue distinct from its size, needed a comprehensive restructuring. Separately, but in direct communication with this secretariat, Robert de Cotret, then minister of the environment, formed an advisory group in 1992 to examine this question and presented its report to Mulroney. De Cotret's report was seemingly given little attention by the prime minister or cabinet, but its ideas were, of course, available for others to consider.[7] It is not public knowledge exactly how much, if any, of the Machinery of

Government Secretariat's advice was taken from De Cotret's report. However, it is not unreasonable to think that his experience as minister of the environment and his knowledge of the relationship between parks and the rest of the department would have influenced his thinking and, in turn, prompted similar views in the secretariat. However, at the time (1992), Mulroney was busy with the failure of the Charlottetown Accord and with deciding his own future.[8]

In 1993, the accession of Kim Campbell to the position of prime minister presented a more suitable opportunity to change the machinery of government, especially by allowing her to establish her own mark on its organization.

Ideas and the Transfer to the Department of Canadian Heritage
National parks, as outlined in earlier chapters, have been lodged in several departments during their existence, none of which has been a perfect fit. In the 1970s, the Parks Branch was in the Department of Indian Affairs and Northern Development even though national parks were neither "Indian" nor northern (since at that time most parks were south of the sixtieth parallel). However, as a land management concern, they did coincide somewhat with similar federal government concerns in the North. In addition, there was a trustee responsibility that paralleled the trustee mandate with respect to Aboriginal lands. Nevertheless, parks, and their sibling mandate, historic sites, were somewhat unusual in that department. Many thought that the move to the Department of the Environment in 1979 provided a more suitable setting. While this may have been true for national parks, with their growing environmental protectionist references, it was distinctly not true for national historic sites and monuments. While some commentators remarked that protecting the environment and protecting historic sites sometimes called upon similar skills and concepts, there was a wide breadth of policy understanding needed to bridge the management of industrial pollution in the Environment Protection Services Directorate, on the one hand, and the public presentation of historic buildings, on the other, which were all within the same department.

Indeed, the extensive process of rewriting the parks policy statement in the late 1980s and early 1990s, the successor to the 1979 policy statement, which became the official 1993 *Guiding Principles* document, was undertaken expressly to try to find a way to unify the diverse mandates for national parks and national historic sites and monuments. To that end, it was easier to identify "heritage" in parks than it was to find "environment" in historic sites. Therefore, it seems reasonable that more unity could be found by redefining parks than by reinterpreting historic sites.

In the early 1990s, Parks Canada, in consultation with the public, was preparing its new policy document, *Guiding Principles*, within the Department of the Environment. As minister, Robert de Cotret was, no doubt, aware of the concerns that Parks Branch officials had in unifying the mandate's two principal parts. Whatever role De Cotret might have had in the decision to transfer parks, in June 1993, just as Campbell took office, the Treasury Board Secretariat (TBS) described the mission of the department as "drawing on Canada's rich and diverse cultural and natural heritage[;] the Department of Canadian Heritage is committed to fostering the development of a strong Canadian identity based on shared values and goals in order to strengthen the foundation upon which Canada can grow and prosper."[9] Two things relevant to parks are immediately evident in this statement. First, they are referred to as "natural heritage," an expression that had been in official use for at least two decades but whose prominence is placed in tandem with "cultural heritage." Second, it is brought into service for Canadian identity and prosperity alongside, one might add, Canadian citizenship and cultural development. Clearly, national parks were no longer an element of environmental policy. Indeed, their preservation is no longer aimed at environmental purposes but at nation-building ones. Returning, thus, to the nation-building objectives of the first parks in the nineteenth century, national parks have, in a sense, gone full circle.

Implications of the Transfer

In its June 1993 perspective on the new department, the TBS briefly described the parks program and noted, in parentheses, that it was "largely unchanged."[10] In another previously secret document released by the Privy Council Office in February 2003 (although its precise provenance is not known), the assessment was made after the transfer had taken place that the move was "not yet a public issue (i.e., no public campaign criticising move to Heritage or seeking return to Environment)." The word *yet* seems to suggest that the writers of this brief had anticipated some criticism about what must have been seen as a new identity for parks. This document continues by saying,

> Parks can fit into either department:
> – national parks are an essential part of Canada's heritage and identity
> – yet Parks can be seen as closely tied to environment objectives and close
>   to hearts of environmental groups.[11]

These internal assessments show that government decision makers saw the transfer as more or less routine and not requiring any substantial reconsideration of parks policy. Yet there was recognition, at least in the latter document, that the mandate was not quite the same. For the parks themselves, there was not significant change, especially in view of recent legislation to strengthen both management autonomy and the provisions for ecological integrity. What alteration occurred was more in terms of the role played by parks in a network of expressly environmental policies and the withdrawal of resources from that network.

This shift in emphasis has not occupied decision makers, however. Rather, the rest of the decade, until the passage of Bill C-29 and the creation of the Parks Canada Agency in 2001, was marked by conflict and turmoil wherein officials sought both to maintain the definition of parks and redefine their organizational setting. Further experimentation with market-oriented ideas caused serious tensions with the Parks Branch, although it had nearly lost that organizational identity within the department, and the eventual solution to those problems was the creation of a special operating agency to become the parks' administrative vehicle. These were the tasks that occupied decision makers through the 1990s and that are addressed below.

Banff-Bow Valley Study

Banff is Canada's oldest, most famous, and most popular national park. However, it is also a very complex one. Its central feature is the narrow Bow River valley, which functions as a vital wildlife migration pathway and prime wintering ground. But this valley also serves as the principal corridor for two of the country's major transportation routes, and, just where it debouches into the prairies, it is also the location of the town of Banff. When the park was established in 1885, human presence was on a relatively small scale and therefore not in serious conflict with the natural environment. Over its long history, however, road and rail transport has become more intense, the town of Banff has expanded, and the number of visitors has virtually exploded. Today the human presence has, according to scientific and naturalist observers, pushed the park to the brink of ecological collapse.

Concerns about the effects of human activity began to be expressed as early as the late 1950s, and several unsuccessful attempts, accompanied by much controversy, have been made to address the worsening problems. However, while Banff town had been growing steadily but slowly since World War II, from 1986 to 1994 there was a sudden increase in the rate of construction of commercial space, almost doubling the amount of floor space already in existence.[12] This and other increases in human use led environmental groups and some scientists to argue that Banff National Park needed immediate help to protect the natural environment. To assess these claims and to take into account the interests of businesses, visitors, residents, and others, the minister responsible for parks appointed the Banff-Bow Valley Study in 1994. This task force conducted an open, public inquiry that sought to determine the ecological condition of the park and make recommendations to the minister.

Background to the Banff-Bow Valley Crisis

The foundation of Banff's present problems was laid in the 1880s when the park was first created. As outlined in Chapter 2, the government of Sir John A. Macdonald envisioned the park as a "pleasuring ground for a better class of people." Macdonald, in conjunction with the CPR, sought to achieve this by establishing fine hotels, a genteel community, and well-designed homes. To encourage the development of this upper-class character, Macdonald's government leased park land in the Banff townsite on twenty-one-year terms, renewable in perpetuity.

As long as Banff town remained relatively small and, in any event, consistent with early national park objectives, no conflict was seen between the perpetually renewable leases and park management. However, this changed with the development of the 1964 *National Parks Policy*. When that document was released, its most controversial element was the statement of intention to limit residency rights to those people whose work required them to live in parks and to remove the option of perpetual lease renewal. Although other elements of the 1964 policy were generally adopted, those features, after public consultations by the Standing Committee on Northern Affairs and Natural Resources in 1966 and much further debate, were never implemented.

The matters of residency and the leases were pursued further through the courts in 1967. Following a recommendation by the standing committee, the Parks Branch allowed its proposed non-renewal policy to be tested by the judiciary, and George Steer, an Edmonton lawyer, took the matter before the Exchequer Court (now the Federal Court) on behalf of two lease-holders in Jasper townsite. He argued that a lease in a national park should be renewable indefinitely as long as its terms were met. The court agreed and stated that, since Parliament had not explicitly removed the right of renewal, the minister, on the basis of the general policy statement, did not have the right to do so.[13]

Despite this resolution of the lease issue (unfavourably from the minister's view), conflicts over the status of Banff town continued to be an administrative problem for the Parks Branch. In particular, Banff was not a municipality like other towns in Alberta but was managed exclusively from Ottawa through the resident park superintendent. Agitation for municipal status under the jurisdiction of the Alberta government dominated the relationship between the townsfolk and the branch until eventually, in 1989, an incorporation agreement was signed between the Government of Canada and the Government of Alberta, establishing Banff town as an Alberta municipality.[14] Achievement of municipal status included the definition of boundaries for the town inside of which the locally elected council has substantial authority to govern land use and to legislate on the size and nature of buildings (like other municipalities). However, even after Banff gained this status, the minister responsible for national parks retained some authority with respect to townsite decisions in order to ensure that they did not conflict with federal parks policy. Therefore, in the late 1980s and early 1990s, when there was a rapid expansion of commercial space, the ultimate responsibility for the decisions and for finding a solution to this long-standing problem continued to fall to the minister.

Ideas and the Banff-Bow Valley Study

While Banff is the oldest and most famous national park, it is also the one where the conflict between ideas about environmental protection and those about economic use and development converge. The legacy of past decisions concerning transportation, land tenure, and settlement has meant that Banff is the most developed park and the one where development interests are strongest and have become most deeply institutionalized. The rise in prominence of environmental concerns in the postwar era resulted, therefore, in a conflict of ideas that has remained unresolved, sometimes even avoided. Indeed, in 1988, when interest groups appeared before the parliamentary committee debating amendment to the National Parks Act (Bill C-30), there was a de facto separation between the objectives of environmental groups that wanted to entrench preservationist language in the act, for parks in general, and those of business groups that sought to maintain their specific position in Banff (and some other parks with established internal communities, such as Jasper). That effective truce had ended by 1994, and the BBVS was the forum in which policy discussants, both state and societal, sought the resolution that had eluded them for thirty years. However, the ideas at issue were not only about Banff but would also affect the whole national parks system. If the recommendations of the task force favoured business, then they would signal a permissiveness for commercial development in all other parks, whereas if they focused on environmental protection then these ideas would be reinforced throughout the system.

In addition to concepts about use and development, a crucial idea present in the BBVS was about the central role of the public in an open participatory process. While the minister held final decision-making authority, the breadth and openness of the process gave the panel's recommendations great legitimacy.

The central motivating concern that gave rise to the BBVS was the sense that Banff had become unmanageable, from an administrative perspective, not only in terms of the relationship between environmental protection and human settlement but also simply in terms of the demands of the human population. Commercial expansion and building activity in the first few years of the 1990s continued apace with a multitude of individual problems to be solved. Many of these were referred to senior management in Ottawa. To the new assistant deputy minister, Thomas Lee, appointed in

1993, it quickly became apparent that the details of management for Banff were overwhelming the branch's capacity to manage the rest of the parks system. Therefore, Lee recommended to the minister of Canadian heritage that a panel of inquiry be established to find a long-term and orderly solution to the problems that plagued Banff.

Moreover, the sense of crisis resulting from the steady expansion of human activity in the park, and the scientifically documented decline in animal populations and restriction on wildlife movements, made such a long-term solution imperative. Indecision could not continue if Banff were to maintain its rank as Canada's premier national park and to hold a similar recognition in international circles.

The Study Process and Its Conclusions

The BBVS, drawing on two decades of experience with public participation in the national parks arena, and following the guidelines expressed in various parks policy documents, was organized in an elaborate way to allow a wide diversity of views to be represented by a multitude of interests and groups. Chairpersons representing First Nations, adjacent municipalities, local and national environmental groups, and others met in round-table discussions where scientific, demographic, economic, and social information was fed into a four-phase inquiry that took two years to complete.

When the report was released in October 1996, it made 500 recommendations, the main thrust of which was to reorient Banff National Park along stronger environmental lines. The task force's ideas included limiting the growth of Banff town, curtailing commercial development, especially that not directly linked with national park values, and in some instances closing access and removing structures (e.g., dams, buildings, and campgrounds) to allow environmental rehabilitation. For example, the grass-surfaced airstrip adjacent to the town was ordered closed, along with corrals, barns, and a cadet camp, all more or less adjacent to one another, which blocked an important wildlife migration route. It was further recommended that the Town of Banff, now incorporated, and several hotels be fenced to reduce human-wildlife conflict and to limit human interference with migration corridors. On these topics, the report is strongly worded: if fencing the hotels turns out to be ineffective, it says in plain language, then "the hotel(s) may have to be phased out." For one hotel, the Timberline, it is more terse: "remove hotel."[15]

The report does recognize the important role of business in providing services to visitors, however. In its statement on a vision for Banff National Park, the report acknowledges that "a healthy economic climate, based on the heritage values of the Park, contributes to national, provincial and local business. Businesses evolve and operate along aesthetically pleasing and environmentally responsible lines. Innovative ideas, designs and technology are emphasized when providing services including education, transportation, waste management and other infrastructure."[16] Despite this recognition of business values, the objective of the report and its recommendations "is to create a very special kind of tourism destination [that] fully respects the ecological integrity of its unique setting [and] provides authentic rather than artificial experiences."[17] The task force flatly disagrees with the proposition that tourism and commerce are not sustainable without continued growth and argues that, with the right approach, business will prosper.[18] Moreover, it argues that operating a business in a national park is a privilege, not a right, and that opportunities in Banff are simply not the same as in (the rest of) a national economy.[19] Unequivocally, then, the study's authors, while acknowledging a role for business, direct the application of national parks policy toward ecological protection and environmental restoration in Banff.

While the priority of the environment over commerce is clarified, in the eyes of the task force the Town of Banff presents a special challenge. As a result of gaining a degree of municipal autonomy, the town represents a potent political force with enhanced power. The report says,

> By fixing the Town's annual rent for municipal land at $550,000, Parks Canada gave away any opportunity to benefit from economic growth in the Town. They also forgave an opportunity to participate in Town affairs by not insisting on a seat on Council, and by creating instead a much weaker liaison committee. The Town has also become more autonomous than either originally intended or desirable. Moving away from the intent of the *Incorporation Agreement* with regard to development, the Town is becoming a significant political force unto itself. Re-establishing a more structured role in relation to Parks Canada, one which conforms with Park values, promises to be challenging.[20]

The concerns raised by the BBVS panel, and by others, about the Banff agreement clearly led the minister and other key decision makers to see it as a mistake. In the updated and expanded legislation, the Canada National Parks Act, passed in 2000, Parliament made clear that the Banff agreement would not be repeated in any of the other six resident park communities. In this way, Parliament had come back to deal with an issue that it had first encountered in 1964 when it considered the policy statement of that year.

The Aftermath and the Implications of the Study
Banff has been something of an anomaly in the modern parks system because it embodies so strongly the economic development model while, progressively, the policy and most of the rest of the system have been aligned in favour of environmental protection. Some of the other older parks resemble Banff in this respect, but none has reached the same level of

urban and commercial development. It is, therefore, in Banff where the conflict between the nineteenth-century view of parks as instruments of economic development and the late-twentieth-century view of parks as reflections of environmental protection is most acute. The task force recommendations, and the minister's acceptance of the majority of them,[21] therefore, attempt to bring Banff within the ambit of formal parks policy and, finally, to resolve the essential ambiguity of national parks in favour of environmental protection.

The conflict was not over, however. Eight months after the report was released and just two months after the minister, Sheila Copps, tabled it in the House of Commons, the Banff Town Council approved a municipal plan that would see commercial space increase by 25 percent. Also, early in 1997, CP Hotels (now Fairmont Hotels and Resorts), which owns properties in several national parks, discussed a possible deal wherein it would be given permission to expand its convention facilities at Lake Louise (in Banff National Park) in exchange for surrendering title to some of the other properties that it owns. These events, and others on a smaller scale, demonstrate that the problems of managing Banff National Park, while given greater clarity and new direction by the Banff-Bow Valley Study, will continue to confound parks policy makers.

Market Orientation and National Parks

In contrast to the continuity concerning ideas about environmental protection and about the role of interest groups, as reflected by the World Wildlife Fund initiative and the Banff-Bow Valley Study, the 1990s also saw the innovative application to parks of neo-conservative ideas that had become prominent in the 1980s and that in many policy fields dramatically redefined the interaction among institutions, interest groups, and ideas themselves. When applied to the details of national parks policy, the market orientation inherent in these new ideas appears in a revised and expanded approach to revenue generation and, through the creation of a special operating agency, an extensive redesign of the Parks Branch's administrative arrangements. When these ideas, or some of them, were first applied, they suggested a radical business model approach to parks management, but in less than a decade these ideas were modified for the purpose of protecting the relative independence of Parks Canada. Since its mandate is to protect parks, this redirection of market-oriented ideas had the effect of further strengthening the ecological objectives of parks.

Market-oriented ideas appeared (in newly reconstituted form) in national parks as the result of the Treasury Board's 1989 statement "External User Charges for Goods, Services, Property, Rights, and Privileges,"[22] directing departments and their various agencies to seek ways to generate additional revenue through fees and other dues that might be levied on their clients.[23]

Following this, in 1994, the Parks Branch introduced its own revenue management policy. While the details of this policy[24] were developed within the branch and at the direction of senior management, the policy fitted well with the program review authorized by Minister of Finance Paul Martin and the Department of Finance. Martin's review was mainly in response to the federal government's fiscal needs in the 1990s, but it was also partly the result of an adoption of market-oriented ideas about who should pay for services received by individuals. Both ideas were present in the actions taken by parks management.

The second application of market-oriented ideas was the creation of the Parks Canada Agency, the latest incarnation of the historically mutable Parks Branch. Through the agency, parks will function somewhat autonomously, outside the lines of hierarchical authority within the Department of the Environment (since the agency returned to the responsibility of the minister of the environment from Canadian Heritage in 2003). Special operating agencies are part of an approach to government management that stems from the 1980s neo-conservative impetus to make government administration more efficient and more responsive by organizing parts of it along private-sector lines or at least along lines where government organizations will function according to and in response to market or market-like signals.

Ideas and the Reinvention of Government

During the 1980s, ideas about a revolution in government spread through many Western industrialized democracies, particularly the English-speaking ones. This revolution consisted of a broadly based attack on the size of government and the steady expansion of the state that occurred in the 1950s, 1960s, and 1970s. Partly ideological, in terms of opposition to government intervention in the economy, and partly pragmatic, in terms of the perceived need to eliminate government budget deficits and public debt, these ideas favoured policies aimed at producing smaller government through privatization of public enterprise, deregulation of private industry, and commercialization of many government services.

While these ideas were present in various settings prior to the 1980s, it was, according to Donald J. Savoie, the election of Margaret Thatcher's Conservative government in the United Kingdom in 1979 that marked the beginning of this revolution. Thatcher, whose views are by now famous, came to office convinced that government interfered too much in the economy and was less efficient than the private sector at allocating economic resources and in contributing to economic growth. Immediately on taking power, Thatcher began to change the methods and the machinery of British government, at first by inviting Sir Derek Raynor to examine the efficiency with which government resources were used. The Efficiency Unit, a seven-person team created by Raynor within the Prime Minister's Office, became an important instrument in the examinations, the so-called scrutinies, of departments and other government agencies that led to a reorganization of financial management and a redirection of departmental attention toward management and away from policy development.[25]

In 1987, after eight years in government and with some sense of success, Thatcher began to realize that more was needed to further improve the efficiency of government and to further reorient departments toward an emphasis on management.[26] Recommendations for new changes flowed from the Efficiency Unit in the form of a report entitled *Improving Management in Government: The Next Steps*.[27] This report argued that, although progress had been made, the message to emphasize management over policy development had not been widely assimilated. The proposal that followed was aimed at restructuring government agencies so that they would operate at greater distance from ministers and from the policy development process. While long-standing issues of public administration such as personnel management, accountability, and ministerial responsibility had to be addressed, the recommendations of the *Next Steps* report led to the creation of "executive agencies." These agencies had broadly delegated authority allowing them to be highly independent from the minister and to manage their day-to-day administrative activities as required by law or regulation at the direction of a self-reliant chief executive officer.

Thatcher's revolution in government gave inspiration and direction to both Ronald Reagan in the United States and Brian Mulroney in Canada. Ideas about expenditure reductions, privatization, deregulation, and other elements of the conservative agenda circulated freely among the three leaders and the governments that they led. For example, when first elected in 1984, Mulroney quickly established the Ministerial Task Force on Program Review[28] under the direction of Deputy Prime Minister Erik Nielsen. Aware of recent reviews in Britain and the United States, Nielsen structured Canada's process halfway between the different concepts used in the other two countries.[29] The so-called Nielsen Task Force (1984-86) did not have a strong direct effect on government administration, however, as numerous commentators have observed.[30]

By 1989 and his second mandate, Mulroney wanted, like Thatcher in 1987, a powerful instrument to effect administrative reform in the Canadian federal government. In early 1989, therefore, the Treasury Board Secretariat began to float the ideas of a *Next Steps* initiative, modelled on the British program, for this country, and it sent staff to London to examine the UK experience more closely. The British approach was adopted almost without alteration (the executive agencies were named special operating agencies [SOAs] in Canada), although its adoption in Canada was less extensive than in Britain. In the United Kingdom, these agencies were seen as the single most effective solution to administrative inertia, and as early as 1994 more than 60 percent of public servants were engaged in them.[31] In Canada, SOAs were seen in more modest terms, and their introduction was more partial and experimental. For example, whereas British agency chief executives had a high level of responsibility and reported directly to the relevant minister, the Canadian SOA chief executive generally reported to the deputy minister.[32] The Treasury Board of Canada's description of SOAs confirms this view of more limited independence by depicting the agencies as partially within line departments and, by way of comparison, having less autonomy than a departmental corporation. This limited autonomy has resulted in some internal criticism that suggests that nothing has changed despite the advent of SOAs. Savoie quotes a mid-level agency official as saying that "the rules are the same and the senior executives are the same. We have seen no new blood coming from outside. If anything, the home department has made things more difficult, perhaps because they do not like part of their empire hived off. For me and my colleagues, SOA no longer stands for Special Operating Agencies; it stands for Screwed Once Again. If anything we have less freedom than before."[33] Rather than being a radical departure, therefore, SOAs can be seen as only one measure in an ever-expanding menagerie of administrative instruments.

In the form that has been adopted in Canada, SOAs provide several new features to the delivery of public policy compared to existing departmental agencies. First, they increase the visibility of an administrative unit and its public purposes in a way that would not be possible for an agency buried within a larger organization. This was an important aspect of Parks Canada as it sought to maintain its public profile when it was at risk of being submerged within the bureaucracy of the Department of Canadian Heritage. Second, SOAs have provisions for new financial management systems, such as revolving funds, which allow for the allocation and management of budgets over two or more years, thus enabling expenditures to be made more in accordance with practical requirements rather than in response to rigid fiscal year rules. Some SOAs are also fiscally independent from their home departments and are permitted to retain revenues generated from fees and service charges rather than having to submit these monies to the consolidated revenue fund. Third, some SOAs have been granted autonomy over personnel management compared to departmental units. While few have fully independent employer status, as is the case for many executive agencies in the United Kingdom, and are still subject to Treasury Board oversight, greater consideration is given to allowing agencies to reach their own employment contracts, including bargaining separately with labour unions. Fourth, in addition to financial and personnel matters, there is a general release from centrally determined rules, thus permitting greater management flexibility. Fifth, the separation from departments and centralized structures results in a change of values and organizational culture that, early evidence suggests, results in a better service to the public and more efficient use of government resources.[34]

In addition to these administrative changes, there is potential for a more institutionalized and closer working relationship with the public since many SOAs are structured with advisory boards comprising client, customer, and so-called stakeholder groups. These boards may simply provide information and customer/client responses to the chief executive, but they may also participate in developing an operating strategy for the agency.

While some of the mechanisms and practices of SOAs are becoming clearer in the Canadian setting, how they will fit within the government over the long term is less certain. In the *Next Steps* measures in Britain, Thatcher was determined that, if privatization was feasible, then those agencies would be sold.[35] In Canada, Ian Clark, then secretary of the Treasury Board, said in 1991 that, while there was "no guarantee that an agency ... is forever immune to privatization, ... ministers ... have been very clear that the SOA initiative is not about improving government services so that they can be sold to the private sector."[36] The task force that prepared the 1994 report for the auditor general and the secretary of the Treasury Board wrote that the ambiguity surrounding SOAs and privatization weakened the agencies' effectiveness. The task force went on to suggest that government re-emphasize the relevance of these agencies to public purposes. However, these authors did not discount privatization either. More recently, in a 1995 report, the Treasury Board continued this ambiguity by identifying SOAs as essentially parts of departments while, at the same time, generalizing about privatization of government assets. Thus, while there is some public anxiety that SOAs may lead to privatization, government officials in Canada have not yet been clear about the government's long-term strategy with respect to these agencies. This concern of privatization was one of the fears expressed by interest groups around the development of the Parks Canada Agency. The minister, the assistant deputy minister, and others were at pains to show that national parks would always remain in the government domain.

Interestingly, the independent agency idea, while new in the general context, is not new to national parks but, in fact, repeats a recommendation made by the (Glassco) Royal Commission on Government Organization in 1962. That commission recommended "that the operation of the national parks should be vested in an autonomous commission [whose] terms of reference should include a clear definition of public policy and its senior management should be appointed on the recommendation of the commissioners."[37]

The earlier proposal was also made in the image of the private sector since the royal commission was appointed by the Diefenbaker Conservative government and was made up of people selected from the private sector. J.E. Hodgetts observed in the early 1970s that "well over half the staff of some 170 investigating officers were associated with management consultant firms and most of the remainder were drawn from executive positions in private industry."[38] Recommendations in the commission's report "reflect," says Hodgetts, "the thinking of the business oriented community on problems of managing and organizing large enterprises."[39] Given the prevalence of business opinion among its staff, it is not surprising that for national parks the royal commission concluded that "it is not unreasonable to set as a goal for these parks ... a condition of financial self-sufficiency."[40]

It is striking that the present establishment of the Parks Canada Agency is a near, but not perfect, parallel with ideas from the 1960s. In both decades, a Conservative government initiated an evaluation of and changes to the federal public service using principles of business management for guidance and to establish, what was in their view, a more efficient government. In both cases, the changes were incomplete when Conservatives were replaced by a Liberal government, but in both cases the Liberals continued to adopt many of the ideas and to implement the changes of the previous administration. Indeed, in 1967 Liberal Treasury Board President E.J. Benson said that his government had implemented thirty-six of the forty-eight recommendations made by the Glassco Commission.[41] Similarly, in the 1990s, the Chrétien Liberal government continued and extended the budget control and privatization policies begun by its predecessors.

In the 1960s, however, the recommendation for an autonomous parks management commission was not acted upon, whereas in the 1990s and early 2000s such an agency was created. The difference can be explained by the variation in contextualizing ideas between the two periods. For governments in the 1960s, there was a challenge to improve management practices but not necessarily to reduce the government's size, especially not its fiscal scope. In fact, the Pearson and Trudeau Liberals of the period presided over a significant expansion of government. In the 1990s, however, not only were management issues in question, but, more importantly, the role of the state and its use of economic resources were also being re-evaluated.

The combination of questions about management issues and about the role of the state, together with those about user fees and the delivery of services, has therefore led to a more vigorous and far-reaching application of market-oriented ideas in the 1990s than was attempted in the 1960s. In fact, despite strong parallels, there does not appear to be any direct link between the Glassco recommendations and the present attention to SOAs. The current thrust almost certainly comes from ideas imported more recently from the United Kingdom.

Cost Recovery and Revenue Generation in National Parks

Parks Canada, or its predecessor organizations, notes the 1995 business plan, has been charging fees in parks since the 1880s, so by itself revenue generation in the 1990s is not new. In the earliest case, the charge was for access to Banff hot springs, but over the following century various fees were applied for general access to most parks and for different services within them. While it is not entirely correct to say that there was no systematic basis for their application, there was great variation about the earlier placement of fees. In particular, they were seen as part of general revenue generation for government rather than a tool specifically for parks management. In this conception, there was no direct relation between the demand for and the supply of services, nor was an explicit relationship drawn between the fee level, the price in other words, and competition with other recreational activities. Most significantly, however, in the first century, all monies raised were vested in the consolidated revenue fund and not available to parks either for direct expenditure or for management.

Development of the Treasury Board's 1989 external-user-charges policy not only provided a rationale for the raising of additional revenue but also introduced a major shift in philosophy. That policy explains that user charges will shift the financial burden from taxpayers as "the Canadian public is prepared to invest in Parks Canada operations and pay market rates for services having a personal benefit."[42] While these principles were articulated during a Conservative administration, they were retained by the incoming Liberals in 1993.

Parks Canada's own 1994 revised revenue generation policy was the first measure to introduce these new ideas. Then, in 1995, the Parks Branch released its five-year business plan, in which it asserts that "the future success of Parks Canada is contingent upon managing its operation in a business-like, market-responsive manner."[43] This did not mean that parks were to be entirely self-financing. In fact, the business plan points out that parks establishment, protection, and general maintenance, what it refers to as the "public good component,"[44] will be financed from the government treasury. On the other hand, services that benefit individuals directly, including basic access to parks, will be subject to fees to cover the costs of providing them. Under these new arrangements, Parks Canada was also able to retain the revenues derived from its charging policies. With this opportunity, the organization was now able to use charging policy as a management tool to administer, through a price signal, the demand for certain parks services. Moreover, it somewhat re-emphasized its self-perception as (partly) a recreation-providing organization in competition with other such organizations. Its fees, therefore, were seen within a context of market prices, and thus their determination would have to take into account the context of private-sector operators and their prices.

Although these plans initially derived from the 1989 Treasury Board position, they were dramatically reinforced by Liberal Minister of Finance Paul Martin's attempts to deal with the federal government budget deficit.

Martin's request to his fellow ministers and their departments to identify areas where spending could be reduced led to a 30 percent reduction in Parks Branch appropriations between 1993 and 1998.[45] One of the consequences of this was to put added pressure on the branch to raise its own revenues to cover, as much as possible, its own costs. This responsibility was, however, desirable for many parks administrators since it gave them greater control over revenue policy and the opportunity to use it for their own management purposes.

Since various fees have been in place for over a century, the presence of a revenue-raising plan was not revolutionary. However, its deliberate organization around market-oriented principles was an important change from the basis of past policies and offered a framework for a new set of priorities for parks management. As a demand management tool and as a measure seen in the context of providing recreational services, charging policies subtly shift the conception of park users from citizen-visitors to consumers. While the idea that parks belong to the people of Canada remains entrenched in legislation and in the public's mind, the fee structure and its comparison with prices for other types of recreation and entertainment detaches Canadians from them in terms of a sense of public ownership or belonging.

The presence of these new ideas about governance within the parks program is really an interplay between the market-oriented context during the Conservative government years, initiatives taken by senior management within the Parks Branch, and, finally, later directives given by Paul Martin and the Department of Finance. While this background of cost recovery and fiscal restraint provided an atmosphere for adoption of these ideas, the branch itself, under the direction of the newly appointed assistant deputy minister, drew up a business plan in 1993 with the objective of changing the fee structure and doubling revenue by 1995. This plan predates and was distinct from the program review initiated by Martin in 1995[46] and thus illustrates continuity between the governments of the period.

The revenue-generating rules do more than outline the means by which to raise money, however. They also offer a framework for a new set of priorities for parks management. First, this policy makes an essential distinction between general policy objectives concerning parks on the one hand (their establishment, planning, protection, and broad public education about them), and states that these objectives will continue to be supported by tax-based budgets, while on the other hand the cost of personal services provided by parks (e.g., opportunities for hiking, visiting, viewing, and picnicking) must be borne by the individual using them. Second, the policy redefines the park system's broad goals by declaring three key mandates. One, the long-term protection of park resources, is well established, while the other two, meeting market demand for client services and maintaining cost efficiency, are new expressions, for parks, of market-oriented ideas. Third, according to the new rules, revenues from one source will not be used to cross-subsidize unrelated activities. In other words, there is no implicit judgment that one activity is worth supporting on general policy grounds while others are not. For example, hiking is consistent with national park values but it may not always be feasible, from a revenue perspective, to offer such opportunities, while golfing is not consistent but may be more practicable in revenue terms. An injunction against cross-subsidization could, in the extreme (and hypothetical) case, lead to parks where one could golf but not hike. Fourth, consistent with this theme of activity-specific accountability, all field units[47] will be able to retain funds earned by them, and thus there will be little or no cross-subsidization between popular parks and lesser-known ones. Finally, these points make it clear that, as the policy states, "fees [shall] promote a market discipline in the supply of services, rights, and privileges."[48]

The general picture that emerges from these points is one of a highly regulated business in which parks will have to meet stringent environmental conditions set down in legislation but will otherwise respond to consumer demand. Societal objectives such as family recreation or the appreciation of natural history have ceased to be public policy choices and have become individual consumer choices. Even symbolic messages about Canada's natural heritage and a shared identity based on that heritage are now matters of consumer choice. This new role, therefore, has the effect of turning parks into instruments of revenue generation and fiscal guardianship, thus modifying the centrality of their social meanings.

Bill C-29: An Act to Establish the Parks Canada Agency

The relationship between parks and the idea for a special operating agency is an intriguing one and casts a new light on the role of contextualizing ideas. It might be expected that the market-orientation that informs SOAs would shift parks in a commercial or commercial-like direction, but this was not the purpose for the agency, nor thus far has it been the result. Indeed, commercialization was one of the fears expressed by some parks protection advocates at the time that the agency was being created. However, while the organizational or structural characteristics of SOAs may facilitate a private-sector mode of operation, they are also suitable for establishing organizational independence and administrative coherence irrespective of whether or not the agency pursues commercial-like practices. In this sense, they replicate the roles of some Crown corporations as established in previous policy periods. For parks, it was the organizational characteristics that provide coherence and management autonomy that appealed to senior decision makers, not necessarily the opportunity to increase revenue, and it was these characteristics that were critically behind this policy decision. In fact, rather than create a quasi-commercial agency, the consequence of the legislation was to strengthen the parks protection mandate by creating greater distance between management decisions and political ones (including the small "p" political ones within a large departmental structure).

The relationship between parks and the idea of a special operating agency powerfully demonstrates the interaction between the existing framework of established ideas, institutions, and interests on the one hand and new and forceful conceptions such as those that condition the policy context on the other. Given the zeal with which neo-conservative ideas were adopted by policy makers in the late 1980s and early 1990s, one might have expected national parks policy to change substantively toward increased market orientation. However, as in other instances where contextualizing ideas have influenced policy development, there was a dynamic interaction between the established framework and new ideas about management and policy, the consequence of which is that some of the ideas in the new context, but not all of them, were adopted. The appropriateness of the SOA did not become apparent until after 1993 and the relocation of the Parks Branch within the Department of Canadian Heritage. More important, however, these ideas were adopted in a way that was consistent with and, indeed, reinforced existing policy ideas.

Three factors contributed to the adoption of the SOA model for parks. First, contemporary neo-conservative ideas provided the idea for and the vehicle of these agencies. Second, the chaos wrought within the parks program by the transfer to Canadian Heritage created the need for a new administrative mechanism. Third, the precipitous budget reductions resulting from program review necessitated a different approach to the management of the financial resources within Parks Canada.

Throughout its long history, from its beginnings as the Dominion Parks Commission in 1911, the Parks Branch existed (most of the time) as a coherent, identifiable organization even though it was located in many different departments at different times. In 1993, however, with the creation of the Department of Canadian Heritage and the inclusion of parks within it, the branch risked losing that coherence for the first time. In its new location, also a new department wherein the structure of the department was just being established, the administrative functions for parks were melded and blended with the parallel functions for other activities within the department. Routine roles such as budgeting, accounting, planning, hiring, and management were brought within a single supervisory framework for the department whether for parks, multiculturalism, amateur sport, or other mandates. Thus, Parks Canada, as an organization, lost effective control of its own budget, personnel decisions, long-term planning, and other administrative activities. The management concepts that underlay these organizational decisions also led to the realignment of parks-specific functions. In the most severe cases, parks were stripped of their resident superintendents (not all parks lost them), and the role of these officials was carried out by people in regional centres instead of by those located within the park, as had been done for more than a century. The responsible officials, however, also had other duties, so that park duties were only part of, rather than all of, their functions. These organizational changes affected the jobs of everyone in the branch, from the senior administrative officials in Ottawa to staff members at the field level.

In the field, the effects of the new organization were felt especially strongly. Here a matrix model of responsibilities for field staff resulted in specialists being responsible for their subject areas in several parks, but no one held overall responsibility for the conditions of any single park. Managing out of regional centres, these staff specialists risked becoming detached from the intricate ecological and human processes within and characteristic of each park.

As these reorganizational decisions accumulated, it quickly became apparent that no single person was responsible for any specific park, and in general personnel had no attachment to individual parks but were responsible for general functions spread over several parks. Moreover, these roles were brought under the same single supervision as other components of the department whereby the managers had no special professional commitment to or necessarily experience with parks. The consequence was that no one, nominally, was in charge of any particular park, and the assistant deputy minister's ability, or anyone else's for that matter, to provide unimpeded direction to the parks program had dissolved. In turn, this led to a breakdown of accountability in the parks program since there was no clear chain of responsibility from the field staff to the ADM.

This increasing formlessness was a dramatic change from preceding practices and sharply contradicted the organizational culture of the Parks Branch. Historically, the branch was organized along lines of clear hierarchical command, the use of uniforms, and, before modern telecommunications, highly autonomous park superintendents. Moreover, in the past, while personnel did occasionally move from one park to another, they usually had a detailed and intricate knowledge of, and often a personal attachment to, the individual parks in which they worked. In terms of organizational culture, this attachment led parks personnel to have high levels of personal commitment to ideas about parks, to the objective of ecosystem management, and to presenting "their" parks to the public. What these personnel were not were infinitely interchangeable generic managers. Therefore, the changes, in organization and activities brought upon the branch (indeed, it had ceased to be a "branch") caused significant anxiety among the parks staff and were met with strong internal criticism and staunch resistance.

Concurrent with these changes and, indeed, contributing to employee unease was the department's program of employee takeover (ETO) whereby certain park functions and activities were to be contracted to private-sector operators with the expectation that existing parks staff would establish themselves as private firms and bid for these contracts. While the specific proposal for this program came from the department, the impetus for it was from the program review process instituted by the Department of Finance.

The Liberals were under no illusions about the serious conditions of the government's finances when they assumed office. Despite repeated attempts at restraint by Brian Mulroney's Conservative government, the federal debt had continued to grow during its nine years in office, and by 1994 the annual deficit was $42 billion. Although Minister of Finance Paul Martin's first budget introduced some relatively strong measures in an attempt to address the fiscal problems, it was coolly received by the private sector and the business media, which described it as equally ineffective as the Conservative efforts that preceded it. Both private-sector commentators and Martin's own finance department officials argued that more needed to be done in order to have a signal effect on the deficit. Martin took these admonitions seriously through the summer and autumn months of 1994 by ensuring that program review, which had been announced in that year's budget, would have a serious effect on the deficit.

Following that budget, the cabinet established its own ad hoc committee, the Co-ordinating Committee of Ministers and, at the administrative level, the Steering Committee of Deputy Ministers to lead the review. While it was conducted among peers, the rules were strict, with both the finance minister and the prime minister ready to enforce them. The review required each department to develop business plans and to identify those programs that could be eliminated or whose budgets could be substantially cut. The size of the cuts required was significant, and many departmental officials were uneasy about making them. Some ministers sought exemptions and allowances in order to avoid having to make drastic reductions to programs that they thought were critical to their departments. Program review leaders thought, however, that there was no room for exceptions. When departments or ministers failed to make the necessary reductions, decisions were made for them. For example, when then Minister of Industry John Manley sought to protect the $144 million Defence Industry Productivity Program by, among other things, appealing directly to the prime minister, he found that, while the program was retained, all of its funding was removed.[49] Other programs were treated with similar directness. Ministers and senior officials quickly learned that the prime minister was solidly behind the program review process.

While the decisions about program cuts were being made in the autumn of 1994, the urgency for action was dramatically illustrated in December when the Mexican peso was abruptly devalued and other currencies, including Canada's, lost confidence on international markets. This development was followed by an editorial in the *Wall Street Journal* in January 1995 that opined about the risk of Canada following the Mexico example into financial crisis. If there had been some reluctance to pursue the strong measures of program review in earlier months, these events dispelled them, and the 1995 budget introduced a dramatically reduced spending agenda for the federal government.

One of the central features of the review was a six-part set of tests that committees used to examine programs and activities. The test asked of programs the following questions:

1 Does it serve a public interest?
2 Is it a necessary role for government?
3 Should it be a federal government role?
4 Should the program be transferred to the private or voluntary sector?
5 Can efficiency be improved?
6 Is the program affordable within the scope of fiscal restraint?[50]

This test not only provided the committees with a means for evaluating programs but also gave officials some indication of measures that could be taken to realign programs to satisfy the review objectives.

This budgetary imperative set the context in which the Parks Branch, along with other components of the Department of Canadian Heritage, was required to make substantial adjustments to programs and spending. There were several immediate consequences for parks. One was a 24 percent reduction in funding in the 1995 budget. A significant effect of this cut was the substantial reduction in interpretation programs throughout the parks system. These activities, familiar to park users as guided tours explaining the natural or historical phenomena of the park, are educational and are seen as a key element in making parks meaningful to their visitors.

More important as an influence on future decisions, however, the budgetary requirements led to proposals for employee takeover. Contracting out was a major plank in the neo-conservative agenda as advocates sought to reduce the size of the state. Numerous governments, at all levels, saw contracting out as a means to stabilize their budgets, reduce their costs, contain union demands, or merely remove items from their books by transferring them out of government. Since many observers believed that the private sector is necessarily more efficient than state employers, there was a strong motivation to transfer many service activities from the public to the private sector. Within the Parks Branch, there was already considerable variation across the country as to which activities were provided by employees and which were supplied by private contractors. Standardizing and expanding on these contracting experiences fit well both with ideas to reduce the size of government and with the specific requirements of program review.

The results of employee takeover would not be neutral for staff, however, since, in addition to moving these tasks outside the branch, fewer people would be required. Therefore, staff members faced a high degree of uncertainty in what was in fact a dismissal, a competitive bidding process with which most were unfamiliar, the possibility of not winning an available contract, and consequently seeking a new job entirely, or, if they won the contract, the need to establish a business with procedures that, for many, were unfamiliar.

In addition to the concerns of individuals, the Public Service Alliance of Canada (PSAC), the union representing most Parks Branch workers, was strongly opposed to employee takeover. It is, of course, the union's job to protect its members, so the layoff and probable unemployment for some was of grave concern. PSAC also, as reflecting its environment, supports the idea of public-sector employment and does not necessarily believe that the private sector provides superior service. Indeed, the association strongly supported national park values and the role of public servants in sustaining and promoting these values. Thus, from both an individual and an organized perspective, the employee takeover proposal faced considerable resistance.

The combination of the measure to integrate the Parks Branch into the new Department of Canadian Heritage and the proposals flowing from program review devastated employee morale across the parks system. In July 1996, this concern came to the attention of officials when a staff member at Riding Mountain National Park sent an e-mail across the Parks Canada system saying that *"the problem* is the network of control-hungry, self-serving bureaucrats who live in hierarchies and care more about power and personal status than they do about national parks."[51] This outburst caused an enormous and sustained response by Parks Canada personnel as Rick Searle, a former Parks Canada employee at Riding Mountain and author of *Phantom Parks: The Struggle to Save Canada's National Parks,* explains. To respond to the flood of e-mails, the department had to establish a dedicated electronic bulletin board to serve as the forum in which employees could register their concerns.[52] The discussion that followed was wide ranging, though not all of it was directly opposed to the new arrangement; however, there was enough opposition to make it clear that there was a serious morale problem and potential management difficulties in the new plan.

At the same time, there was discontent among external groups who work co-operatively with parks. As part of Parks Canada's planning activities and its co-ordination with local communities adjacent to parks, there are various committees at the respective parks comprising both officials and local volunteers. It became increasingly difficult for these volunteers to work with parks officials who were located in distant regional centres and who may not have had an immediate familiarity with the local circumstances. These volunteers also registered their concerns with local, regional, and Ottawa officials and in some cases directly to politicians.

Three sources of concern animated the evaluation of the Parks Branch's new situation. First, the ADM thought that the system was becoming unmanageable and that accountability for the legislated mandate was being diffused and even lost. Second, employee morale was at its nadir and seriously complicated the management challenges. Third, the branch was at risk of losing support among local volunteers who not only assist the parks program but are the essential public participants required by official policy. These issues contributed to a sense that the reinvention of parks arising from the branch's incorporation into the Department of Canadian Heritage and from the neo-conservative agenda was unsuccessful.

Central to the resolution of these tensions was Thomas Lee, appointed as the assistant deputy minister responsible for parks in 1993 when the transfer to the heritage department took effect. Lee had previously worked for the Ontario provincial parks branch and, more recently, for the BC government, where he had been in charge of the management of Crown lands.[53] In these roles, he gained substantial experience in the administrative principles and mechanisms with respect to large land management programs. In particular, in British Columbia, the operations allowed him, as manager, a degree of autonomy in financial and personnel decisions of a type that would later be among the features of the special operating agency. One of the issues of concern to him was the nature of accountability for specific mandates and programs through a department's administrative structure such that a minister can be realistically answerable to Parliament.

After the 1993 transfer, and as the process of integration took place, Lee – as the senior official responsible for parks – realized he was losing his capacity to manage and, as outlined above, be accountable for the parks program. Furthermore, with Parks Canada facing program-review reductions in the order of 100 million dollars per year, there was no room, if the program were to survive, for complex and bureaucratic hierarchies. The organizational structure would need to be highly efficient in order to accommodate the scale of these changes. These concerns led him to consider alternative administrative mechanisms in order to ensure the continuing integrity and accountability of the program. In the years immediately prior to program review and to assuming the role of head of Parks Canada, Lee had been extensively involved in various activities examining the organizational nature and delivery of government services. He had been selected to participate in a senior executive development program with the Canadian Centre for Management Development (CCMD), a federal crown agency that offers specialized programs aimed at providing management development and administrative proficiency within the federal public service. This program permitted Lee to study alternative delivery mechanisms in other countries, including Britain's executive agencies. It also provided intensive contact with senior bureaucrats in Ottawa, including those in the Privy Council Office (PCO).

In the early period of his new responsibilities with Parks Canada, Lee participated in a number of informal sessions sponsored by PCO and CCMD to explore ideas about possible structures and powers that might apply to agencies that could be established in order to assist in minimizing the fiscal constraints of program review. Out of these informal sessions grew the ideas and impetus toward the establishment of three new special operating agencies, of which the Parks Canada agency was one.

His contact with PCO officials also aided Lee in providing the right kind of advice to the minister, who in turn understood that something needed to be done to restore the organizational coherence of parks. This process provided some initial impetus for the creation of the agency as early as 1995 such that the March 1996 budget speech announced that the government would establish a separate agency for parks reporting to the minister of Canadian heritage. As an internal draft discussion paper from Lee's office to parks employees in July 1996 explains, the rationale for the agency was that it "will enhance, not reduce, Parks Canada's accountability to Canadians, to Parliament and to the Minister for the conservation and protection of Canada's heritage. It is the opportunity to put in place visible and transparent processes to enhance accountability."[54] Specifically, creation of the agency would require the Parks Branch to "confirm and strengthen the mandate," "to reinforce accountability," and to "create a climate which facilitates the management of investments, income and assets."[55] While these words are meant to be general, as a discussion paper requires, they nevertheless directly address many of the concerns that both Lee, as senior official, and the staff of the branch had in the post-1993 arrangements.

While some early progress was made toward establishing the agency, it was not yet in place by the election in June 1997. However, national parks and their protection received prominent mention in the Liberal Party's campaign "Red Book" presented to the electorate.[56] While the agency proposal was not mentioned specifically, it must have been part of the prime minister's agenda since, in constructing his cabinet following the election, Jean Chrétien specifically appointed a junior minister to the short-term position of secretary of state responsible for parks. His principal responsibility was to oversee the preparation and passage of Bill C-29, An Act to Establish the Canadian Parks Agency. While the secretary of state took responsibility for other parks activities besides guiding the legislation through Parliament, the position lasted only until the legislation had passed, and in a cabinet shuffle in 1999 the position was not renewed, and the full ministerial roles returned to the minister of Canadian heritage. The legislation was tabled on 5 February 1998 and received royal assent on 3 December of that year.

Although interest groups and others outside government had been watching these developments keenly, the main thrusts of policy development had occurred inside government. Throughout the process, from the transfer of parks to the creation of the agency, Thomas Lee was the assistant deputy minister. In this capacity, he advised the minister (or the secretary of state), sought alternatives to the departmental administrative arrangements, and helped to guide Bill C-29 through Parliament. Finally, Lee was the first chief executive officer of the agency in its initial years of operation. It is impossible to say whether other individuals, such as the ADM, would have addressed these issues the same way he did. Nevertheless, there is some contingency in Lee's being the ADM, with a particular set of experiences and ideas about parks administration, at this crucial time. There is even some serendipity in Lee's invitation to participate in the executive program at CCMD and the enhanced contact with PCO officials there, although ideas about SOAs were already extant elsewhere within the federal government.

An Agency for Protection
In the development of the Parks Canada Agency, the policy context provided both a challenge and a solution. The contextual challenge was the neo-conservative agenda and the programmatic fiscal requirements to reduce the size and to redefine the role of government. At the same time, one of the solutions arising from this agenda was the special operating agency with its foundation in a business model of organization but which, for parks, became a vehicle for autonomy and coherence for the program. By doing so, the agency is the result of an analysis and a rationale about the kind of organization necessary to protect parks. After an interval of three decades, the agency parallels the 1970 System Plan by providing a rational and coherent basis for administration and management in the way that the plan redefined parks according to a set of rational and scientific principles for selection. Both are attempts to protect the long-term coherence of the parks system from the short-term vagaries of ambitious tinkerers, both elected and appointed.

To understand the genesis of the agency, it is necessary, first, to appreciate the contextualizing market-oriented ideas of the period and their various manifestations in reducing the size of government, increasing internal revenues, proposing employee takeover, and creating the special operating agency. Second, the tectonic shifts within government revealed fracture lines in the principles of parks management that prompted rethinking and redefining of the organization. Contextualizing ideas did not wholly determine this outcome, though they were important in influencing the shape of the result. Not only did they provide opportunities for policy choices, but they also motivated decision makers to pursue certain directions and not others. While it may not be realistic to try to separate budget challenges from neo-conservative ideas, the consequences of these ideas for parks are considerable. They also contribute significantly to understanding why certain decisions were made. However, to fully understand the creation of the agency, it is essential also to acknowledge the institutions of the parks and their deep meaning for employees, local volunteers, and the general public. At its creation, then, although the agency did provide a degree of fiscal autonomy, it was the autonomy, not the opportunity to increase revenue, that was critically behind this policy decision. In fact, rather than create a quasi-commercial agency, the legislation established a stronger foundation for parks management and protection. In contrast, when similar ideas about structure and administration were presented by the Glassco Commission in the early 1960s, neither the neo-conservative agenda nor the fiscal imperative was present, and the ideas were not adopted.

Bill C-27: A New National Parks Act

The legislation creating the Parks Canada Agency was only one of three acts passed in the early 2000s by means of which the federal government aimed to streamline and strengthen its ability to manage and protect the ecological integrity of national parks. Having established the agency as the administrative vehicle for effective parks management, the government then set about writing a new national parks act. While this legislation, Bill C-27, introduced some new elements to those in the extant laws and policies, the new act mostly combined existing legislation, streamlined park-establishment procedures, strengthened enforcement, and clarified the legal position of communities, such as Jasper and Wakasui, within some parks. The new act thus confirmed and enhanced the existing ecological integrity provisions that had been included in 1988 and, taken together with the administrative coherence of the agency, allowed for the strongest protection for parks so far.

The new National Parks Act is the further extension of the four-decade-long process of defining and strengthening this body of legislation. Its specific provenance is the result of efforts to reorient some to the directions taken in the 1990s. The relative activism of the minister at the time, Sheila Copps, and the assistant deputy minister responsible for parks, Thomas Lee, also contributed to these legislative actions. However, this new act was not otherwise the product, even in its minor innovations, of a new set of contextualizing ideas. It was, as described by the Library of Parliament, a piece of housekeeping legislation that was to tidy up some loose ends of policy.[57]

The third piece of legislation in this suite, and one not addressed further in this account, is the Canada National Marine Conservation Areas Act.

Ideas and a New National Parks Act

While the new legislation consolidates ideas already present in the laws and regulations, it also incorporates the conclusions of two deliberative processes. Neither came to radical or surprising conclusions, but both confirmed and updated the values already inherent in the system.

The first was the *Guiding Principles and Operational Policies* document, which renewed the earlier policy statements of 1964 and 1979. While this document sought to reconcile and combine the differences and similarities of the wilderness aspects of national parks and the cultural features of historic sites (as described earlier), at the same time its public consultations demonstrated the strong commitment of many Canadians to the ecological and commemorative integrity, as the document describes them, of the two types of protected areas. In common with its two predecessors, this statement specified the way in which parks legislation would be implemented and outlined the interpretation of the parks mandate for public understanding. This document had been tabled in the House of Commons in March 1994 and, like its predecessors, spanned governments of different political parties, thus demonstrating its broad support.

The second process was the Panel on the Ecological Integrity of Canada's National Parks, a body appointed by Minister of Canadian Heritage Sheila Copps in November 1998 shortly after her receipt of the report of the Banff-Bow Valley Study. The panel, comprising eleven members with scientific and resource management backgrounds, was charged with examining the ecological integrity of the parks and recommending actions needed to protect it. Its formal report, in February 2000, came just as Bill C-27 was about to receive its first reading (on 1 March 2000), but, because of the openness of the process, including a series of interim publications, the panel's conclusions and recommendations were already well known to legislative drafters. The report offers 127 recommendations, many of which are more detailed than was likely to be reflected in legislation. For example, recommendations about dealing with invasive species are generally more specific than the broader powers provided for in legislation. In addition, implementation of many of the panel's recommendations is dependent on budget allocations, some of which may be the result of priorities within the agency, while others would require increased appropriations from the treasury. In some instances, the panel challenges the directions recently taken by the department and the agency. For example, the panel recommends that the agency abandon the language of business, as promoted by the market orientation of recent years, and suggests that the agency refer to its main planning document as an implementation plan rather than a business plan.[58] On the other hand, the panel recommended the redesign or removal of buildings and infrastructure from parks to reduce their ecological footprint. This, in some respects, is consistent with the provision in the new legislation to prohibit the extension of municipal government powers to other park communities beyond the single instance of Banff.

While the Panel on Ecological Integrity conducted its work at the same time as the new legislation was being prepared, there are no obvious links between the two. The legislation, while it served to increase protection for parks, was more modest than the sum of the panel's recommendations.

The New Amendments to Policy

The new National Parks Act is reminiscent of earlier policy documents and the initial bill of amendments introduced in 1988 in that it seeks to address several of the management issues that had arisen for parks administration. For example, while protecting the agreed-upon rights of Aboriginal people with respect to park resources, there were new provisions to combat the collection of or the trafficking in fossils, plants, or other resources from parks. In addition, penalties for poaching vulnerable species were increased. Furthermore, measures to make park establishment more efficient and to increase the regularity and scope of management plans are included in the new act. In this sense, the act met the needs of park administrators and was consistent with the "management tool" concept of earlier documents. Perhaps the most significant addition, however, was that which constrains the growth of park communities. This long-standing issue had bedevilled policy makers since the 1964 policy statement attempted to limit residency in parks and to constrain the prerogatives of leaseholders. While the new act did not return to the 1964 ideas, it does prevent the establishment of municipal powers in the other six intrapark communities, unlike those granted to Banff in 1989.

The Process of Participation

By the end of the twentieth century and the beginning of the twenty-first, the relationship between several principal interest groups and the Parks Canada Agency, together with the Department of Canadian Heritage (and now the Department of the Environment) and Parliament, had become so highly institutionalized that the boundaries that defined participation a decade or more earlier had become steadily blurred. In recent years, individuals who have been strong advocates in interest groups have worked in exchange and other programs within the department, and there is regular communication between government and interest group personnel. Interest group ideas, therefore, become a constant part of the deliberations about policy. In addition, these experienced and institutionalized groups regularly appear before parliamentary committees, and they did so again as Bill C-27 was before the Heritage Committee.

The role of groups' appearance before the committee can be seen in the changes made to the centrally important clause on ecological integrity. In the first reading of the bill, clause 8(2) read, "maintenance of ecological

integrity through the protection of natural resources shall be the first priority of the Minister in the consideration of park zoning and visitor use."[59] As
passed, the clause reads: "Maintenance of ecological integrity, through the
protection of natural resources and natural processes, shall be the first priority of the Minister when considering all aspects of the management of
parks."[60] The Canadian Parks and Wilderness Society (CPAWS), the Sierra
Legal Defence Fund (SLDF), and the Canadian Nature Federation all recommended word changes for this clause to the committee. All three suggested
the addition of the words *natural processes*, and all proposed phrasing the
limited "park zoning and visitor use" variously as "all actions" or "all aspects" of management and decision making.[61] Other additions to the bill,
such as a clause requiring the designation of wilderness areas within one
year of the preparation of the management plan, came almost verbatim
from the brief by Kevin McNamee of the Canadian Nature Federation.[62] In
addition, the SLDF provided one of the links between the legislation and
the Panel on Ecological Integrity as it, the SLDF, served as the legal adviser
to the panel and made specific reference to the panel's report in its submission to the Heritage Committee.[63]

In contrast to the contributions of these three advocates for parks protection, several groups, such as the Association for Mountain Parks Protection
and Enjoyment (AMPPE), the Jasper Town Committee, and the Jasper Chamber of Commerce, all advocating greater human access and recreational use
of parks, were unable to persuade the committee of their views. AMPPE, for
example, cautions the committee that there is "tremendous pressure both
from within the Parks Canada and the Minister's office and powerful environmental lobby groups to 'rewild' the parks, [which] will result in the
interests of people in the parks being unduly trammelled upon."[64] Meanwhile, the Jasper Town Committee expressed its discomfort with the restrictions on Jasper ever having the municipal status once conferred upon Banff.

While the decision to accept or reject proposals made to it is the committee's, the role of environmental groups is unmistakable. All stages in the
policy process are influenced by their ideas and their presence, from the
marshalling of public support, to the presentation of detailed policy proposals, to the specific recommendations for the wording of the legislation
about national parks.

Implications

The combined effect of the creation of the Parks Canada Agency, which secured administrative coherence for parks, and enhanced powers in the new
act is that Canada's national parks are, in formal policy, more strongly protected than at any time in their history. Nevertheless, at the time of writing,
it is too early to tell what the long-term consequences will be. Although
early impressions are that the agency will act to stabilize the bureaucratic

environment, the business model and the marketing style of communication do cause concern among some interest groups and did for the now-concluded Panel on Ecological Integrity. Since the National Parks Act provides the mandate for the agency, one may conclude that its conservationist strengths become the agency's too. However, that analysis cannot yet be made.

The recommendations of the Panel on Ecological Integrity constitute another body of ideas, the full consequences of which also await future analysis. Since many proposals require the conclusion of some practices before new ones can be implemented, while others require additional monies, several years will be needed before one can conclude whether the proposals are adopted or ignored. It can be said, however, that they are consistent with the main currents of the discourse about national parks over the past forty years. On the other hand, it is not unknown for task force recommendations to be ignored or to be used selectively by the government. Whatever the precise outcome of many of the panel's recommendations, they will almost certainly be part of the continuing dialogue about how to manage the national parks system.

Conclusion

The fourth period of national parks policy development was the most turbulent in the past half century. At its end, however, a new management structure and new legislation gave parks the potential for the strongest and most coherent protection in their history. Interestingly, almost all the conflict, and its resolution, happened with the state itself. While non-state participants were involved at times, their contribution was modest. An understanding of these events and the eventual outcomes for policy requires an appreciation of two sets of ideas that provide the context and the justification for the decisions of the period. It is the collision of these two sets of ideas that caused the turmoil in this period but that also caused a creative tension out of which their fusion now provides for a stronger, or the potential for a stronger, parks system.

The first set of ideas was, as in earlier policy periods, relatively stable and provided the background against which new policy formats were constructed. They are, by this time, deeply embedded in the parks system. Important among them are the parks mandate as set out in legislation, in numerous policy documents, and in operational procedure. The requirement to protect parks from impairment on behalf of future generations had been, as argued in this analysis, the central feature of the policy debate for thirty years (by the early 1990s) and was thoroughly subscribed to both inside and outside the Parks Branch. Within the branch, it was more than straightforward management procedure, however. It was also part of the organizational culture in which a large number of parks personnel had strong individual commitments.

The second set of ideas was more recent and external to the branch. Some of these ideas were about the fiscal crisis of the Canadian state, while others were about market orientation and were seen as a means to resolve that crisis. While national opinion overwhelmingly held that the fiscal circumstances constituted an emergency, it was a body of ideas about fiscal management that undergirded that opinion. To address this problem, ideas about market orientation such as business models of management, market-like price signals, deregulation, and privatization were enlisted. These ideas were deployed across the breadth of the Canadian government, including within the national parks system.

With respect to the first set of ideas, as if to foreshadow its new assertiveness toward defining the parks system, the branch took only passing interest in the World Wildlife Fund's Endangered Spaces Campaign. Other concerns were more immediate. Primary among them were Banff and the Bow Valley, where the ecological imperatives of a narrowly confined but critical corridor confronted relentless commercial development pressures. To reasonably meet its mandate, the branch had to find a solution to that confrontation. The public consultation process of the Banff-Bow Valley Study, and the resulting report, were therefore the continuation of a series of efforts that the branch had undertaken since drafting the 1964 policy statement aimed at dealing with its responsibilities. The public nature of the process also employed the mandated policy to consult the public on management matters of this type. In turn, the Banff-Bow Valley Study gave rise to the Panel on Ecological Integrity, a forum for public discourse that served to restate and confirm the environmental side of the branch's mandate. These processes, together with other management needs, ultimately led to a new act.

The second set of ideas, those about fiscal prudence, partly contributed to the branch's transfer from the Department of the Environment to the Department of Canadian Heritage. While there were other considerations in this move, the occasion was the comprehensive reorganization of government departments and the shrinking of cabinet, by Prime Minister Kim Campbell, to reduce the size of and streamline the procedures of the state. The new organization was not the result of either the reduction in government or the transfer itself, but it gave an opportunity to organizational careerists who had no a priori interest in parks.

Another consequence of the response to the fiscal crisis was the introduction of market-oriented ideas. For parks, this meant new revenue-generating practices and new management priorities. Critically, however, it included the attempt at employee takeover and contracting out. For many parks personnel, these were alien ideas that, when combined with the organizational changes brought about as a result of the transfer to the heritage department, collided with the deeply embedded organizational culture and strongly held individual views about parks that were rooted in the background set of ideas. This collision led to a rebellion against the new organizational framework, including its market-inspired components, and eventually to a search for a different management model altogether.

This search led, perhaps serendipitously, to the creation of the Parks Canada Agency. The agency conveniently bridges the divide between traditional ideas about parks and the newer market-oriented ones. As a product of new management techniques, the agency itself is part of the market-oriented wave of ideas. At the same time, it is a self-contained management device through which the traditional, contextual ideas about parks can be applied. Thus, the outcome of this turbulent decade turns out to be a union between the long-standing, background ideas about parks and new ideas about management practices. It is yet too early to know whether this will be a long-term success, but it does have strong potential.

7
National Parks and the Giving of Meaning

National parks are about meaning. They are expressions of collective attitudes about the natural environment both in the sense of what it actually
means to people as well as, more normatively, what they want done to
protect it. Since parks are focused on the use or protection of selected tracts
of the natural environment, they are manifestations of Canadians' feelings
about those environments. But they are also about who may use the resources within those tracts and even who may participate in making decisions to determine those uses. Therefore, parks are also statements about
what sorts of relationships exist among the groups of people who participate in environmental decision making. They represent normative positions about who ought to be involved in defining and deciding what parks
are. For example, as public parks, they express a claim for societal involvement in decisions affecting them. And, increasingly, as Aboriginal people
experience a renaissance in their identities and a renewal of their rights,
parks enunciate Aboriginal claims to a fuller recognition in the Canadian
polity. In these ways, parks reflect not only Canadians' attitudes toward
their wilderness areas but also reveal positions about the nature of political
relations among different groups of Canadians.

The meanings of parks are not static but varied and complex. Meanings
have been in nearly constant flux over the century (and slightly more) of
parks' existence. In the beginning, when national parks were first established in the United States in the nineteenth century, they symbolized that
country's desire to declare its sense of present or imminent national greatness. Canada's national project in the same period was one of economic
development as one means to bind this country together. The Canadian
government established its first parks for economic reasons, a set of objectives that has continued to make itself felt in various guises through to the
present. Despite this relative continuity, there has been a major reduction
in parks' economic purposes in the post-World War II period, and parks
have since come to represent environmental protection and preservation.

More recently, they have come to embody new understandings about humanity's place in the natural world, especially with respect to Aboriginal peoples. Finally, from the 1960s at least, but accelerating in the 1990s, parks came to be seen as objects of heritage. In 1993, this conception was formalized as they were included in the new department with a mandate to promote heritage.

At the beginning of the twenty-first century, the meaning of parks may be changing again. Environmental and Aboriginal components remain deeply embedded in modern parks policy and within the community of policy participants. It seems unlikely that there will be a sudden change with respect to them. However, new ideas about the connection between parks and their clientele have shifted the relationship toward a more commercial one in which park users are expected to pay a fee to appreciate Canada's natural splendour.

To understand and account for these transformations in meaning, it is helpful to analyze parks within relatively discrete periods and to chart the vectors of political influence together with their domains of intersection. Therefore, policy development and amendment can be understood as the result of interaction among substantive policy ideas, interest groups, and state institutions. While these elements are crucial in explaining policy, the nature of the interaction itself changes and thus, by affecting the relative weights of these elements, influences the contribution that they make and, in turn, the policy outcomes that result. It is ideas, usually short term in nature, that effect changes in the nature of the interaction and thus in the context of decision making. Revised contexts then condition policy outcomes and thus affect the evolution of meanings. Post-World War II national parks policy, therefore, can be largely explained by examining the interaction of substantive ideas, interest groups, and state institutions within the conditioning effects of short-term or contextualizing ideas.

The Historic Basis of National Parks

National parks were intended as instruments of nation building when they were first established, initially in the United States and shortly after in Canada. In the United States, they were meant as symbols of national greatness as that country sought an expression of national pride. In Canada, the government unambiguously created them in order to generate revenue for the newly constructed transcontinental railway and for the federal treasury. Although there were some expressions of national pride in recognizing the grandeur of the Rocky Mountains, early national parks in this country were singularly instrumental in their economic purposes.

Whatever the initial agenda, parks were quickly seized upon as vehicles to convey ideas about environmental protection and wilderness preservation, first in the United States and later in Canada. In the United States, members of the public made this claim, whereas in Canada the newly established parks bureaucracy and dominion parks commissioner, J.B. Harkin, quietly introduced some of the environmental ideas then being debated in the United States. Harkin saw national parks as an opportunity to protect disappearing wildlife as part of a broader strategy for preserving Canada's natural heritage. This development led to a natural conflict between ideas about utility and those about preservation, resulting in nearly a century of struggle about the essence of national parks and the policies that should govern their administration.

At the time, Harkin's own views and his adoption of American ideas, together with his adroit use of his position, explain the inclusion of an early expression of environmental ideas in Canadian parks policy. Even with this influence, ideas about economic development remained predominant, and Harkin had to satisfy Parliament that economic and revenue potential was present in the parks that he was proposing and administering. Nevertheless, the blending of economic and environmental ideas in administrative practice served to protect endangered wildlife and examples of magnificent scenery, thus embedding in the public imagination the belief that national parks were about Canadian wilderness. Harkin's influence went further than the mere establishment of administrative practices since he was also instrumental in the drafting and promoting of the National Parks Act (1930). With its admittedly ambiguous phrasing, this act ultimately provided the legislative foundation on which later policy change and a shift toward concepts of environmental protection were constructed.

The Era of State Initiative

Despite the environmental component in the 1930 legislation, economic development remained the predominant meaning for national parks in the early post-World War II period. New parks reflected this meaning in Newfoundland, where Terra Nova National Park was designed as an economic incentive to encourage that British colony to join Canada, and in New Brunswick, where Kouchibouguac National Park was also conceived to promote tourism and create jobs in a low-income region of that province. In addition, in Diefenbaker's "Vision," the Roads to Resources program, the Resources for Tomorrow Conference, and the Agricultural and Rural Development Agency (ARDA), national parks were taken simply as one means among many to extract some economic utility from Canada's vast hinterland. Both governments and the Canadian public saw national parks as instruments of government policy and government officials as virtually the sole decision makers.

At the same time, tourism, the engine behind the economic development ideal, fostered two additional elements in national parks planning. First, in the 1950s, as families flocked to national parks for recreational purposes, Canadian parks began to reflect the democratic ideas that had been expressed in the United States in the nineteenth century but were conspicuously absent in this country. Second, the Parks Branch undertook, as part of its mandate, to provide programs in nature education. These two pursuits essentially added a social policy dimension to parks whereby, unlike the elite ideals of the nineteenth century, parks were now instruments of broad public well-being. They also foreshadowed future changes in meaning with respect to popular ownership of parks and an emphasis on environmental meanings.

By the mid-1950s, however, parks officials increasingly saw existing policy directions and administrative practices as inadequate. There was little guidance about how to manage the throngs of visitors or the inconsistencies in management practices across the country. Growing misunderstandings with the provinces over what objectives and what locations were desired for new national parks also occurred in this period. These uncertainties and tensions led parks officials to draft the 1964 policy statement and the 1970 System Plan as means of clarifying their mandate and redirecting their management activities. Both documents, while not intended for this purpose, had the effect of reorienting parks toward environmental protection and of redefining them, at least partly, as environmental policy instruments.

The parks bureaucracy, aware of the growing management needs resulting from the increasing urbanization and automobility of the population, initiated deliberations around policies and practices. Although the bureaucracy was the dominant actor, it was not able to get Parliament's authorization for its policy ideas without the support of newly created environmental interest groups. In this task, however, it also had considerable manoeuvrability in influencing the policy environment to provide the needed support. In addition, in the 1950s, environmental interest groups were only beginning to develop, and the public interest in the environment was still mostly latent. The enhanced environmental component in the policy statement was therefore not simply the initiative of parks officials but was the somewhat unintended outcome of a policy approach dependent on the features of the National Parks Act, taken by the relatively autonomous Parks Branch.

In addition to dependence on the legislative framework, the 1930 resources transfer agreements and the postwar resurgence of provincial ambitions forced the federal government to follow precepts of co-operative federalism in order to establish new national parks. The provinces' own desire to benefit directly from the growing economic importance of outdoor, automobile-based recreation, combined with the co-operative relations between the two levels of government, led to the subdivision of the parks field between the two, with the federal government focusing on wilderness parks located at a distance from the main urban centres.

Taken together, relative bureaucratic autonomy and co-operative federalism motivated the shift toward a more naturalist and environmental identity for national parks, and in this they were assisted by the influence of rationalism in government. These ideas, which permeated policy making in the federal government during the 1960s and 1970s, led to, among other things, the 1970 System Plan that redefined the character of the national parks by emphasizing ecological criteria over the formerly predominant economic or recreational ones.

For both the policy statement and the System Plan, therefore, the bureaucracy was the principal actor. Ministers were rarely directly involved in parks policies except to arrange for their formal approval in cabinet or Parliament and in the 1950s and 1960s, while public interest groups did not yet have the capacity for active participation.

Three principal contextualizing ideas – bureaucratic autonomy, co-operative federalism, and rationalism in government – combined in a unique way in the 1960s to link substantive ideas, nascent interest groups, and state institutions. Although all persisted into the 1970s in varying degrees, none would prevail during that decade.

The Growth of Public Participation

Meanings for national parks changed dramatically in the 1970s. At the beginning of the decade, when officials were still discussing the design and application of the System Plan within the exclusive forum of the annual federal-provincial parks conferences, parks remained instruments of government policy. While the emphasis of policy and administration was by now changing in favour of environmental concerns and away from economic development, these new ideas were still seen largely as government decisions. Despite some requirement to manoeuvre around public interests, the relative autonomy of Parks Branch officials, combined with ministerial authority, continued to be reflected in practices that had been in place since parks were first established and to illustrate the long-standing idea that parks were instruments of government policy intended to meet state needs.

By the end of the 1970s, the meaning of national parks had changed significantly to one where they had become articles of public identity and popular ownership. Although the Parks Branch continued to control the official channels of policy discourse, the general public intervened so energetically in the policy process and pressed its ideas so strongly on parks officials, including the minister, that by the decade's end these lands had become truly public parks. Relationship to the land had taken on new associations, both for southern Canadians and for Aboriginal people in the North. Not simply recreational opportunities, parks, and the natural environment in general, were now intimately bound up with questions of survival. For

southern Canadians concerned with global climate change, ozone deple-
tion, and biodiversity, these questions are somewhat matters of conjecture.
For northern Aboriginal Canadians, these can be immediate concerns of
food and shelter.

These two publics (southern Canadians and northern Aboriginal people)
emerged during the 1970s. First, organized interest groups mainly represented
the general public. By being actively and vigorously involved in opposing
Village Lake Louise in western Canada and by objecting to the methods
used to establish Kouchibouguac National Park in New Brunswick, this public
forced the Parks Branch to take account of their concerns. This, in turn, led
to the development of procedures, such as commissions of inquiry, solicita-
tions of briefs, and town hall meetings, as a means to include the public in
all major parks decisions. The 1979 Parks Canada policy adopted these procedures, recognizing officially the public's right to be involved.

Second, as a separate public, Aboriginal people began to reclaim their
land in the late 1960s and early 1970s and to regain rights set out in the
Royal Proclamation of 1763, rights that were being upheld in modern court
decisions. With respect to national parks, Aboriginal spokespersons appeared
before Parliament in 1974 to argue that, until treaties were signed to clarify
ownership, the creation of parks in northern Canada would violate their
rights and claims to this land. As a result of their interventions, an interim
category, called national park reserves, was created to await the resolution
of claims. While this arrangement did not, at the time, change the character of existing parks or even of the national park reserves themselves, it did
set a precedent for having Aboriginal people involved in policy deliberations, and they, like the general public, subsequently became regular participants in the policy process.

Changes in meaning and in the state's approach toward including the
public can be explained almost entirely by ideas about the legitimacy of
public participation. At the conceptual level, the Trudeau Liberals championed the concept of "participatory democracy," while at the operational
level the federal government funded a wide range of social activism. At the
same time, governments were indecisive about their own objectives for parks
and about their relationship with the public. Meanwhile, interest groups,
while more decisive, had few resources and had limited capacity to develop
a nationally coherent program of policy intervention. The changes in meanings emerged out of a very confusing decade in which one of the few points
of agreement was that public participation had become a "public good,"
and governments and interest groups alike sought to adopt it into continuing political and administrative practice.

While the substantive elements in parks policy did not change significantly (policy became only slightly more environmentally sensitive), ideas

about public involvement, including Aboriginal claims to northern lands, changed relations between state and society with respect to parks and transformed the sense of ownership of them. Public participation, as a contextualizing idea, conditioned the interaction among nascent groups, substantive ideas, and state institutions (especially the bureaucracy).

Policy Initiatives by Interest Groups

In the 1980s, the meanings about public ownership, already established in the 1970s, became more deeply entrenched. The environmental importance of parks also intensified as interest groups, the courts, and the minister responsible saw ecological protection of parks as a priority over other approaches to their management. An additional, almost revolutionary new meaning for parks was the recognition of the reality of human presence within natural ecosystems. This view, combined with acceptance of Aboriginal claims, led to a new conception of parks wherein they have come to reflect the traditional and eternal relationship between the land and the people who live directly on it. Thus, both for the public in general and for Aboriginal people in particular, national parks were taken further away from their identity as government instruments and closer to the idea that they are really landscapes held in public trust. These changes placed both publics near the very centre of policy discourse. Interest groups monitored the Parks Branch's behaviour and, sometimes contrary to the minister's wishes, forced the branch to act. Aboriginal groups also shared key decision-making roles through co-management committees with parks officials.

This transformation in favour of public meanings actually took place around several events during this period. First, chronologically speaking, there was the dramatic increase in the sophistication and national coherence of interest groups. Partly this was the result of their natural evolution, and partly it was the outcome of the vigorous national campaign to protect South Moresby Island as a national park. Second, the courts recognized public interest standing for private participants in instances where the courts thought that attorneys general were not likely to act in (what might be) the public interest. Third, the National Parks Act (1988) was amended to, among other things, give first priority to ecological protection within parks. Fourth, through the signing of Aboriginal land claims treaties across northern Canada, the continuing right of Aboriginal people to be present on the lands within national parks and to use the resources of those lands for their own use, including limited commercial purposes, was recognized. Included in the treaties are terms that provide for co-management of resources whereby Aboriginal people and Parks Branch officials will share responsibilities. All of these events served to entrench more deeply the "public ownership" meanings that had emerged in the 1970s.

The institutional changes that took place in the 1980s can be explained by the interaction of state institutions, substantive (though evolving) ideas about the environment, and highly institutionalized organizations of environmental advocates and Aboriginal people. The primary catalyst of this interaction, however, was the set of ideas that legitimized active public participation in policy deliberation and determination. Ideas about the right of citizens to be intimately involved in policy development influenced politicians, including the federal cabinet, the courts, and the participants in the land claims treaty process. Essential state institutions such as Parliament, the courts, and, through treaty negotiations, the Constitution[1] became available to environmental groups and Aboriginal organizations because of the widespread acceptance of public participation.

This belief in public participation, as it was in the 1970s, was the principal contextualizing idea of the 1980s and early 1990s. Unlike the 1970s, however, where the concept was manifest in small-scale terms of protest, town hall meetings, and solicited briefs, in the 1980s public involvement was on a different plane, now focused on the most powerful of state institutions. Enabling this activity were highly sophisticated societal organizations with high degrees of expertise in fields of science, law, and government procedure. They also had a strong, coherent national presence, were able to form effective coalitions with other groups, and were able to use the channels of communication to government and to the public through the media. Finally, they were able to marshall sufficient financial resources to sustain advocacy campaigns over extended periods. Most of these resources came from voluntary contributions, a fact that indicates a strong measure of popular support. Therefore, both through acceptance of public involvement by key state institutions and through the co-ordinated and sophisticated participation of societal organizations, together with popular support, the idea of public participation provided the context in which substantive ideas about environmental protection and Aboriginal claims, authoritative state institutions, and environmental and Aboriginal organizations interacted.

Market-Oriented Solutions for Management

At present, the previous objectives for national parks, articulated over the past forty years, continue to define the outward meanings of parks. However, in the mid-1990s, new ideas appeared to change meanings for parks once again. At least within the federal government itself, a new, or perhaps reinvented, objective for parks emerged. Instead of presenting them in terms of relations between people and their natural environments, or local communities and the use of resources, or even pan-Canadian identity and unity, the Parks Branch now offers them as vehicles to satisfy recreational choices, to "purchase," briefly, some wilderness space, and to adopt the identity of customer rather than one of participant or even "owner."

These new meanings are related to, but not the same as, economic ideas from the past. In 1885, Sir John A. Macdonald argued that the creation of Rocky Mountain National Park (Banff) would benefit the federal treasury. Today parallel arguments are being used to justify the adoption of cost recovery user charges, the elimination of cross-subsidization, and the development of special operating agencies as a means to organize the new fiscal regime. Although the government had collected revenue in parks for decades (and deposited it in the consolidated revenue fund), in the 1990s this practice was expanded to new sources, with the intention of raising more income (which is now retained by parks) to cover a greater portion of the budget for parks.

Complementing this broadening of revenue options, the administrative framework for parks has been reconstructed to separate it from the personnel, fiscal, and management requirements of the department and the direct control of central agencies. The most important developments in this period, and those that define the period, are the expansion of revenue sources and the creation of the Parks Canada Agency.

In contrast to the renovations made to the fiscal and management structure, little has changed for the public itself with respect to the public ownership of and environmental meanings for parks. The Banff-Bow Valley Study continued comprehensive public involvement in its decision making, thereby pursuing the concepts of popular ownership of parks. The study also confirmed the ecological priorities set out in the 1988 amendments to the act, thus deepening environmental meanings, although not dramatically. However, the relative inattention given to the Group of Eight coalition and the Endangered Spaces Campaign tends to undermine the role that interest groups have built up over the past quarter century.

The alterations to the fiscal and administrative framework for parks management can be explained almost entirely by the presence of market-oriented ideas. Cabinet authority, as applied through the central agencies of the Treasury Board Secretariat and the Department of Finance, was instrumental in ensuring that these rising ideas were adopted by individual departments and government agencies and by the Parks Branch in particular. Other policy participants, such as interest groups and Parliament (especially through the standing committee), were involved in the process but made no substantive contribution to the outcome.

Inasmuch as cabinet may promote any of an infinity of ideas, the critical contribution to the 1990s was the presence of market-oriented ones, which dominated the policy context. Indeed, they created the context. Ideas about the market, individual consumer choice, and utility maximization both for individuals (park users) and for organizations (the Parks Canada Agency) suffused policy deliberations since the early part of the decade. Former ideas about parks remain embedded in legislation, treaties, and other policy documents that continue to provide the fundamental character and principal direction for parks. However, the current focus for policy discussion and the attention from most participants are directed at market-oriented concepts, while other extant principles remain in the background of early-twenty-first-century deliberations.

The Role of Contextualizing Ideas

The principal argument of this analysis is that national parks policy, at any given time, can be explained by understanding the interaction among substantive ideas, institutions, and organized interest groups. Over extended periods of time, however, the confluence of these three tributary factors changes, and with it so does the nature of national parks policy. Indeed, the adaptations of policy over time make it difficult to define exactly what the policy is since past ideas are usually embedded or institutionalized within individual parks, and therefore within the system or within administrative practices, thus resulting in an agglomeration of features in more recent periods. To understand how parks policy changes, therefore, it is necessary to examine, for each time period, the most recent increment or layer of ideas added to the national parks corpus. This approach of analyzing policy ideas at the margin, as it were, allows one to examine the time-specific relationship among substantive ideas, institutions, and interest groups. Since this relationship changes over time, so do the policy outputs and outcomes for parks.

Ultimately, then, to understand the long-term accretion of parks policy, it is necessary to understand these temporally different relationships. The contrasting interactions among the contributing factors at different times can, in their turn, be explained by shifting contextualizing ideas. These ideas influence the way in which decisions are made, who will be influential, which kinds of substantive ideas will be considered, and which sorts of forums will be used to make decisions. Unlike substantive ideas that (may) become actual policy content, contextualizing ideas usually are not expressed in policy itself but only condition its formation. In short, although it may be too deterministic to say it in quite this way, contextualizing ideas shape the environment in which decisions are made. Understanding them, and the way in which they affect the decision-making context, leads to an explanation of the increments in parks policy, which in turn become part of the totality of that policy.

New or newly emergent ideas do not exist in a vacuum but interact with existing ideas already contained in legislation, policy guidelines, practices, and attitudes that make up the corpus of national parks policy. That body of policy elements is highly complex and incorporates the economic development ideas that prevailed in the relatively distant past along with public participation concepts of more recent periods. These extant ideas, in turn, both interact with market-oriented ones of the present in such a way that local business groups and national environmental organizations are widely consulted with respect to changes to administrative practices. Thus, multiple meanings coexist (not always peacefully) and influence the application of new ideas to national parks.

For national parks, the meanings embedded in them are the outcome of policy decisions. Therefore, transformations in meanings can also be understood by following the evolution of contextualizing ideas. In the beginning, Canadian national parks were indisputably instruments of economic development (in the interests of national expansion). Despite the efforts of J.B. Harkin over his twenty-five-year tenure and his important contribution to the passage of the National Parks Act (1930), this approach did not fundamentally change until well after World War II, nearly seventy years after the first park was established. Then, in the post-World War II period, because of the needs of the bureaucracy, parks policy began to change. Through this early period of adjustment, the principal contextualizing idea was that it was right and proper for government officials to make the defining policy decisions for parks. Where there was some conflict over whether they had made the correct decisions, it became necessary to win public support for them, but ideas about who should make these decisions were never seriously challenged. At this stage, parks remained instruments of government policy wherein government officials made the defining decisions.

The tentative elicitation of support from a segment of the public in the 1960s gave way to a fundamentally new, even radical, contextualizing idea in the 1970s when public participation in parks decision making was accepted as critical and essential. While the substantive policy did not change significantly in this period, the meaning of parks altered dramatically from the concept of government instrument to one of popular ownership. Moreover, while policy substance was not amended all that much, the change in meaning and in the locus of decision making laid the ground for a more consequential evolution in the next phase of policy development.

Public participation remained the contextualizing idea in the 1980s, but with a difference. In this decade, it became more institutionalized as Parliament, the courts, and treaty making became the forums for policy articulation. Moreover, as public participants increased their sophistication, they too became more institutionalized. No longer were spontaneous outbursts of public feeling the means by which government and public interacted. Strengthening the role of groups in this period was their ability, both learned from experience and granted by institutional decision makers, to use the institutions of the state to force government officials to apply the terms of the act and, essentially, to strengthen the environmental character of national parks, now redefined to recognize a human presence.

At the end of the twentieth century, a new contextualizing idea appeared in the form of market-oriented approaches to reforming government. These approaches have led to the radical restructuring of the administrative framework for national parks and created a setting inside of which concepts about utility maximization may gain favour over those about popular ownership, national symbolism, or environmental protection. While this has been taking place, the initiatives of environmental interest groups, with increasingly sophisticated approaches to environmental protection, have been largely ignored.

Throughout the post-World War II period, economic ideas persisted in parks, but at the margins, where new policy ideas are discussed and implemented, changing contextualizing ideas have given rise to a shifting domain of interaction among substantive ideas, institutions, and interest groups. This interaction, in turn, has changed policy direction and thereby the meanings of national parks throughout the same period. At the end of the previous century and the beginning of a new one, however, changing contextualizing ideas have once again reconfigured the framework for national parks, effectively re-emphasizing economic ideas and returning them to the role of government instrument.

Time and Ideas: The Changing Locus of Interaction

The focus of attention in this analysis has been on four identified periods of policy development since 1955. Thus, ideas, processes, and participants have been viewed mostly within each of these stages. However, neither the periods nor their contents are discrete; each flows from the previous one and into the next. In this way, then, the main factors influencing policy are ever-present even if also in flux. Therefore, some consideration needs to be given to how these factors work across time.

Four observations can be made about the status of the key policy factors. First, the main framework of ideas, interests, and institutions remains constant across all periods. Second, none surpasses the other two to become the dominant variable; all remain, in their ways, integral to the process, although their relative roles may vary. Third, despite the consistency of the basic framework, there is nearly constant change within the main factors, and in the contextualizing ideas, across all four periods. Finally, decisions taken in one period become influences on strategies and decisions taken in subsequent ones.

Within this general outline, three general effects can be seen. First, over time one can see the changing relative importance of the key factors. For example, in the 1960s, the bureaucracy as one of the institutional branches of the state took the leading role with interest groups in support. In the 1970s, in contrast, bureaucracy and groups were sometimes in conflict. Here, groups played a stronger and more independent role, although they somewhat depended on state institutions to make relevant forums available. Both were guided by contextualizing ideas about the value of public participation. In the next period, the 1980s, groups remained important, but institutions were critical to the process by providing access to their authority.

Second, each of the main policy factors has changed over the period of analysis and may be said, at least for substantive ideas about parks and about the network of environmental interests, to have matured over the half century of consideration. The idea about parks expressed in the National Parks Act (1930), that of keeping them "unimpaired for future generations," has grown in scope and detail through this long half century of deliberation. Although ecological sensitivities were already present in some locations in the 1930s and 1940s, most of the articulation of that core idea happened in the postwar decades. By discussing parks in terms of ecological integrity, the concept of keeping them unimpaired was defined and given operational meaning (to a degree). While the word *unimpaired* remains in the legislation, "ecological integrity" is the idea around which serious discussion now occurs.

The concept of maintenance has also changed rather dramatically from one where parks were expected to be devoid of resident humans and park resources left untouched (since scenic resources were the focus of attention anyway) to one where, after the mid-1970s, ideas about the presence of humans in natural ecosystems changed to accommodate the presence of and resource use by Aboriginal people. In these ways, and in others perhaps more modest, ideas about what is meant by impairment, or its lack, have been defined, had details added, and even had some of the core conceptions changed. While lack of impairment remains a central objective for government, the idea has grown and matured since the mid-1950s.

In a similar manner, the role and character of interest groups have matured over this time. At the period's beginning, the National and Provincial Parks Association of Canada was coaxed into existence partly at the initiative and with the assistance of the Parks Branch itself. Over the succeeding decades, this group became more firmly established, and its participation is a regular practice for policy input. In turn, it was joined by other groups so that, by the 1990s, eight national environmental organizations could participate in the Group of Eight. If that was a short-lived coalition, its presence, and the continuing separate presence of each member, demonstrates the dramatically expanded field of environmental associations with interests in national parks. At the same time, there has been an enormous expansion of regional and local groups. While new groups will, no doubt, continue to emerge, and probably some will disappear, it is likely that a kind of equilibrium has been reached in the network of groups and their relations with the state. Thus, in a manner parallel to the evolution of substantive ideas about parks, the network of interest groups has grown, become more institutionalized, and established routine relations with state agencies in a process that, in hindsight, is readily understandable.

Third, this maturing process is influenced by the path of previous development. While the phrase "path dependent" might be used here, it would be better to describe the relationship as "influence" rather than "dependence" since the choices, especially over shorter time periods, were not always as tightly determined as the word *dependent* implies. Decisions may be made with little or no direct relationship to a previous policy. For example, the decision to create national park reserves in the 1974 legislation was influenced not by previous *park* policy but by other decisions (specifically the 1973 Supreme Court decision on the Nisga'a Tribal Council's land claims) outside the parks arena. Indeed, the value of conceiving of contextualizing ideas is to demonstrate the effect of ideas and decisions from outside the immediate policy arena on those inside.

Despite this qualification on the concept of dependence, policy decisions at one time are heavily influenced by those taken at an earlier time. The reciprocal relationship between the invention of human constructions and the subsequent effect that they have on behaviour has been a frequent observation. Perhaps the most famous is Winston Churchill's remark that "we shape our buildings, and afterwards our buildings shape us."[2] More recently, in the specific context of political analysis, Robert Jervis has said that "individuals shape the environments to which they will later respond."[3] These comments indicate well the interactive dynamic of decisions and their following effects. Again, the example of the NPPAC illustrates how the decision, by the Parks Branch, to promote such an organization was a relatively small one at the time but turned out to be more significant in the long run as that group helped to shape a new policy environment. In a similar way, use of the phrase "ecological integrity" in the formal but non-legislated 1979 policy statement created the precedent and the argument for including it in the 1988 legislation. Numerous other examples can be found to show how the decisions taken at one time may be the result of those taken at an earlier stage. In this way, changes in the ideas, interests, and institutions are made as precedents are set, and responses and advances are made as a consequence of them.

Some Implications for Policy Analysis

This analysis of the post-World War II development of national parks policy and its attention to contextualizing ideas has several implications for policy analysis. First, it supports the principal neo-institutional arguments about the importance of ideas, interest groups, and institutions for explaining policy outputs. Class analysis, public choice, and state-centred theories provide valuable conceptions for the examination of parks policy, but in the end they are not persuasive in explaining developments in this arena.

Second, consistent with observations made in other policy arenas, this study shows that relations among ideas, interest groups, and institutions are not static but change over time. This inquiry reveals, as others do, that there are multiple factors affecting these changes, among which are contextualizing ideas. These ideas also change over time and, as a result, bring different influences to bear on policy deliberations at different times.

Third, the argument presented here suggests that, as an explanation of policy outputs, ideas are pre-eminent. Where reasoned and negotiated policy processes occur, an understanding of interest groups and institutions is essential to explaining policy. However, to fully understand the layers or sequences of policy explanation, ideas occupy the primary position.

Fourth, although the policy community/policy network model was not the focus of this study, this work has shown that, in loosely structured networks, the relationships among and between interest groups and with state agencies are highly variable. Groups will seek advantage where they can, using the media, the courts, formal public processes, and other avenues to persuade or pressure authoritative decision makers. Although alliances will form (and dissolve), groups in this arena, and probably in others wherein networks are loosely structured, have not been able to draw on an integrated, hierarchical associational system as a source of political strength.

Finally, by showing how the bureaucracy, interest groups, and Aboriginal people have all drawn on existing quasi-constitutional, legislative, and administrative factors, this study reinforces the claims of historical institutionalists that existing institutions shape objectives and incentives for policy participants and therefore influence subsequent decisions.

Notes

Chapter 1: Introduction

1 Roderick Nash, *Wilderness and the American Mind* (New Haven: Yale University Press, 1967), 74.
2 Alfred Runte, *National Parks: The American Experience* (Lincoln: University of Nebraska Press, 1987), 32.
3 The name of the federal government agency responsible for national parks has changed many times since its creation in 1911. For simplicity, the generic term "Parks Branch" will be used throughout this text. In Chapter 6, this term will be used interchangeably with "Parks Canada," the current and well-known name for the agency.
4 "Park," *Oxford English Dictionary*, vol. 11 (Oxford: Clarendon Press, 1989), 234-35.
5 Nash, *Wilderness and the American Mind*, 106-7.
6 Ann MacEwen and Malcolm MacEwen, *National Parks: Conservation or Cosmetics?* (London: George Allen and Unwin, 1982), 6.
7 Robert Craig Brown, "The Doctrine of Usefulness: Natural Resources and National Park Policy in Canada, 1887-1914," in *Canadian Parks in Perspective*, ed. J.G. Nelson and R.C. Scace (Montreal: Harvest House, 1970), 50.
8 J.A. Kraulis and Kevin McNamee, *The National Parks of Canada* (Toronto: Key Porter, 1994), 17.
9 Brown, "The Doctrine of Usefulness," passim.
10 Aubrey Haines, *The Yellowstone Story: A History of Our First National Park*, vol. 1 (Wyoming: Yellowstone Library and Museum Association, 1977).
11 The World Commission on Protected Areas, a branch of the IUCN, defines protected areas as follows:

> Strict Nature Reserve/Wilderness Areas managed for the science of wilderness areas;
> National Park managed for ecosystem protection and recreation;
> Natural Monument managed for the conservation of specific natural features;
> Habitat/Species Management Area for conservation through management intervention;
> Protected Landscape/Seascape managed for landscape/seascape protection and recreation;
> Managed Resource Protected Area managed for the sustainable use of natural ecosystems.

> See the WCPA website: http://iucn.org/themes/wcpa/wcpa/protectedareas.htm.

12 MacEwen and MacEwen, *National Parks*, 64-68.
13 Janet Foster, *Working for Wildlife: The Beginning of Preservation in Canada* (Toronto: University of Toronto Press, 1978), 30, 239 note 58.
14 In April 1998, when appearing before a House of Commons committee, Chief Dwayne Black-bird pointed out the irony that, while his people were being evicted from the park, a resort community at Wasagaming for "whites" was being created at the park's other end. Canada,

House of Commons, Standing Committee on Canadian Heritage, 36th Parliament, 1st session (22 April 1998).

15 Raphael Samuel, *Theatres of Memory: Volume I: Past and Present in Contemporary Culture* (London: Verso, 1994), 205.

16 David Lowenthal, *Possessed by the Past: The Heritage Crusade and the Spoils of History* (New York: Free Press, 1996), 3.

17 Samuel, *Theatres of Memory,* 209-10.

18 J.E. Tunbridge and G.J. Ashworth, *Dissonant Heritage: The Management of the Past as a Resource in Conflict* (Chichester, NY: John Wiley and Sons, 1996), 1-2.

19 Robert Hewison, *The Heritage Industry: Britain in a Climate of Decline* (London: Methuen, 1987), 9.

20 Ibid., 10.

21 Lowenthal, *Possessed by the Past,* 88.

22 See, in particular, the detailed account of local administrative choices in Alan MacEachern, *Natural Selections: National Parks in Atlantic Canada, 1935-1970* (Montreal and Kingston: McGill-Queen's University Press, 2001).

23 Because of the attention they get from humans, parks may become managed environments. In the 1950s and 1960s, for example, the Parks Branch used to cull predators, the "bad animals," to enhance the survival of "good animals," usually large ungulates.

24 There are also theories that can be used to explain the existence of meaning, but they are not the central focus of this work. In any event, theories in communication (i.e., the transmittal of meaning) are not the same as theories about policy. This book's analysis may help to understand meaning, but it is not intended to be a full explanation of the meanings extant in national parks.

25 Ronald Manzer, *Public Schools and Political Ideas: Canadian Educational Policy in Historical Perspective* (Toronto: University of Toronto Press, 1994), 5.

26 Judith Goldstein, *Ideas, Interests, and American Trade Policy* (Ithaca: Cornell University Press, 1993), 3.

27 Margaret Weir, cited in *Structuring Politics: Historical Institutionalism in Comparative Analysis,* ed. Sven Steinmo, Kathleen Thelen, and Frank Longstreth (Cambridge, UK: Cambridge University Press, 1992), 188.

28 Manzer, *Public Schools and Political Ideas,* 5.

29 A policy community is defined as including "all actors or potential actors with a direct or indirect interest in a policy area or function who share a common 'policy focus' and who, with varying degrees of influence, shape policy outcomes over the long run," whereas a policy network describes "the properties that characterize the relationships among the particular set of actors that forms around an issue of importance to the policy community." William D. Coleman and Grace Skogstad, "Policy Communities and Policy Networks: A Structural Approach," in *Policy Communities and Public Policy in Canada: A Structural Approach,* ed. William D. Coleman and Grace Skogstad (Mississauga: Copp Clark Pitman, 1990), 25-26.

30 A. Paul Pross, *Group Politics and Public Policy* (Toronto: Oxford University Press, 1986), 246-47.

31 Ibid.

32 James G. March and Johan P. Olsen, "The New Institutionalism: Organizational Factors in Political Life," *American Political Science Review* 78 (1984): 734-49.

33 Theda Skocpol, "Bringing the State Back In: Strategies of Analysis in Current Research," in *Bringing the State Back In,* ed. Peter Evans, Dietrich Rueschemeyer, and Theda Skocpol (Cambridge, UK: Cambridge University Press, 1985), 3-38.

34 Peter Hall, *Governing the Economy: The Politics of State Intervention in Britain and France* (New York: Oxford University Press, 1986).

35 Ibid., 19.

36 Bertrand Russell, *A History of Western Philosophy* (London: Unwin, 1984), 63.

37 Kenneth H.F. Dyson, *The State Tradition in Western Europe* (Oxford: Martin Robertson, 1980), 1.

38 Robert D. Putnam, *Making Democracy Work: Civic Traditions in Modern Italy* (Princeton: Princeton University Press, 1993), 8. The social context that Putnam refers to is the density of networks among volunteer organizations.

39 R. Kent Weaver and Bert A. Rockman, eds., *Do Institutions Matter? Government Capabilities in the United States and Abroad* (Washington, DC: Brookings Institution, 1993), 6.
40 James Farr, "Democratic Social Engineering: Karl Popper, Political Theory, and Policy Analysis," in *History and Context in Contemporary Public Policy*, ed. Douglas Ashford (Pittsburgh: University of Pittsburgh Press, 1992), 167-88.
41 Douglas Ashford, "Introduction: Of Cases and Contexts," in *History and Context in Comparative Public Policy*, ed. Douglas Ashford (Pittsburgh: University of Pittsburgh Press, 1992), 4-5.
42 Carolyn Tuohy, "Social Policy: Two Worlds," in *Governing Canada: Institutions and Public Policy*, ed. Michael Atkinson (Toronto: Harcourt Brace Jovanovich, 1993), 287.
43 Ibid., 289. See also Carolyn Tuohy, "Federalism and Canadian Health Policy," in *Challenges to Federalism: Policy-Making in Canada and the Federal Republic of Germany*, ed. William Chandler and Christian W. Zollner (Kingston: Institute of Intergovernmental Relations, 1989), 142-44.
44 Rodney S. Haddow, *Poverty Reform in Canada, 1958-1978: State and Class Influences in Policy Making* (Montreal and Kingston: McGill-Queen's University Press, 1993), 19.
45 Ibid., 191.
46 George Hoberg, *Pluralism by Design: Environmental Policy and the American Regulatory State* (New York: Praeger, 1992), 10-12.
47 Ibid.
48 Ibid., 2.
49 Manzer, *Public Schools and Political Ideas*, 5.
50 Hugh Heclo, *Modern Social Politics in Britain and Sweden: From Relief to Income Maintenance* (New Haven: Yale University Press, 1974), 9.
51 Ibid.
52 Ibid., 313.
53 Ibid., 305.

Chapter 2: Background to the Postwar Era

1 Alfred Runte, *National Parks: The American Experience* (Lincoln: University of Nebraska Press, 1979), 14.
2 Ibid., 19.
3 Ibid., 21, 22.
4 Ibid., 29.
5 Ibid., 47.
6 John Ise, *Our National Park Policy: A Critical History* (Baltimore: Johns Hopkins University Press, 1961), 54.
7 Marilyn Dubasak, *Wilderness Preservation: A Cross-Cultural Comparison of Canada and the United States* (New York: Garland Publishing, 1990), 20.
8 George Catlin may have been the first to use a version of the term that later became "national park." In 1832, he proposed "a nation's park containing man and beast, in all the wild and freshness of their natures' beauty." Cited in Runte, *National Parks*, 26.
9 Ise, *Our National Park Policy*, 56.
10 Roderick Nash, *Wilderness and the American Mind* (New Haven: Yale University Press, 1967), 132.
11 Runte, *National Parks*, 60.
12 Dubasak, *Wilderness Preservation*, 48. See also Norman Henderson, "Wilderness and the Nature Conservation Ideal: Britain, Canada, and the United States Contrasted," *Ambio: Journal of the Human Environment* 21, 6 (1992): 395.
13 Robert Craig Brown, "The Doctrine of Usefulness: Natural Resources and National Park Policy in Canada, 1887-1914," in *Canadian Parks in Perspective*, ed. J.G. Nelson and R.C. Scace (Montreal: Harvest House, 1970), 58.
14 Leslie Bella, *Parks for Profit* (Montreal: Harvest House, 1987), 2.
15 Canada, *House of Commons Debates* (29 April 1887), cited in Brown, "The Doctrine of Usefulness," 50.
16 Ibid.

17 Bella, *Parks for Profit,* 13, 14.
18 Ibid., 14-18.
19 Ibid., 25-39; Brown, "The Doctrine of Usefulness," 53.
20 A detailed discussion of this subject is given in Chapter 5.
21 Harold Eidsvik, senior policy adviser, Parks Canada, personal interview, Ottawa, October 1991.
22 Janet Foster, *Working for Wildlife: The Beginning of Preservation in Canada* (Toronto: University of Toronto Press, 1978), 34-35.
23 Ibid., 1-5.
24 Brown, "The Doctrine of Usefulness," 56-57. See also Foster's discussion (38-42 and 210-16) of the (Canadian) Commission of Conservation (1909-21), including Clifford Sifton's view that "conservation means the utilization of our resources in a proper and economical way." Cited in Foster, *Working for Wildlife,* 41.
25 Dubasak, *Wilderness Preservation,* 48. Despite Bella's account of the influence of the Canadian Alpine Club and its executive director, Arthur Wheeler, on the National Parks Act (1930), this statement is probably apt. See Bella, *Parks for Profit,* 39-58.
26 Foster, *Working for Wildlife,* 75, 76.
27 Ibid., 77, 82.
28 James B. Harkin, *The History and Meaning of the National Parks of Canada,* compiled by Mabel B. Williams (Saskatoon: H.R. Larson Publishing, 1957), 5.
29 Foster, *Working for Wildlife,* 75-83.
30 Alan MacEachern, *Natural Selections: National Parks in Atlantic Canada, 1935-1970* (Montreal and Kingston: McGill-Queen's University Press, 2001), 28.
31 Foster, *Working for Wildlife,* 13.
32 W.F. Lothian, *History of Canada's National Parks,* vol. 2 (Ottawa: Minister of Supply and Services Canada, 1977), 16.
33 Statutes of Canada, 20-21 George V, c. 33, part 1, s. 4, *An Act Respecting National Parks* (1930).
34 Harkin, *The History and Meaning of the National Parks of Canada,* 9.
35 Bella, *Parks for Profit,* 58. Bella is not uncritical, however. She acknowledges that the 1930 National Parks Act gave greater protection to parks from traditional resource exploitation such as mining, forestry, and hydroelectric development, but she charges that it opened parks to another kind of exploitation, that of tourism, especially automobile-based tourism.
36 Canada, *House of Commons Debates,* 16th Parliament, 4th session (9 May 1930), pp. 1932, 1934.
37 Ibid., 1935.
38 Only three small national parks, comprising less that one-tenth of 1 percent of the total area in national parks, had been created outside western Canada (in Ontario).
39 In the nineteenth century, northern and western Canada were named the North-West Territories (with a hyphen), but after the removal of lands for the creation of Saskatchewan and Alberta in 1905 the remaining area was titled the Northwest Territories (no hyphen). For consistency, only the modern form will be used herein.
40 Alberta, because of mineral and other resources, probably gave up more potential provincial revenue than Saskatchewan or Manitoba and was willing to settle for a reduced compensation package as early as 1920. Chester Martin, "Dominion Lands Policy," in *Canadian Frontiers of Settlement,* vol. 2, ed. W.A. Mackintosh and W.L.G. Joerg (Toronto: Macmillan of Canada, 1938), 490.
41 For a good account of the areas excluded and the surrounding debate, see Bella, *Parks for Profit,* 50-58.
42 Bill Waiser, *Park Prisoners: The Untold Story of Western Canada's National Parks, 1915-1946* (Saskatoon: Fifth House, 1995), 4.
43 For a detailed discussion of work and prison camps in national parks, see ibid. See also Bella, *Parks for Profit,* Chapter 5.

Chapter 3: National Parks and the Era of State Initiative
1 Canada, Department of Indian Affairs and National Resources, National Parks Branch, *National Parks Policy (1964),* 1.

2 Although some minor amendments were made, the proposed policy statement in 1964 was largely unchanged from its original 1957 wording.
3 *National Parks Policy (1964)*, 4.
4 Ibid., 8.
5 Ibid., 21.
6 Ibid., 22.
7 Ibid., 3.
8 They may also have been carried forward by individuals with the Parks Branch. Only twenty years separated the retirement of J.B. Harkin and the reconsiderations of policy resulting in the 1964 paper, yet many national parks personnel had long service with the branch over-lapping these events. For example, R.A. Gibson retired as director in 1950, and he had been with the parks service for forty-two years. W.F. Lothian, *History of Canada's National Parks*, vol. 2 (Ottawa: Minister of Supply and Services Canada, 1977), 19.
9 *National Parks Policy (1964)*, 4.
10 Correspondence from Harold Eidsvik, former senior policy adviser, Canadian Parks Service, 27 August 1994.
11 Leslie Bella, *Parks for Profit* (Montreal: Harvest House, 1987), Chapter 3.
12 Cited in A. Paul Pross, *Group Politics and Public Policy* (Toronto: Oxford University Press, 1986), 49.
13 Ibid.
14 Stephan J. Dupré, "Reflections of the Workability of Executive Federalism," in *Perspectives on Canadian Federalism*, ed. R.D. Olling and M.W. Westmacott (Scarborough: Prentice-Hall, 1988), 235.
15 Ibid.
16 Ibid.
17 Ronald Inglehart, *The Silent Revolution: Changing Values and Political Styles among Western Publics* (Princeton: Princeton University Press, 1977), 42.
18 Ibid., 72.
19 Thomas Trump has compared recent American and (West) German high school students with ambiguous results. He concludes with the caution that postmaterialist values "may be short term attitudes that will rise and fall at different times in different nations depending on their national political climates." Thomas Trump, "Value Formation and Postmaterialism: Ingle-hart's Theory of Value Change Reconsidered," *Comparative Political Studies* 24, 3 (1991): 383.
20 Oddbjørn Knutsen, "Materialist and Postmaterialist Values and Social Structure in the Nordic Countries," *Comparative Politics* 23, 1 (1990): 100.
21 Hans-Georg Betz, "Value Change and Postmaterialist Politics: The Case of West Germany," *Comparative Political Studies* 23, 2 (1990): 245.
22 Herman Bakvis and Neil Nevitte, "In Pursuit of Postbourgeois Man: Postmaterialism and Intergenerational Change in Canada," *Comparative Political Studies* 20, 3 (1987): 382.
23 While the Parks Branch was able to act autonomously in developing a proposed policy statement, it was not able to proceed independently in the more complicated processes involved in its adoption and formalization.
24 Lothian, *History of Canada's National Parks*, 18-21.
25 Ibid., 22.
26 Canada, *Report of the Royal Commission on Government Organization* (the Glassco Commission) (Ottawa: Queen's Printer, 1962), 38. Since this report was published in 1962, the parks recommendation may have been based on knowledge that such a policy statement was in fact already in draft form.
27 Library and Archives Canada (LAC), RG 84, vol. 1815, PS 28, vol. 3, part 2, letter from Patrick Hardy, managing director, Canadian Audubon Society, to The Rt. Hon. Lester B. Pearson, prime minister of Canada, 18 January 1965. See also *Park News* (the journal of the NPPAC), July 1965.
28 Cited in Patrick Kyba, *Alvin: A Biography of the Honourable Alvin Hamilton, P.C.* (Regina: Canadian Plains Research Center, 1989), 138.
29 LAC, RG 84, vol. 1813, PS 28, vol. 2, Memorandum from Lloyd Brooks, Chief, Planning Section, to J.R.B. Coleman, Branch Director, 26 March 1962.

30 Kyba, *Alvin*, 100-1.
31 Canada, *House of Commons Debates*, 24th Parliament, 3rd session (23 July 1960), 6857.
32 LAC, RG 84, vol. 1813, PS 28, vol. 3.
33 Baker wrote the Parks Branch's presentation for the Resources for Tomorrow Conference.
34 J.L. Granatstein, *The Ottawa Men: The Civil Service Mandarins, 1935-1957* (Toronto: Oxford University Press, 1982), 41.
35 The name ARDA originally derives from the Agricultural Rehabilitation and Development Act (1961).
36 Peter C. Newman, *The Distemper of Our Times* (Toronto: McClelland and Stewart, 1968), 79.
37 Ibid.
38 Canada, *House of Commons Debates*, 26th Parliament, 2nd session (18 September 1964), 8192.
39 LAC, RG 84, vol. 1815, letter from Canadian Audubon Society to Prime Minister Pearson in support of the minister of northern affairs and national resources, January 1965.
40 On 5 July 1994, the minister of Canadian heritage, in which department the Parks Branch was then located, announced a five-member panel to make recommendations with respect to the Bow Valley, the location of both Lake Louise and Banff townsite, in Banff National Park. The process and report are discussed in Chapter 6.
41 Canada, Department of Indian Affairs and Northern Development, *National Parks System Planning Manual* (Ottawa: Information Canada, 1972), 3.
42 Monte Hummel, "The Upshot," in *Endangered Spaces*, ed. Monte Hummel (Toronto: Key Porter Books, 1989), 272.
43 LAC, RG 84, vol. 1812, PS 2-3, part 2, vol. 1, J.C. Jackson, Branch Director, "Requirements of a National Park," 31 January 1961, 3.
44 Harold Eidsvik, senior policy adviser, Parks Canada, personal interview, Ottawa, October 1991.
45 See Jackson, "Requirements of a National Park."
46 For example, LAC, RG 84, vol. 1814, PS 28, vol. 7, unlabelled draft document, "National Parks and Outdoor Recreation," circa 1965.
47 Robert Boardman, *International Organization and the Conservation of Nature* (London: Macmillan, 1981), 35-44.
48 United States, Department of the Interior, National Parks Service, "National Park System Plan Handbook," typescript, March 1961, 1-1.
49 Ibid., 3-1.
50 Ronald A. Foresta, *America's National Parks and Their Keepers* (Washington, DC: Resources for the Future, 1984), 112.
51 Canada, Proceedings, Annual Federal-Provincial Parks Conference, 1963.
52 *National Parks System Planning Manual*, 2.
53 Peter Aucoin, "Organizational Change in the Management of Canadian Government: From Rational Management to Brokerage Politics," *Canadian Journal of Political Science* 19 (1986): passim.
54 Pierre Elliott Trudeau, *Federalism and the French Canadians* (Toronto: Macmillan, 1968), 203.
55 G. Bruce Doern, "Recent Changes in the Philosophy of Policy-Making in Canada," *Canadian Journal of Political Science* 4 (1971): 243-64.
56 *National Parks System Planning Manual*, 3.
57 Lloyd Brooks studied at Michigan State University, and Harold Eidsvik did his degree at the University of Michigan (though they did so at different times).
58 Canada, Proceedings, Annual Federal-Provincial Parks Conference, 1970, 18.
59 They were John Carruthers and Gerry O. Lee.
60 Gerry O. Lee, Canadian Wildlife Service, personal interview, Ottawa, February 1993.
61 *National Parks System Planning Manual*, 3.
62 Al Davidson, former assistant deputy minister, Parks Canada, personal interview, Ottawa, January 1992.
63 Garth Stevenson, *Unfulfilled Union: Canadian Federalism and National Unity*, rev. ed. (Toronto: Gage, 1982), 190.

64 For Dupré, co-operative federalism is more likely to occur when (a) bureaucrats from both levels of government have shared values and a common vocabulary; (b) the commonalities of intergovernmental relations are reflected at the deputy minister and minister levels; (c) departments and their ministers are independent enough to reach stable agreements with provinces; (d) these relations create an investment in future co-operation; (e) these relations are aided by financial transfers from the federal government to the provincial governments; and (f) societal interests form network ties with appointed and elected officials. Dupré, "Reflections of the Workability of Executive Federalism," 236-37.

65 This council has transformed itself several times and is today the Canadian Council of Ministers of the Environment (CCME).

66 For example, the CCRM provided funding for the National Parks Today and Tomorrow Conference in 1968 that was sponsored by NPPAC and the University of Calgary.

67 Canada, Proceedings, Annual Federal-Provincial Parks Conference, 1973 and 1974 respectively.

68 The idea of a "path" is discussed together with the concept of "path dependence" in Kathleen Thelen and Sven Steinmo, "Historical Institutionalism in Comparative Politics," in *Structuring Politics: Historical Institutionalism in Comparative Analysis,* ed. Sven Steinmo, Kathleen Thelen, and Frank Longstreth (Cambridge, UK: Cambridge University Press, 1992), 1-32.

69 *National Parks Policy (1964),* 1.

70 Eidsvik, correspondence, 1994.

71 Charles E. Lindblom, "The Science of Muddling Through," *Public Administration Review* 19 (Spring 1959): 79-88; Graham T. Allison, "Conceptual Models and the Cuban Missile Crisis," *American Political Science Review* 63 (September 1969): 689-718.

72 Robert S. Montjoy and Laurence J. O'Toole Jr., "Toward a Theory of Policy Implementation: An Organizational Perspective," *Public Administration Review* 39, 5 (1979): 465-76.

73 National parks budgets had declined from 1949 to 1954, but they rose sharply after 1955, such that in 1959 they were four times what they had been six years earlier, as the following figures show:

Year	$ 000s	Year	$ 000s	Year	$ 000s
1949-50	10,337	1953-54	6,587	1957-58	16,934
1950-51	9,125	1954-55	7,510	1958-59	21,950
1951-52	6,358	1955-56	9,304	1959-60	24,948
1952-53	6,536	1956-57	15,283		

Source: National Parks and Historic Sites Services, Expenditures Canada, *Public Accounts* (Ottawa: Receiver General for Canada, 1949-50 to 1959-60).

74 For more on social and governmental learning, see, for example, Peter Hall, "Policy Paradigms, Social Learning, and the State: The Case of Economic Policymaking in Britain," *Comparative Politics* 25 (1993): 275-96; Hugh Heclo, *Modern Social Policies in Britain and Sweden: From Relief to Income Maintenance* (New Haven: Yale University Press, 1974); Paul Sacks, "State Structure and the Asymmetrical Society: An Approach to Public Policy in Britain," *Comparative Politics* 12 (1980): 349-76; Jack L. Walker, "The Diffusion of Knowledge, Policy Communities, and Agenda Setting: The Relationship of Knowledge and Power," in *New Strategic Perspectives on Social Policy,* ed. John E. Tropman, Milan J. Dluhy, and Roger M. Lind (New York: Pergamon Press, 1982), 75-96.

Chapter 4: National Parks and Public Participation

1 Alastair R. Lucas, "Legal Foundations for Public Participation in Environmental Decision-making," *Natural Resources Journal* 16 (1976): 75. See also Norman Wengert, "Citizen Participation: Practice in Search of a Theory," *Natural Resources Journal* 16 (1976): 23; Paul Emond, "Participation and the Environment: A Strategy for Democratizing Canada's Environmental Protection Laws," *Osgoode Hall Law Journal* 13 (1975): 783-817; and David E. Smith, *The Regional Decline of a National Party: Liberals on the Prairies* (Toronto: University of Toronto Press, 1981), Chapter 5.

2 See George Hoberg, "Environmental Policy: Alternative Styles," in *Governing Canada: Institutions and Public Policy,* ed. Michael M. Atkinson (Toronto: Harcourt Brace Jovanovich,

1993), 307-42. See also Michael Howlett, "The Judicialization of Canadian Environmental Policy, 1980-1990: A Test of the Canada-United States Convergence Thesis," *Canadian Journal of Political Science* 27, 1 (1994): 99-127.

3 Jon O'Riordan, "The Public Involvement Program in the Okanagan Basin Study," *Natural Resources Journal* 16 (1976): 177-96.

4 Sherry R. Arnstein, "A Ladder of Public Participation," *Journal of the American Institute of Planners* 35 (1969): 217.

5 Harold K. Eidsvik, "Involving the Public in Park Planning: Canada," *Parks* 3, 1 (n.d.): 3-4. This model was initially published in "Canadian Participation," *Resources* 2, 9 (1973).

6 George B. Priddle, "Role of the Public," in *People and Environment: Proceedings of the Conference on Public Participation in Environmental Assessment,* University of Guelph, 4-5 November 1977, ed. Dennis Kuch and O.P. Dwivedi (Guelph: University of Guelph, 1977).

7 Marilyn Dubasak, *Wilderness Preservation: A Cross-Cultural Comparison of Canada and the United States* (New York: Garland Publishing, 1990), 79.

8 See, for example, Wilson A. Head, "The Ideology and Practice of Citizen Participation," in *Citizen Participation: Canada – A Book of Readings,* ed. James A. Draper (Toronto: New Press, 1971), 14; W.R. Derrick Sewell and Timothy O'Riordan, "The Culture of Participation in Environmental Decisionmaking," *Natural Resources Journal* 16 (1976): 1; and Lucas, "Legal Foundations," 75.

9 Head, "The Ideology and Practice of Citizen Participation," 14-15.

10 James A. Draper, "Evolution of Citizen Participation in Canada," in *Involvement and Environment: Proceedings of the Canadian Conference on Public Participation,* 2 vols., ed. Barry Sadler (Edmonton: Environment Council of Alberta, 1979), passim.

11 This idea seems to derive from De Tocqueville's comments about democracy in the United States and Arthur Bentley's early-twentieth-century work on interest groups. More recent work by Robert Putnam on Italy and Gertrude Himmelfarb on Victorian England suggests that voluntary organization was, and remains, commonplace in those countries also. America may not be an exception. See Robert D. Putnam, *Making Democracy Work: Civic Traditions in Modern Italy* (Princeton: Princeton University Press, 1993); and Gertrude Himmelfarb, *The De-Moralization of Society: From Victorian Virtues to Modern Values* (New York: Vintage, 1996).

12 Marcus E. Ethridge, "Procedures for Citizen Involvement in Environmental Policy: An Assessment of Policy Effects," in *Citizen Participation in Public Decision Making,* ed. Jack DeSario and Stuart Langton (New York: Greenwood Press, 1987), 116.

13 Ibid.

14 Head, "The Ideology and Practice of Citizen Participation," 16-17; Sewell and O'Riordan, "The Culture of Participation in Environmental Decisionmaking," 4.

15 Dubasak, *Wilderness Preservation,* 164.

16 Lucas, "Legal Foundations," 102.

17 Ethridge, "Procedures for Citizen Involvement," 121.

18 While the existence and the basic structure of the legislature, both national and provincial, are included in the Constitution Act (1867), its role in terms of practices and relationships is not specified. On this point, Andrew Heard says that "the formal provisions of the Canadian constitution are curiously silent on the operation of the national and provincial legislatures." Legislative practice, he says, "is determined by an amalgam of a few provisions of positive law fleshed out by usage, binding convention, and what has come to be called the 'law and custom of Parliament.'" Andrew Heard, *Canadian Constitutional Conventions: The Marriage of Law and Politics* (Toronto: Oxford, 1991), 76. In a similar vein, David E. Smith observes that "the other constitution – the one to do with everything but the structure of federalism – is not found in the Act of 1867." By "the other constitution," Smith means responsible government, "which came to Canada not by changes to the law but by the governors of the different colonies adopting new rules of practice." David E. Smith, *The Invisible Crown: The First Principle of Canadian Government* (Toronto: University of Toronto Press, 1995), 137.

19 This situation has changed somewhat since the introduction of the Charter of Rights and Freedoms in 1982 but would certainly have been the case in the 1960s unless the courts were involved in questions of jurisdiction.

20 Lucas, "Legal Foundations," 77, lists the following legislation: British Columbia Pollution Control Act (1967), Alberta Clean Air Act (1971), Alberta Clean Water Act (1971), Ontario Environmental Protection Act (1971), National Energy Board Act (1970), and (Canada) Fisheries Act (1970).

21 Gerald Killan, *Protected Places: A History of Ontario's Provincial Park System* (Toronto: Dundurn Press, 1993), 170.

22 Ibid., 170-74.

23 J.A. MacDonald was deputy minister for the whole department but had been assistant deputy minister in charge of parks until earlier that year.

24 This account was given, in interviews, by two different Parks Canada officials on separate occasions.

25 T.L. Green, "The Role of the Public in National Park Planning and Management," in *The Canadian National Parks: Today and Tomorrow. Conference II: Ten Years Later,* vol. 2, ed. J.G. Nelson et al. (Waterloo: University of Waterloo, 1979), 736.

26 Rodney Touche, *Brown Cows, Sacred Cows: A True Story of Lake Louise* (Hanna, AB: Gorman Brothers, 1990), 54. Touche was the president of Village Lake Louise in the 1970s.

27 Ibid., 73; see also Robert C. Scace, "The Visitor Service Centre and Developments at Lake Louise, Banff National Park," *Park News,* July 1971: 16.

28 Touche, *Brown Cows, Sacred Cows,* 102-3.

29 Canada, Department of Northern Affairs and National Resources, Natural and Historic Resources Branch, "Winter Recreation and the National Parks: A Management Policy and a Development Program," typescript, March 1965.

30 Scace, "The Visitor Service Centre," 21.

31 Touche, *Brown Cows, Sacred Cows,* 137.

32 Documentation for the Four Mountain Parks management plan contained only a single line mentioning the plans for the Lake Louise VSC. See Stephen Herrero, "Parks Canada and Public Participation: The Case of Village Lake Louise and Sunshine Village," in *Involvement and Environment: Proceedings of the Canadian Conference on Public Participation,* 2 vols., ed. Barry Sadler (Edmonton: Environment Council of Alberta, 1979), 255.

33 Touche, *Brown Cows, Sacred Cows,* 137.

34 Ibid.

35 Herrero, "Parks Canada and Public Participation," 59.

36 Touche, *Brown Cows, Sacred Cows,* 144.

37 Ibid., 142-44; Leslie Bella, *Parks for Profit* (Montreal: Harvest House, 1987), 125; Aileen Harmon, "Village Lake Louise," *Nature Canada* 1 (1972): 33.

38 Herrero, "Parks Canada and Public Participation," 260. Herrero has a long association with national park issues. A professor at the University of Calgary and an expert on grizzly bears, he is currently chair of the Eastern Slopes Grizzly Bear Project, which is studying the effects of development on grizzly bears in Banff National Park generally and in the Bow Valley specifically. Sid Marty, "Homeless on the Range: Grizzlies Struggle for Elbow Room and Survival in Banff National Park," *Canadian Geographic* 117 (1997): 28-39. In the 1970s, Herrero was active with the NPPAC in opposing Village Lake Louise.

39 Touche, cited in Sadler, ed., *Involvement and Environment,* 274.

40 Unless otherwise noted, all the events and substantive facts in this section are condensed from Gerald V. La Forest and Muriel Kent Roy, *Report of the Special Inquiry on Kouchibouguac National Park* (Ottawa: Government of Canada and Government of New Brunswick, 1981).

41 This was the term used by La Forest and Roy to refer to the people whose lands were expropriated.

42 La Forest and Roy, *Report of the Special Inquiry,* 15.

43 Anthony G. Careless, *Initiative and Response: The Adaptation of Canadian Federalism to Regional Economic Development* (Montreal and Kingston: McGill-Queen's University Press, 1977), 80.

44 La Forest and Roy, *Report of the Special Inquiry,* 48.

45 John C. Courtney, "Franchise," in *Canadian Encyclopaedia,* 2nd ed. (Edmonton: Hurtig Publishers, 1988). See also Sally M. Weaver, *Making Indian Policy: The Hidden Agenda, 1968-70* (Toronto: University of Toronto Press, 1981), 45. Although Aboriginal people now had some standard political rights, such as the right to vote, their individual lives still were

highly circumscribed by the Indian Act and the Department of Indian Affairs, particularly with respect to fiscal matters and the oversight of Indian agents.

46 C.E.S. Franks, *The Parliament of Canada* (Toronto: University of Toronto Press, 1987), 162-63.

47 Quoted in Thomas R. Berger, *A Long and Terrible Shadow: White Values and Native Rights in the Americas, 1492-1992* (Vancouver: Douglas and McIntyre, 1991), 75.

48 Ibid., 80.

49 In 1990, the Supreme Court of Canada adopted Marshall's arguments when it ruled in favour of Aboriginal title in *R. v. Sparrow.* Berger, *A Long and Terrible Shadow,* 83.

50 Paul Tennant, *Aboriginal Peoples and Politics: The Indian Land Question in British Columbia, 1849-1989* (Vancouver: UBC Press, 1990), 111-12.

51 Douglas Sanders, *Native Rights in Canada,* cited in Weaver, *Making Indian Policy,* 18.

52 Harry B. Hawthorn, ed., *A Survey of the Contemporary Indians of Canada: A Report on Economic, Political, Educational Needs and Policies* (Ottawa: Indian Affairs, 1966).

53 Because of the overtones of European ("white")–Indian relations, the government attempted to call this a green paper, but it was clearly a statement of policy, not an explanation, and Indian spokespersons correctly referred to it as a white paper. See Tennant, *Aboriginal People and Politics,* 149-50.

54 Cited in Weaver, *Making Indian Policy,* 21.

55 See ibid., 4; and Tennant, *Aboriginal People and Politics,* 149-50.

56 Weaver, *Making Indian Policy,* 183-87.

57 Of the seven justices who decided the case, one ruled against the Nisga'a on a technicality. The remaining six, however, ruled unanimously that pre-existing Aboriginal title had in fact existed, although they did so for differing reasons, thus denying one of the province's principal arguments. On the question of extant Aboriginal title, the six were evenly divided, three arguing that without explicit extinguishment title continued, while the remaining three accepted the province's argument that title had been implicitly extinguished. Although the Nisga'a lost their case, the support of three Supreme Court justices on continuing title changed the nature of the argument for both the Nisga'a and the province.

58 Bill S-4, An Act to Amend the National Parks Act, 1st Session, 29th Parliament, 1973.

59 Canada, House of Commons, Standing Committee on Indian Affairs and Northern Development, Minutes, no. 29 (Whitehorse, Yukon, 12 December 1973), 31.

60 Ibid., 35.

61 Indian leaders held the forefront of this campaign, but they had many supporters. One of these was Professor Peter Cumming, who, at a Liberal Party conference in British Columbia, called for a co-operative effort to develop an Indian policy. Weaver, *Making Indian Policy,* 181.

62 An Act to Amend the National Parks Act, c. 11, 2nd Session, 29th Parliament, 1974, clause 11(2).

63 More explicit attention was paid to the other elements of the Parks Branch mandate – national historic parks, national historic sites, and heritage canals. In addition, new initiatives for Canadian landmarks, heritage rivers, and heritage buildings were included in the 1979 policy statement. However, national parks (those mostly large, mostly natural tracts of land, set aside and protected to represent elements of the country's biophysical heritage) command a major share of the policy attention and remain the sole focus of this analysis.

64 Canada, Minister of the Environment, *Parks Canada Policy* (Ottawa: Supply and Services Canada, 1982), 38. This policy was authorized by cabinet and is universally known as the 1979 policy (although sometimes as the 1978 policy since it was prepared and finalized in that year) even though the formal publication was 1982. The idea of maintaining national parks unimpaired finds its basis in the National Parks Act (1930). The concept of protecting representative natural areas was developed along with the System Plan in the 1970s.

65 Ibid., s. 1.3.1, 39.

66 Ibid.

67 Since these towns exist within national parks, they have no municipal government, a provincial responsibility. Municipal services were handled by the Parks Branch, often from Ottawa itself, sometimes at great delay and frustration for the residents.

68 Comments by J.A. MacDonald, senior assistant deputy minister, Standing Committee on Northern Affairs and National Resources, Minutes, no. 24 (28 February 1967), 1001-2.

69 See Nelson et al., eds., *The Canadian National Parks*.

70 Ibid., 639-40.

71 Parks Canada, *The Response to Public Comments on the Parks Canada Policy* (Ottawa: Parks Canada, 1979). The view that few changes were made is supported by Bella, *Parks for Profit*, 119.

72 Parks Canada, *The Response to Public Comments*, 3.

73 The protectionist theme is further illustrated by the response to the single contribution by the minister, who had suggested a designation of "wilderness" parks for those parks north of the sixtieth parallel, implying that parks south of sixty were not therefore seen as wilderness. To dispel this interpretation, the policy deleted the minister's suggestions and henceforth treated all national parks by the same criteria. Confidential interview.

74 Another important event for national parks under the brief Joe Clark government was that the Parks Branch was moved from the Department of Indian Affairs and Northern Development to the Department of the Environment, although there does not appear to be any direct policy consequences resulting from the move.

75 Canada, Federal Environmental Assessment Review Office, *Public Review: Neither Judicial, Nor Political, but an Essential Forum for the Future of the Environment: A Report* (Ottawa: Supply and Services, 1988), 12.

76 Gavin Henderson, former executive director, NPPAC, personal interview, Toronto, June 1994.

Chapter 5: National Parks and the Initiatives of Organized Interests

1 For details on Grasslands National Park, see Keith Neufeld, "Ranching and Grasslands National Park: An Historical and Institutional Analysis" (master's thesis, University of Waterloo, 1984).

2 Arlin Hackman, "Endangered Spaces: Ten Years for Wilderness in Canada," *Borealis* (January 1990): 27-29; and Arlin Hackman, director, Endangered Spaces Campaign, World Wildlife Fund Canada, personal interview, Toronto, 28 June 1994.

3 For a discussion of containment, see Jeremy Wilson, "Wilderness Politics in B.C.: The Business Dominated State and the Containment of Environmentalism," in *Policy Communities and Public Policy in Canada: A Structural Approach,* ed. William D. Coleman and Grace Skogstad (Mississauga: Copp Clark Pittman, 1990), 141-69.

4 The IPC was a private interest group, not a government committee, as the name might suggest.

5 In fact, the Haida do not see their position as a "claim": "It is Canada which claims Haida land," says one Haida, cited in Elizabeth May, *Paradise Won: The Struggle for South Moresby* (Toronto: McClelland and Stewart, 1990), 59.

6 Paul Tennant, *Aboriginal Peoples and Politics: The Indian Land Question in British Columbia, 1849-1989* (Vancouver: UBC Press, 1990), 111, 122.

7 In little more than half a century following the 1850s, the Haida suffered a loss of over 90 percent of their population, so that in 1915 there were only 588 Haida individuals, where there had been between 6,000 and 8,000 sixty-five years earlier. The population had grown considerably by the 1950s, although it was still less than 2,000. Trisha Gessler, "Haida," in *Canadian Encyclopaedia*.

8 May, *Paradise Won*, 63.

9 Tennant, *Aboriginal Peoples and Politics*, Chapter 9.

10 See Douglas MacDonald, *The Politics of Pollution: Why Canadians Are Failing Their Environment* (Toronto: McClelland and Stewart, 1991); and Samuel E. Hays, *Beauty, Health, and Permanence: Environmental Politics in the United States, 1955-85* (Cambridge, UK: Cambridge University Press, 1987). The public and official attention paid to these issues constitutes what has been referred to as the first wave of environmentalism. See George Hoberg, "Environmental Policy: Alternative Styles," in *Governing Canada: Institutions and Public Policy*, ed. Michael M. Atkinson (Toronto: Harcourt Brace Jovanovich, 1993), 312 and passim.

11 Anna Bramwell, *Ecology in the 20th Century: A History* (New Haven: Yale University Press, 1989). Bramwell, 104-5, distinguishes ecologism and environmentalism in much the same

way as American writers make the distinction, respectively, between preservationism and conservationism; ibid., 15.

12 Ibid., 35.
13 The material in this section draws principally from *Paradise Won,* by Elizabeth E. May, who was a special adviser to federal Minister of the Environment Tom McMillan when the South Moresby area was made a national park reserve.
14 Wilson, "Wilderness Politics in B.C.," 150.
15 While the IPC did not appear before the commission, the Skidegate Band Council did. See British Columbia, *Report of the Royal Commission on Forest Resources* (Victoria: Queen's Printer, 1976).
16 May, *Paradise Won,* 99-100.
17 See Islands Protection Society, *Islands at the Edge: Preserving the Queen Charlotte Islands Wilderness* (Vancouver: Douglas and McIntyre, 1984).
18 May, *Paradise Won,* 62.
19 Wilson, "Wilderness Politics in B.C.," 150.
20 May, *Paradise Won,* 143.
21 In the 1950s and 1960s, Haida culture received a dramatic boost from the work of artist Bill Reid (whose mother was Haida), who became interested in Haida arts while studying at Ryerson Polytechnic Institute in Toronto in 1951. Later (after returning in 1968 from further arts study in England) Reid participated in a monumental Haida sculpture at the University of British Columbia. His work quickly became a powerful stimulus and contribution to the cultural renaissance of the Haida. Carol Sheehaan, "William Ronald Reid," in *Canadian Encyclopaedia.*
22 May, *Paradise Won,* 194. Specifically, Reid was commissioned by the federal government, but his influence on that government was meant also to affect the BC provincial government.
23 Wilson, "Wilderness Politics in B.C.," 145.
24 May, *Paradise Won,* Chapter 6.
25 This was a bureaucracy special to the Environment and Land Use Committee of the provincial cabinet and was not related to the BC Ministry of the Environment.
26 The WAC proposal was accepted in principle in May 1986, but in the fall of that year, after an election in which the Social Credit Party retained power, the government went ahead with yet more logging permits.
27 Technically, in the mid-1970s, fisheries was a "service" within the Department of the Environment. However, prior to 1970, it had been a department in its own right, and it became so again after 1978.
28 John A. Carruthers, chief, National Parks System Division, Parks Canada, "Presentation to South Moresby Resource Planning Team," Queen Charlotte City, 28-29 January 1980 (mimeograph, National Parks Documentation Centre, Ottawa).
29 John Fraser had also been minister of the environment in the brief Joe Clark Conservative government, 1979-80.
30 Active consideration for this park had begun in the 1960s, although the first considerations for a Pacific coast national park were made in the 1930s. See Melanie Miller, "Origins of Pacific Rim National Park," in *Pacific Rim: An Ecological Approach to a New Canadian National Park,* ed. J.G. Nelson and L.D. Cordes (Waterloo: n.p., 1972), 5-25. Agreement between the two governments to establish a park was reached in 1969. However, the exact boundaries, including a contentious area of old-growth timber and compensation for logging companies with holdings in the area, dragged on into the 1980s. To begin negotiations regarding South Moresby, the BC government wanted to clear up the $25 million the federal government still owed for Pacific Rim National Park.
31 Officially, An Act to amend the National Parks Act and to amend An Act to amend the National Parks Act.
32 There had, however, been many limited and specific amendments to create new national parks or to make boundary changes to existing ones.
33 As late as 1984, when Charles Caccia was minister of the environment, discussions for proposed amendments had not reached the minister's office.
34 The citizens' heritage fund was later removed after discussion in the legislative committee, however. Nevertheless, the general protectionist ideals of the task force contributed to the climate of environmental ideas in national parks management.

35 Task Force on Park Establishment, *Our Parks: Vision for the 21st Century* (Waterloo: Heritage Resources Centre, University of Waterloo, 1987), 4.

36 Actually, two governments approved the 1979 policy statement since it was authorized by the Trudeau cabinet in March 1979 and again by the Clark cabinet in September 1979.

37 Canada, Environment Canada, Parks Canada, *Parks Canada Policy* (Ottawa: Minister of Supply and Services, 1982), ss. 1.1, 1.2. The actual phrasing is "ecological and historical integrity" since the branch's mandate included national and historic parks and sites (which are not of concern to the present analysis).

38 Canada, Parks Canada, *Response to Public Comments on the Parks Canada Policy* (Ottawa: Minister Responsible for Parks Canada, 1979), 3.

39 Canada, *Report of the Royal Commission on Government Organization* (the Glassco Commission) (Ottawa: Queen's Printer, 1962), 40.

40 See Task Force on Park Establishment, *Our Parks – Vision for the 21st Century*.

41 In discussions surrounding the amendments to the act, the Alberta provincial government specifically proposed a joint federal-provincial management regime of those parks to promote tourism, especially skiing, as part of the overall promotion of the 1988 Calgary Olympics (*Calgary Herald*, 28 November 1987, B12). In particular, from the first reading of the proposed legislation, Bill C-30, in December 1986, the Alberta caucus of government MPs tried hard to persuade McMillan to relax proposed restrictions on the expansion of Banff and Jasper townsites and on the land available to the Sunshine Village ski facilities in Banff National Park.

42 On committees, James Gillies and Jean Piggott have argued that, "while special interest groups do appear with regularity before House committees, such appearances ... seldom result in any major changes in legislation." James Gillies and Jean Piggott, "Participation in the Legislative Process," *Canadian Public Administration* 25 (1982): 259-60. On the other hand, Grace Skogstad concluded, with respect to standing committees on agriculture and transport in the 32nd Parliament, that "veteran members' direct links to and considerable familiarity with the concerns of regional clientele groups ... led them to press especially hard for their right to be heard. The fact that they prevailed was the consequence both of their success and that of the interest groups in focusing media attention on their efforts and of the government's political vulnerability." Grace Skogstad, "Interest Groups, Representation, and Conflict Management in the Standing Committees of the House of Commons," *Canadian Journal of Political Science* 28 (1985): 770. The experience of the legislative committee on the national parks bill was similar to Skogstad's account of the agriculture committee in that interest groups (with some media support) were instrumental in influencing the outcome of the committee deliberations.

43 In fact, Aboriginal concerns formed a small part of the discussion. In general, national park policy was not changed to meet their views except that traditional activities would be allowed in a limited manner in Pukaskwa National Park in Ontario.

44 No representatives of national tourist or recreational organizations, or any resource extraction advocates, appeared before the committee.

45 National Parks Act (1988), clause 4, subsection 1.2. The management plan is the means by which national policy is translated into action for the individual national park. Prior to 1988, management plans were expected to reflect national policy and were approved by the minister, but there were few specific requirements to follow.

46 House of Commons, Legislative Committee on Bill C-30, 33rd Parliament, 2nd Session, "The National Parks Act: Expanding and Preserving Canada's System of National Parks and Protected Areas: A Position Paper of the Canadian Parks and Wilderness Society [CPAWS] on Bill C-30: An Act to Amend the National Parks Act and to Amend an Act to Amend the National Parks Act," May 1988, 1.

47 See *Calgary Herald*, 15 June 1988, D15.

48 Not to be confused with "Dené," a name for the Aboriginal people in this area.

49 W.F. Lothian notes that in the early 1950s several changes were made to timber regulations for the parks, and "by 1970 the cutting of timber in national parks had been substantially reduced." W.F. Lothian, *History of Canada's National Parks*, vol. 2 (Ottawa: Minister of Supply and Services Canada, 1977), 34.

50 D.P. Emond, "Environmental Law and Policy: A Retrospective Examination of the Canadian Experience," in *Consumer Protection, Environmental Law, and Corporate Power,* ed. Ivan Bernier and Andrée Lajoie (Toronto: University of Toronto Press, 1985), 106.

51 *McNeil v. Nova Scotia Board of Censors* (1976), cited in Andrew J. Roman and Mart Pikkov, "Public Interest Litigation in Canada," in *Into the Future: Environmental Law and Policy for the 1990s,* ed. Donna Tingley (Edmonton: Environmental Law Centre, 1990), 171.

52 *Finlay v. Canada (Minister of Finance),* [1986] 2 S.C.R. 607 at 625.

53 The material on the four cases has been condensed from Roman and Pikkov, "Public Interest Litigation in Canada," 170-74, and Canada, *Supreme Court Reports,* 1986, 607-36.

54 Cited in Stuart Elgie, "Injunctions, Ancient Forests, and Irreparable Harm: A Comment on *Western Canada Wilderness Committee vs. A.G. British Columbia," UBC Law Review* 25 (1991): 390 note 15.

55 The SLDF is not connected to the Sierra Club or the US-based Sierra Club Legal Defense Fund, although the founder of the SLDF did work with the latter organization before returning to Canada.

56 There were other parks established in this period for the explicit protection of wildlife, but they were later disbanded after the relevant population recovered. Only Wood Buffalo survived as a park for environmental protection (albeit focused on one species).

57 See Janet Foster, *Working for Wildlife: The Beginning of Preservation in Canada* (Toronto: University of Toronto Press, 1978), Chapter 3.

58 Barry Potyondi, "Wood Buffalo National Park: An Historical Overview and Source Study" (Internal Manuscript Report, Environment Canada, 1979), 82, 103, 107, and passim.

59 Ibid., 95-96.

60 Ibid., 102.

61 "Statement of Claim" in the Federal Court of Canada, Trial Division (File No. T-272-92), by Canadian Parks and Wilderness Society, paragraph 2.

62 Ibid., paragraph 29.

63 The information in this section is condensed from Canadian Environmental Law Reports, "Sunshine Village Corp. v. Canada (Minister of Canadian Heritage)," *Canadian Environmental Law Reports (CELR)* 20: 171-208.

64 Ibid., 187.

65 Ibid., 191.

66 This act succeeds the Environmental Assessment Review Process Guidelines Order under which the proceeding applications, permits, and court hearings had been conducted.

67 *CELR,* "Sunshine Village Corp.," 192.

68 Ibid., 193.

69 Sunshine appealed the Federal Court of Appeal's decisions to the Supreme Court of Canada but was denied. See *Globe and Mail,* 21 February 1997, A4.

70 Bryan H.C. Gordon, *Of Men and Herds in Barrenland Prehistory* (Ottawa: National Museum of Canada, 1975), cited in Raymond Chipeniuk, "The Vacant Niche: An Argument for the Re-Creation of a Hunter-Gatherer Component in the Ecosystems of Northern National Parks," *Environments (Canada)* 20, 1 (1989): 52.

71 Ibid.

72 Jeffrey A. McNeely, "Afterword: People and Protected Areas: Partners in Prosperity," in *The Law of the Mother: Protecting Indigenous Peoples in Protected Areas,* ed. Elizabeth Kemf (San Francisco: Sierra Club Books, 1993), 251.

73 Claude Martin, "Introduction," in Kemf, ed., *The Law of the Mother,* xix.

74 See Chapter 4 with reference to the significance of the *Calder* decision and the intervention by the Inuit Tapirisat in the deliberations over the 1974 amendments to the National Parks Act.

75 Thomas R. Berger, *Northern Frontier, Northern Homeland: The Report of the Mackenzie Valley Pipeline Inquiry,* rev. ed. (Ottawa: Minister of Supply and Services, 1988), 74.

76 Ibid., 76-77.

77 Ibid. It is interesting to note that, in the eastern Arctic, before Auyuittuq ("The Land that Does Not Melt") National Park received its official name, and was referred to simply as Baffin Island National Park Reserve, the local Inuit referred to it as "the place where whiteman

comes to play." Nicholas Lawson, "Where Whitemen Come to Play," *Cultural Survival Quarterly: Parks and People* 9, 1 (1985): 54.

78 Patrick C. West, "Introduction," in *Resident Peoples and National Parks: Social Dilemmas and Strategies in International Conservation,* ed. Patrick C. West and Steven R. Brechin (Tucson: University of Arizona Press, 1991), xviii.

79 Will Weber, "Enduring Peaks and Changing Cultures: The Sherpas and Sagarmatha (Mount Everest) National Park," in *Resident Peoples and National Parks,* ed. West and Brechin, 206-14.

80 Sheila Davey, "Creative Communities: Planning and Comanaging Protected Areas," in Kemf, ed., *The Law of the Mother,* 197.

81 Nancy C. Weeks, "National Parks and Native Peoples: A Study of the Experience of Selected Other Jurisdictions with a View to Cooperation in Northern Canada," in *Contributions to Circumpolar Studies,* ed. Hugh Beach (Uppsala: Department of Cultural Geography, University of Uppsala, 1986), 98.

82 For a comparison of the Berger Inquiry and the (Australian) Ranger Uranium Environmental Inquiry, see Catherine Althaus, "Legitimation and Agenda-Setting: Development and the Environment in Australia and Canada's North," in *Royal Commissions and the Making of Public Policy,* ed. Patrick Weller (Melbourne: Macmillan, 1994), 186-97.

83 Weeks, "National Parks and Native Peoples," 98.

84 Arguably, there were three, the third being that the site of Kakadu was already Aboriginal land under a previous agreement and was merely leased back to the Australian government. This was a change from previous, and common, practice, where governments hold national parks in fee simple. Since jurisdiction over land has been determined differently in Canada, this point is of less interest here than the general involvement of Aboriginal people in park management.

85 Sally Weaver, "The Role of Aboriginals in the Management of Australia's Coburg (Gurig) and Kakadu National Park," in *Resident Peoples and National Parks,* ed. West and Brechin, 311-32.

86 Alaska National Interest Lands Conservation Act, 1980, s. 101(c), cited in Weeks, "National Parks and Native Peoples," 108.

87 Weaver, "The Role of Aboriginals," 311.

88 See note 57, Chapter 4.

89 Chipeniuk, "The Vacant Niche," 50.

90 Gurston Dacks, "The Politics of Native Claims in Northern Canada," in *The Quest for Justice: Aboriginal Peoples and Aboriginal Rights,* ed. Menno Boldt and J. Anthony Long (Toronto: University of Toronto Press, 1985), 258.

91 Arctic Institute of North America and Joint Secretariat–Inuvialuit Renewable Resources Committees, *Circumpolar Aboriginal People and Co-Management Practice: Current Issues in Co-Management and Environmental Assessment,* Inuvik, NWT, 20-24 November 1995, proceedings prepared by Karen Roberts, 40-41.

92 Terry Fenge, "National Parks in the Canadian Arctic: The Case of Nunavut Land Claim Agreement," *Environments (Canada)* 22 (1993): 28.

93 Ibid., 26.

94 When it was established in 1922, Wood Buffalo would have been formally bound by the terms of Treaty 8, signed in 1899, giving Aboriginal people access to traditional resource use.

95 Ken M. East, "Joint Management of Canada's Northern National Parks," in *Resident Peoples and National Parks,* ed. West and Brechin, 341-42; and Barry Olsen and Brendan O'Donnell, "First Nations Involvement in National Park Establishment and Management: Interim Measures," paper presented at the Interim Measures during Treaty Negotiations Conference, Vancouver, 22 April 1994.

96 The Aboriginal use of renewable resources in Wood Buffalo National Park is another way, in addition to continued logging, in which this park had been atypical in the system.

97 *Vuntut Gwitchin First Nation Final Agreement between the Government of Canada, the Vuntut Gwitchin First Nation, and the Government of Yukon* (signed at Whitehorse, Yukon, 29 May 1993), schedule A, clause 1.1.2, 105.

98 Ibid., schedule A, clause 4.1, 109. Capitalized words and phrases in this and following quotations refer to terms officially defined in the glossary of the agreement.

99 Ibid., clauses 4.17, 4.18, 4.19.
100 Ibid., clause 4.5, 110.
101 *Gwaii Haanas Agreement between the Government of Canada and the Council of the Haida Nation* (signed in Old Masset, BC, 30 January 1993), clause 3.2.
102 *Vuntut Gwitchin Final Agreement,* 225.
103 Ibid., 116-18.
104 *Gwaii Haanas Agreement,* 4-5.
105 *Globe and Mail,* 16 July 1997, A1.
106 The term "groups" will be used for convenience. However, environmental groups and Aboriginal organizations are not exactly parallel because of the legal and constitutional position of Aboriginal people. Since many of the activities undertaken by each are essentially the same, even if some of the underlying political resources are different, they will be discussed in tandem in this analysis.
107 Stephen Krasner, "Approaches to the State: Alternative Conceptions and Historical Dynamics," *Comparative Politics* 16 (1984): 235-38, and "Sovereignty: An Institutional Perspective," *Comparative Political Studies* 21 (1988): 66-94.
108 Mark Sproule-Jones, *Governments at Work: Canadian Parliamentary Federalism and Its Public Policy Effects* (Toronto: University of Toronto Press, 1993), 33.

Chapter 6: Repossession by the State

1 As reported by several parks officials in confidential interviews.
2 See Raphael Samuel, *Theatres of Memory,* Volume 1, *Past and Present in Contemporary Culture* (London: Verso, 1994), 209: "In the language of nature conservancy, 'heritage' is represented by unspoiled countryside and wildlife reserves."
3 World Wildlife Fund, *1995-96 Endangered Spaces Progress Report* (Toronto: World Wildlife Fund, 1996), 30.
4 Ibid., 24-27 and passim.
5 Ibid., 23.
6 These groups are the World Wildlife Fund, Canadian Parks and Wilderness Society, Ducks Unlimited, Canadian Nature Federation, Canadian Wildlife Federation, Canadian Arctic Resources Committee, Nature Conservancy of Canada, and Wildlife Heritage Canada.
7 Donald J. Savoie, *Governing from the Centre: The Concentration of Power in Canadian Politics* (Toronto: University of Toronto Press, 1999), 142-44.
8 Ibid., 139-45.
9 From an internal Treasury Board Secretariat memo released by the Privy Council Office under its Academic Access Program, February 2003.
10 Ibid.
11 From a document headed "Canadian Parks Services" but not attributed, released by the PCO under its Academic Access Program, February 2003.
12 Alanna Mitchell, "Banff's Outlook Not a Pretty Picture," *Globe and Mail,* 24 December 1994, A1, 8.
13 W.F. Lothian, *History of Canada's National Parks,* vol. 2 (Ottawa: Minister of Supply and Services Canada, 1977), 71-76. The issue was later appealed by the minister to the Supreme Court, which upheld the initial decision.
14 Government of Canada and Government of Alberta, "Town of Banff Incorporation Agreement," typescript, 12 December 1989.
15 Banff-Bow Valley Study, *At the Crossroads: Summary Report,* submitted to Sheila Copps, Minister of Canadian Heritage, October 1996, 36-37.
16 Ibid., 22.
17 Ibid., 47.
18 Ibid., 55.
19 Ibid., 56.
20 Ibid., 53.
21 "Copps Moves to Save Banff," *Globe and Mail,* 8 October 1996, A1.
22 Canada, Treasury Board of Canada Secretariat, "External User Charges for Goods, Services, Property, Rights, and Privileges," Ottawa, 7 December 1989. It follows a draft guideline

statement from 1985. The earlier document was contemporaneous with the Nielsen Task Force and may have been influenced by it, but that is not clear; it appears to have been developed strictly by the secretariat. The document currently in force is the "Cost Recovery and Charging Policy," December 1997.

23 Canada, Department of Canadian Heritage, Parks Canada, "Parks Canada Revenue Policy," mimeograph, May 1998, 3.

24 Revenue generation had occurred in parks for a long time through lease fees for property and from park entrance fees. However, the revenue generation policies of the 1990s had a more clearly articulated philosophy underpinning them and were more ambitious in terms of the amount of revenue likely to be raised and in the scope of possible sources.

25 Donald J. Savoie, *Thatcher, Reagan, Mulroney: In Search of a New Bureaucracy* (Toronto: University of Toronto Press, 1994), 118-23.

26 Ibid., 204-5.

27 As referenced in ibid., 205.

28 Ibid., 128.

29 Erik Nielsen, *The House Is Not a Home: An Autobiography* (Toronto: Macmillan of Canada, 1989), 228, cited in Savoie, *Thatcher*, 128 note 40.

30 See, for example, Savoie, *Thatcher*, 130-31; and V. Seymour Wilson, "What Legacy? The Nielsen Task Force Program Review," in *How Ottawa Spends 1988/89: The Conservatives Heading into the Stretch*, ed. Katharine A. Graham (Ottawa: Carleton University Press, 1988), 37.

31 Office of the Auditor General of Canada, *Special Operating Agencies: Taking Stock (Final Report)* (Ottawa: n.p., 1994), 2.

32 Savoie, *Thatcher*, 233.

33 Ibid., 241 note 107.

34 This list of features has been compiled from a report prepared for Office of the Auditor General of Canada, *Special Operating Agencies*, passim. See also Savoie, *Thatcher;* Canada, Treasury Board Secretariat, *Framework for Alternative Program Delivery* (Ottawa: Treasury Board, 1995); and Paul Thomas and John Wilkins, "Special Operating Agencies: A Culture Change in the Manitoba Government," in *Alternative Service Delivery: Sharing Governance in Canada*, ed. Robin Ford and David Zussman (Toronto: Institute of Public Administration of Canada, 1997), 109-22.

35 Savoie, *Thatcher*, 209-10.

36 I.D. Clark, "Special Operating Agencies: The Challenges of Innovation," *Optimum: The Journal of Public Sector Management* 22 (1991): 16.

37 Canada, Royal Commission on Government Organization, *Supporting Services for Government*, vol. 2 (Ottawa: Queen's Printer, 1962), 39.

38 J.E. Hodgetts, *The Canadian Public Service: A Physiology of Government 1867-1970* (Toronto: University of Toronto Press, 1973), 25.

39 Ibid.

40 Royal Commission on Government Organization, *Supporting Services for Government*, 39.

41 Cited in Savoie, *Thatcher*, 65.

42 Canada, Department of Canadian Heritage, Parks Canada, *Framework: National Business Plan* (Ottawa: Department of Canadian Heritage, 21 April 1995), 4.

43 Canada, Department of Canadian Heritage, Parks Canada, *National Business Plan 1995/ 1996-1999/2000* (Ottawa: Department of Canadian Heritage, 1995), 46.

44 Ibid., 40.

45 The reduction was, specifically, from $410 million in fiscal year 1993-94 to $287 million in 1998-99: *Public Accounts* (Ottawa: Receiver General for Canada, 1993-94 and 1998-99).

46 See Savoie, *Thatcher*, 181 ff. Also see Edward Greenspon and Anthony Wilson-Smith, *Double Vision: The Inside Story of the Liberals in Power* (Toronto: Doubleday, 1996), passim.

47 "Field units" are a pragmatic new administrative subdivision of the Parks Branch. Each unit operates separately from the rest even when there are apparent overlaps. Some are geographically based: that is, a unit may be a collection of parks in a certain region of the country, sometimes a single park constitutes a field unit, and in one important instance the unit is functionally based. In the last case, a golf course, in Cape Breton Highlands

National Park, and the hot springs at Banff are combined into an exclusively commercial unit (even though these functions take place essentially inside other units).

48 Canada, Department of Canadian Heritage, Parks Canada, *Parks Canada Revenue Policy* (Strategic Policy Direction: 26 November 1997), 4.

49 Greenspon and Wilson-Smith, *Double Vision,* 225.

50 Savoie, *Governing from the Centre,* 175.

51 From the original e-mail provided by a former Parks Canada employee.

52 Richard D. Searle, *Phantom Parks: The Struggle to Save Canada's National Parks* (Toronto: Key Porter, 2000), 119.

53 Tom Lee, personal interview, Ottawa, 10 December 2002.

54 Ibid.

55 Ibid.

56 Liberal Party of Canada, *Creating Opportunity: The Liberal Plan for Canada* (the "Red Book") (Ottawa: Liberal Party of Canada, 1993), 50.

57 Canada, Library of Parliament, "Legislative Summary: Bill C-27 Canada National Parks Act," #LS-365E, 36th Parliament, 2nd Session.

58 Canada, Parks Canada Agency, *Unimpaired for Future Generations,* Volume II, *Setting a New Direction for Canada's National Parks,* report of the- Panel on Ecological Integrity of Canada's National Parks (Ottawa: Minister of Public Works and Government Services, 2000), recommendations 2-3, 3-14.

59 Canada, House of Commons, 2nd Session, 36th Parliament, Bill C-27, An Act Respecting the National Parks of Canada, first reading, 1 March 2000, clause 8(2).

60 Canada, Department of Justice, Canada National Parks Act, 2000, c. 32.

61 Harvey Locke, Canadian Parks and Wilderness Society (CPAWS), "A Summary of the Brief Presented to the Standing Committee on May 16, 2000," 3; Jerry De Marco, Sierra Legal Defence Fund, "Sierra Legal Defence Fund Brief Re: Bill 27," 24 May 2000 (final version), 5; Kevin McNamee, Canadian Nature Federation (CNF), "Expanding and Preserving Canada's National Park System: A Brief on Bill C-27: An Act Respecting the National Parks of Canada," 16 May 2000, 3.

62 See McNamee, "Expanding and Preserving," 3; first reading of Bill C-27; and act as passed.

63 See De Marco, "Sierra Legal Defence Fund Brief," 4.

64 Association for Mountain Parks Protection and Enjoyment, "Submission to the House of Commons Standing Committee on Canadian Heritage Regarding Bill C-27," 18 May 2000, 1.

Chapter 7: National Parks and the Giving of Meaning

1 Once ratified, new treaties are protected by the Constitution Act (1982), ss. 25(b) and 35(3).

2 Winston Churchill, 28 October 1943, on speaking to the British House of Commons to promote the exact reconstruction of the Westminster Parliament buildings after their destruction by Nazi German bombs in 1941.

3 Robert Jervis, "Timing and Interaction in Politics: A Comment on Pierson," *Studies in American Political Development* 14, 1 (2000): 93.

Bibliography

Government Documents and Legislation

An Act to Amend the National Parks Act. 2nd session, 29th Parliament, 1974, c. 11.

An Act to Amend the National Parks Act and to Amend an Act to Amend the National Parks Act. 2nd session, 33rd Parliament, 1988, c. 48.

An Act Respecting National Parks. 20-21 George V, c. 33 (assented 30 May 1930).

Archipelago Management Board (AMB). *Gwaii Haanas: Haida Heritage Site and National Park Reserve*, Public Planning Program, newsletters 1-3. Queen Charlotte City, BC: AMB, 1993-94.

Banff-Bow Valley Study. *An Historical Analysis of Parks Canada and Banff National Park, 1968-1995.* Prepared by Walter Hildebrandt for the Banff-Bow Valley Study Task Force, 1995.

–. *At the Crossroads: Summary Report.* Submitted to Sheila Copps, Minister of Canadian Heritage, by the Banff-Bow Valley Task Force, October 1996.

–. *At the Crossroads: Technical Report.* Submitted to Sheila Copps, Minister of Canadian Heritage, by the Banff-Bow Valley Task Force, October 1996.

Bill C-27, An Act Respecting the National Parks of Canada, first reading, 1 March 2000. 2nd session, 36th Parliament, cl. 8(2).

Bill C-29, An Act to Establish the Canadian Parks Agency and to Amend Other Acts as a Consequence. 1st session, 36th Parliament, 1998.

Bill S-4, An Act to Amend the National Parks Act. 1st session, 29th Parliament, 1973.

British Columbia. *Report of the Royal Commission on Forest Resources.* Victoria: Queen's Printer, 1976.

Canada. *House of Commons Debates.* Various years.

–. *Report of the Royal Commission of Government Organization* (the Glassco Commission). Ottawa: Queen's Printer, 1962.

–. *Resources for Tomorrow: Conference Background Papers.* Ottawa: Queen's Printer and Controller of Stationery, 1961.

–. *Supreme Court Reports.* 1986.

Canada. Canadian Environmental Advisory Council. *Reports of the First and Second Meetings of Public Interest Groups with the Canadian Environmental Advisory Council.* Ottawa: Supply and Services Canada, 1978.

Canada. Department of Canadian Heritage. Parks Canada. *Framework: National Business Plan.* Ottawa, 1995.

–. *Guiding Principles and Operational Policies.* Ottawa: Minister of Supply and Services, 1994.

–. *National Business Plan 1995/1996-1999/2000.* Ottawa: Department of Canadian Heritage, 1995.

–. "Parks Canada Revenue Policy." Mimeograph. May 1998.

–. "Parks Canada Revenue Policy." Mimeograph. November 1997.

–. "Parks Canada to Become Federal Agency" and "Summary of the Canadian Parks Agency Legislation." News releases. Ottawa, 5 February 1988.

–. *State of the Parks: 1997 Report.* Ottawa: Public Works and Government Services, 1998.

Canada. Department of Finance. *Budget Plan.* Ottawa: Department of Finance, 1996.

Canada. Department of Indian Affairs and Northern Development. *Agreement between the Inuit of the Nunavut Settlement Area and Her Majesty in Right of Canada.* 1993.

–. *Gwaii Haanas Agreement between the Government of Canada and the Council of the Haida Nation.* 1993.

–. *National Parks System Planning Manual.* Ottawa: Information Canada, 1972.

–. *Vuntut Gwitchin First Nation Final Agreement between the Government of Canada, the Vuntut Gwitchin First Nation, and the Government of the Yukon.* 1993.

–. *The Western Arctic Claim: The Inuvialuit Final Agreement.* 1984.

Canada. Department of Northern Affairs and National Resources. National Parks Branch. *National Parks Policy (1964).* Ottawa: Minister of Northern Affairs and Natural Resources, 1964.

–. Natural and Historic Resources Branch. "Winter Recreation and the National Parks: A Management Policy and Development Program." Typescript. March 1965.

Canada. Environment Canada. Parks Canada. *National Marine Parks Policy.* Ottawa: Minister of Supply and Services, 1987.

–. *National Parks System Plan.* Ottawa: Minister of Supply and Services, 1990.

–. *Parks Canada Policy.* Ottawa: Minister of Supply and Services, 1982.

–. *State of the Parks: 1990 Profiles.* Ottawa: Minister of Supply and Services, 1991.

–. *State of the Parks: 1990 Report.* Ottawa: Minister of Supply and Services, 1991.

Canada. Federal Court of Canada. Trial Division. "Reasons for Judgment," by Justice W. Andrew MacKay (court file T-272-92). 23 June 1992.

–. "Statement of Claim." In *Canadian Parks and Wilderness Society v. Superintendent of Wood Buffalo National Park, Director of Parks Canada, Prairie and Northern Region, Minister of the Environment, and Her Majesty the Queen in Right of Canada* (court file T-272-92). 31 January 1992.

Canada. Federal Environmental Assessment Review Office. *Public Participation in Environmental Decision Making.* Ottawa: Supply and Services, 1988.

–. *Public Review: Neither Judicial, nor Political, but an Essential Forum for the Future of the Environment: A Report Concerning the Reform of Public Hearing Procedures for Federal Environmental Assessment Reviews.* Ottawa: Supply and Services, 1988.

Canada. House of Commons. Legislative Committee on Bill C-13 (An Act to Establish a Federal Environmental Assessment Process), 3rd session, 34th Parliament, October 1991. Session 3: submission by Richard Lindgren, Canadian Environmental Law Association; and session 4: submission by William J. Andrew, West Coast Environmental Law Association.

Canada. House of Commons. Legislative Committee on Bill C-30, 2nd session, 33rd Parliament. "The National Parks Act: Expanding and Preserving Canada's System of National Parks and Protected Areas: A Position Paper of the Canadian Parks and Wilderness Society [CPAWS] on Bill C-30: An Act to Amend the National Parks Act and to Amend an Act to Amend the National Parks Act." May 1988.

Canada. House of Commons. Standing Committee on Canadian Heritage. Minutes (consideration of Bill C-29). April 1988.

Canada. House of Commons. Standing Committee on Environment and Sustainable Development. *Harmonization and Environmental Protection: An Analysis of the Harmonization Initiative of the Canadian Council of Ministers of the Environment.* Ottawa: The Standing Committee, 1997.

Canada. House of Commons. Standing Committee on Indian Affairs and Northern Development. Minutes, issue 29. Whitehorse, 12 December 1973.

Canada. House of Commons. Standing Committee on Northern Affairs and National Resources. Minutes, comments by J.A. MacDonald, Senior Assistant Deputy Minister, 28 February 1967.

Canada. Library of Parliament. "Legislative Summary: Bill C-27 Canada National Parks Act."

Canada. Minister of the Environment. *Parks Canada Policy.* Ottawa: Supply and Services Canada, 1982.

Canada. Office of the Auditor General, Secretary of the Treasury Board, and Office of the Comptroller General. *Special Operating Agencies: Taking Stock (Final Report)*. Ottawa: n.p., 1994.

Canada. Parks Canada. *Response to Public Comments on the Parks Canada Policy*. Typescript. Ottawa: Minister Responsible for Parks Canada, 1979.

Canada. Parks Canada Agency. *Unimpaired for Future Generations*. Volume II. *Setting a New Direction for Canada's National Parks*. Report of the Panel on Ecological Integrity of Canada's National Parks. Ottawa: Minister of Public Works and Government Services, 2000.

Canada. Public Archives of Canada. RG 84, vols. 1810-23.

Canada. Royal Commission on Government Organization. *Supporting Services for Government*. Vol. 2. Ottawa: Queen's Printer, 1962.

Canada. Special Inquiry on Kouchibouguac National Park. Report submitted to John Roberts by Gerard V. La Forest and Muriel Kent Roy. October 1981.

Canada. Treasury Board Secretariat. "External User Charge for Goods, Services, Property, Rights, and Privileges." 7 December 1989.

–. *Framework for Alternative Program Delivery*. Ottawa: Treasury Board, 1995.

Canadian Environmental Advisory Council. *A Protected Areas Vision for Canada*. Ottawa: Minister of Supply and Services, 1991.

Canadian Environmental Assessment Act. 3rd session, 34th Parliament, June 1992, c. 37.

Canadian Parks Service. Joint Federal-Provincial Committee on the Proposed Grasslands National Park. *A Proposed Grasslands National Park: What Would It Mean?* Regina, 1975.

Liberal Party of Canada. *Creating Opportunity: The Liberal Plan for Canada* (the "Red Book"). Ottawa: Liberal Party of Canada, 1993.

Proceedings, federal-provincial parks conferences. 1963-77.

Saskatchewan. Department of Tourism and Renewable Resources. "Report of the Public Hearings Board on the Proposed Grasslands National Park." 1976.

Task Force on Park Establishment. *Our Parks: Vision for the 21st Century*. Waterloo: Heritage Resources Centre, University of Waterloo, 1987.

United States. Department of the Interior. National Parks Service. *National Parks System Plan Handbook*. Typescript. March 1961.

Books and Articles

Alberta Society of Professional Biologists. *Native People and Renewable Resource Management (Symposium Papers)*. Edmonton, 29 April-1 May 1986. Edmonton: Alberta Society of Professional Biologists, 1986.

Alford, Robert, and Roger Friedland. *Powers of Theory: Capitalism, the State, and Democracy*. Cambridge, UK: Cambridge University Press, 1985.

Allison, Graham T. "Conceptual Models and the Cuban Missile Crisis." *American Political Science Review* 63 (1969): 689-718.

Althaus, Catherine. "Legitimation and Agenda-Setting: Development and the Environment in Australia and Canada's North." In *Royal Commissions and the Making of Public Policy*, ed. Patrick Weller, 186-97. Melbourne: Macmillan, 1994.

Anthony, Brian. "Parks Canada Stands Alone." *Beaver: Exploring Canada's History* 78 (1998): 22-23.

Archibald, Clinton C. "Special Operating Agencies: The Way of the Future or a Smoke Screen?" *Optimum: The Journal of Public Sector Management* 22 (1991): 2-4.

Arctic Institute of North America and Joint Secretariat–Inuvialuit Renewable Resources Committees. *Circumpolar Aboriginal People and Co-Management Practice: Current Issues in Co-Management and Environmental Assessment*. Inuvik, NWT, 20-24 November 1995. (Proceedings prepared by Karen Roberts.)

Armstrong, Jim. "Special Operating Agencies: Evolution or Revolution?" *Optimum: The Journal of Public Sector Management* 22 (1991): 5-12.

Arnstein, Sherry R. "A Ladder of Citizen Participation." *Journal of the American Institute of Planners* 35 (1969): 216-24.

Ashford, Douglas. "Introduction: Of Cases and Contexts." In *History and Context in Contemporary Public Policy*, ed. Douglas Ashford, 3-24. Pittsburgh: University of Pittsburgh Press, 1992.

Association for Mountain Parks Protection and Enjoyment. "Submission to the House of Commons Standing Committee on Canadian Heritage Regarding Bill C-27." 18 May 2000.

Atkinson, Michael, ed. *Governing Canada: Institutions and Public Policy*. Toronto: Harcourt Brace Jovanovich, 1993.

Aucoin, Peter. "Organizational Change in the Management of Canadian Government: From Rational Management to Brokerage Politics." *Canadian Journal of Political Science* 19 (1986): 3-27.

Bakvis, Herman, and Neil Nevitte. "In Pursuit of Postbourgeois: Postmaterialism and Intergenerational Change in Canada." *Comparative Political Studies* 20, 3 (1987): 357-89.

Banting, Keith G. *The Welfare State and Canadian Federalism*. 2nd ed. Montreal and Kingston: McGill-Queen's University Press, 1987.

Bell, David. "The Political Culture of Problem Solving and Public Policy." In *Federalism and Political Community: Essays in Honour of Donald Smiley*, ed. David P. Shugarman and Reg Whitaker, 93-110. Peterborough: Broadview Press, 1989.

Bella, Leslie. *Parks for Profit*. Montreal: Harvest House, 1987.

Berger, Thomas R. *A Long and Terrible Shadow: White Values, Native Rights in the Americas, 1492-1992*. Vancouver: Douglas and McIntyre, 1991.

–. *Northern Frontier, Northern Homeland: The Report of the Mackenzie Valley Pipeline Inquiry*. Rev. ed. Ottawa: Minister of Supply and Services, 1988.

Betz, Hans-Georg. "Value Change and Postmaterialist Politics: The Case of West Germany." *Comparative Political Studies* 23, 2 (1990): 239-56.

Birckhead, Jim, Terry De Lacy, and Laurajane Smith, eds. *Aboriginal Involvement in Parks and Protected Areas*. Papers presented at a conference, Charles Sturt University, Albury, New South Wales. 22-24 July 1991. Canberra: Aboriginal Studies Press, 1996.

Block, Fred. *Revising State Theory: Essays in Politics and Postindustrialism*. Philadelphia: Temple University Press, 1987.

Boardman, Robert. *International Organization and the Conservation of Nature*. London: Macmillan, 1981.

Bramwell, Anna. *Ecology in the 20th Century: A History*. New Haven: Yale University Press, 1980.

Braybrooke, David, and Charles E. Lindblom. *A Strategy of Decision*. New York: Free Press, 1970.

Brown, Robert Craig. "The Doctrine of Usefulness: Natural Resources and National Park Policy in Canada, 1887-1914." In *Canadian Parks in Perspective*, ed. J.G. Nelson and R.C. Scace, 46-62. Montreal: Harvest House, 1970.

Bruce, Christopher, and Don Woytowich. "Delegated Administrative Organizations: Alberta's 'Third Option.'" In *Alternative Service Delivery: Sharing Governance in Canada*, ed. Robin Ford and David Zussman, 208-19. Toronto: Institute of Public Administration of Canada, 1997.

Burch, William R., Neil H. Cheek, and Lee Taylor, eds. *Social Behavior, Natural Resources, and the Environment*. New York: Harper and Row, 1972.

Burnett, J. Alexander. *A Passion for Wildlife: The History of the Canadian Wildlife Service*. Vancouver: UBC Press, 2003.

Burns, Robert J., with Mike Schintz. *Guardians of the Wild: A History of the Warden Service of Canada's National Parks*. Calgary: University of Calgary Press, 2000.

Canadian Environmental Law Reports. "Sunshine Village Corp. v. Canada (Minister of Canadian Heritage)." *Canadian Environmental Law Reports* 20, new series (1996): 171-208.

Careless, Anthony G. *Initiative and Response: The Adaptation of Canadian Federalism to Regional Economic Development*. Montreal and Kingston: McGill-Queen's University Press, 1977.

Carnoy, Martin. *The State and Political Theory*. Princeton: Princeton University Press, 1984.

Carruthers, John A., Chief, National Parks System Division, Parks Canada. "Presentation to South Moresby Resources Planning Team." Queen Charlotte City, 28-29 January 1980. Mimeograph, National Parks Documentation Centre, Ottawa.

Chipeniuk, Raymond. "The Vacant Niche: An Argument for the Re-Creation of a Hunter-Gatherer Component in the Ecosystems of Northern National Parks." *Environments (Canada)* 20, 1 (1989): 50-59.

Clark, I.D. "Special Operating Agencies: The Challenges of Innovation." *Optimum: The Journal of Public Sector Management* 22 (1991): 13-18.

Coleman, William D., and Grace Skogstad. "Policy Communities and Policy Networks: A Structural Approach." In *Policy Communities and Public Policy in Canada: A Structural Approach,* ed. William D. Coleman and Grace Skogstad, 14-33. Mississauga: Copp Clark, 1990.

Connor, Desmond M. "Models and Techniques of Citizen Participation." In *Involvement and Environment: Proceedings of the Canadian Conference on Public Participation,* 2 vols., ed. Barry Sadler, 58-76. Edmonton: Environment Council of Alberta, 1979.

Courtney, John C. "Franchise." *Canadian Encyclopaedia.* 2nd ed. Edmonton: Hurtig, 1988.

Dacks, Gurston. "The Politics of Native Claims in Northern Canada." In *The Quest for Justice: Aboriginal Peoples and Aboriginal Rights,* ed. Menno Boldt and J. Anthony Long, 251-64. Toronto: University of Toronto Press, 1985.

Davey, Sheila. "Creative Communities: Planning and Comanaging Protected Areas." In *The Law of the Mother: Protecting Indigenous Peoples in Protected Areas,* ed. Elizabeth Kemf, 197-204. San Francisco: Sierra Club Books, 1993.

Davidson, A.T. "Canada's National Parks: Past and Future." In *The Canadian National Parks: Today and Tomorrow – Conference II: Ten Years Later,* 2 vols., ed. J.G. Nelson et al., 23-37. Waterloo: Graphic Services, University of Waterloo, 1979.

Dearden, Philip, and Rick Rollins, eds. *Parks and Protected Areas in Canada: Planning and Management.* Toronto: Oxford University Press, 1993.

–. *Parks and Protected Areas in Canada: Planning and Management.* 2nd ed. Toronto: Oxford University Press, 2002.

Deihl, Colin. "Wildlife and the Maasai." *Cultural Survival Quarterly* 9 (1985): 37-40.

De Marco, Jerry. "Sierra Legal Defence Fund Brief Re: Bill 27." 24 May 2000 (final version).

DeSario, Jack, and Stuart Langton, eds. *Citizen Participation in Public Decision Making.* New York: Greenwood Press, 1987.

Doern, G. Bruce. "Recent Changes in the Philosophy of Policy-Making in Canada." *Canadian Journal of Political Science* 4 (1971): 243-64.

Dooling, Peter J., ed. *Parks in British Columbia: Emerging Realities.* Vancouver: Faculty of Forestry, University of British Columbia, 1985.

Downs, Anthony. "Up and Down with Ecology: The 'Issue-Attention Cycle.'" *Public Interest* 28 (1972): 38-50.

Draper, James A., ed. *Citizen Participation: Canada – A Book of Readings.* Toronto: New Press, 1971.

–. "Evolution of Citizen Participation in Canada." In *Involvement and Environment: Proceedings of the Canadian Conference on Public Participation,* 2 vols., ed. Barry Sadler, 26-42. Edmonton: Environment Council of Alberta, 1979.

Dubasak, Marilyn. *Wilderness Preservation: A Cross-Cultural Comparison of Canada and the United States.* New York: Garland Publishing, 1990.

Dupré, J. Stephen. "Reflections on the Workability of Executive Federalism." In *Perspectives on Canadian Federalism,* ed. R.C. Olling and W.M. Westmacott, 233-56. Scarborough: Prentice-Hall, 1988.

Dyck, Rand. "The Canada Assistance Plan: The Ultimate in Cooperative Federalism." *Canadian Public Administration* 19, 4 (1976): 587-602.

Dyson, Kenneth H.F. *The State Tradition in Western Europe.* Oxford: Martin Robertson, 1980.

Eagles, Paul F.J. *Sustainable Tourism in Protected Areas: Guidelines for Planning and Management.* Gland: IUCN-World Conservation Union, 2002.

Eagles, Paul F.J., and Stephen F. McCool, with contributions by Elizabeth A. Halpenny and R. Neil Moisey. *Tourism in National Parks and Protected Areas: Planning and Management.* Wallingford, UK; New York: CABI, 2002.

East, Ken M. "Joint Management of Canada's Northern National Parks." In *Resident Peoples and National Parks: Social Dilemmas and Strategies in International Conservation,* ed. Patrick West and Steven R. Brechin, 333-45. Tucson: University of Arizona Press, 1991.

Eidsvik, Harold K. "Involving the Public in Park Planning: Canada." *Parks* 3, 1 (n.d.): 3-5.

–. "Parks Canada, Conservation, and Tourism: A Review of the Seventies – A Preview of the Eighties." In *Tourism in Canada: Selected Issues and Options,* ed. Peter E. Murphy, 241-70. Victoria: Department of Geography, University of Victoria, 1983.

Elgie, Stuart. "Injunctions, Ancient Forests, and Irreparable Harm: A Comment on *Western Canada Wilderness Committee vs. A.G. British Columbia.*" *UBC Law Review* 25 (1991): 387-99.

Emond, D.P. "Environmental Law and Policy: A Retrospective Examination of the Canadian Experience." In *Consumer Protection, Environmental Law, and Corporate Power*, ed. Ivan Bernier and Andrée Lajoie, 89-179. Toronto: University of Toronto Press, 1985.

Emond, Paul. "Participation and the Environment: A Strategy for Democratizing Canada's Environmental Protection Laws." *Osgoode Hall Law Journal* 13 (1975): 783-817.

Etheredge, Lloyd S. "Government Learning: An Overview." In *The Handbook of Political Behavior*, vol. 2, ed. Samuel L. Long, 73-146. New York: Plenum Press, 1981.

Ethridge, Marcus E. "Procedures for Citizen Involvement in Environmental Policy: An Assessment of Policy Effects." In *Citizen Participation in Public Decision Making*, ed. Jack DeSario and Stuart Langton, 115-31. New York: Greenwood Press, 1987.

Evan, Peter, Dietrich Rueschemeyer, and Theda Skocpol, eds. *Bringing the State Back In.* Cambridge, UK: Cambridge University Press, 1985.

Farr, James. "Democratic Social Engineering: Karl Popper, Political Theory, and Policy Analysis." In *History and Context in Contemporary Public Policy*, ed. Douglas E. Ashford, 167-88. Pittsburgh: University of Pittsburgh Press, 1992.

Fenge, Terry. "National Parks in the Canadian Arctic: The Case of the Nunavut Land Claim Agreement." *Environments (Canada)* 22 (1993): 21-36.

Foresta, Ronald A. *America's National Parks and Their Keepers.* Washington, DC: Resources for the Future, 1984.

Foster, Janet. *Working for Wildlife: The Beginning of Preservation in Canada.* Toronto: University of Toronto Press, 1978.

Franks, C.E.S. *The Parliament of Canada.* Toronto: University of Toronto Press, 1987.

Gardner, J.E., and J.G. Nelson. "National Parks and Native Peoples in Northern Canada, Alaska, and Northern Australia." *Environmental Conservation* 8 (1981): 207-15.

Garson, G. David. *Group Theories of Politics.* Beverly Hills: Sage Publications, 1978.

Gates, Paul W., and Lillian F. Gates. "Canadian and American Land Policy Decisions, 1930." *Western Historical Review* 15 (1984): 389-405.

Gessler, Trisha. "Haida." *Canadian Encyclopaedia.* 2nd ed. Edmonton: Hurtig, 1988.

Gillies, James, and Jean Piggot. "Participation in the Legislative Process." *Canadian Public Administration* 25 (1982): 254-64.

Goldstein, Judith. *Ideas, Interests, and American Trade Policy.* Ithaca: Cornell University Press, 1993.

Goldstein, Judith, and Robert O. Keohane, eds. *Ideas and Foreign Policy: Beliefs, Institutions, and Political Change.* Ithaca: Cornell University Press, 1993.

Granatstein, J.L. *The Ottawa Men: The Civil Service Mandarins, 1935-1957.* Toronto: Oxford University Press, 1982.

Green, T.L. "The Role of the Public in National Park Planning and Management." In *The Canadian National Parks: Today and Tomorrow – Conference II: Ten Years Later*, 2 vols., ed. J.G. Nelson et al., 733-44. Waterloo: Graphic Services, University of Waterloo, 1979.

Greenspon, Edward, and Anthony Wilson-Smith. *Double Vision: The Inside Story of the Liberals in Power.* Toronto: Doubleday, 1996.

Hackman, Arlin. "Endangered Spaces: Ten Years for Wilderness in Canada." *Borealis* (January 1990): 27-29.

Haddow, Rodney S. *Poverty Reform in Canada, 1958-1978: State and Class Influences on Policy Making.* Montreal and Kingston: McGill-Queen's University Press, 1993.

Haines, Aubrey. *The Yellowstone Story: A History of Our First National Park.* Vol. 1. Wyoming: Yellowstone Library and Museum Association, 1977.

Hall, Peter. *Governing the Economy: The Politics of State Intervention in Britain and France.* New York: Oxford University Press, 1986.

–. "Policy Paradigms, Social Learning, and the State: The Case of Economic Policymaking in Britain." *Comparative Politics* 25, 3 (1993): 275-96.

Harkin, James B. *The History and Meaning of the National Parks of Canada.* Papers compiled by Mabel B. Williams. Saskatoon: H.R. Larson Publishing, 1957.

Harmon, Aileen. "Village Lake Louise." *Nature Canada* 1, 2 (1972): 33.

Harrison, Kathryn. "Prospects for Intergovernmental Harmonization in Environmental Policy." In *Canada: The State of the Federation 1994*, ed. Douglas Brown and Janet Hiebert, 179-99. Kingston: Institute of Intergovernmental Relations, 1994.

Hawthorn, Harry B., ed. *A Survey of the Contemporary Indians of Canada: A Report on Economic, Political, Educational Needs and Policies.* Ottawa: Indian Affairs, 1966.

Hays, Samuel E. *Beauty, Health, and Permanence: Environmental Politics in the United States, 1955-85.* Cambridge, UK: Cambridge University Press, 1987.

Head, Wilson A. "The Ideology and Practice of Citizen Participation." In *Citizen Participation: Canada – A Book of Readings*, ed. James A. Draper, 14-29. Toronto: New Press, 1971.

Heard, Andrew. *Canadian Constitutional Conventions: The Marriage of Law and Politics.* Toronto: Oxford University Press, 1991.

Heclo, Hugh. *Modern Social Policies in Britain and Sweden: From Relief to Income Maintenance.* New Haven: Yale University Press, 1991.

Henderson, Norman. "Wilderness and the Nature Conservation Ideal: Britain, Canada, and the United States Contrasted." *Ambio: Journal of the Human Environment* 21, 6 (1992): 394-99.

Herrero, Stephen. "Parks Canada and Public Participation: The Case of Village Lake Louise and Sunshine Village." In *Involvement and Environment: Proceedings of the Canadian Conference on Public Participation*, 2 vols., ed. Barry Sadler, 254-65. Edmonton: Environment Council of Alberta, 1979.

Hewison, Robert. *The Heritage Industry: Britain in a Climate of Decline.* London: Methuen, 1987.

Himmelfarb, Gertrude. *The De-Moralization of Society: From Victorian Virtues to Modern Values.* New York: Vintage, 1996.

Hoberg, George. "Environmental Policy: Alternative Styles." In *Governing Canada: Institutions and Public Policy*, ed. Michael M. Atkinson, 307-42. Toronto: Harcourt Brace Jovanovich, 1993.

–. *Pluralism by Design: Environmental Policy and the American Regulatory State.* New York: Praeger, 1992.

–. "The Politics of Sustainability: Forest Policy in British Columbia." In *Politics, Policy, and Government in British Columbia*, ed. R.K. Carty, 272-89. Vancouver: UBC Press, 1996.

Hodgetts, J.E. *The Canadian Public Service: A Physiology of Government 1867-1970.* Toronto: University of Toronto Press, 1973.

Hodgson, J.S. "Management by Objectives: The Experience of a Federal Government Department." *Canadian Public Administration* 16 (1973): 422-31.

Hoole, Arthur F. "Public Participation in Park Planning: The Riding Mountain Case." In *Involvement and Environment: Proceedings of the Canadian Conference on Public Participation*, 2 vols., ed. Barry Sadler, 239-53. Edmonton: Environment Council of Alberta, 1979.

Howlett, Michael. "The Judicialization of Canadian Environmental Policy, 1980-1990: A Test of the Canada-United States Convergence Thesis." *Canadian Journal of Political Science* 27 (1994): 99-127.

Huel, Raymond. "The Creation of the Alpine Club of Canada: An Early Manifestation of Canadian Nationalism." *Prairie Forum* 15 (1990): 25-43.

Hummel, Monte, ed. *Endangered Spaces.* Toronto: Key Porter Books, 1989.

Inglehart, Ronald. *The Silent Revolution: Changing Values and Political Styles among Western Publics.* Princeton: Princeton University Press, 1977.

Ise, John. *Our National Park Policy: A Critical History.* Baltimore: Johns Hopkins University Press, 1961.

Islands Protection Committee. "Queen Charlotte Wilderness: Unique and Threatened." *Nature Canada* (January-March 1976): 39-43.

Islands Protection Society. *Islands at the Edge: Preserving the Queen Charlotte Islands Wilderness.* Vancouver: Douglas and McIntyre, 1984.

Jervis, Robert. "Timing and Interaction in Politics: A Comment on Pierson." *Studies in American Political Development* 14, 1 (2000): 93-100.

Johnson, Ronald C.A. "The Effect of Contemporary Thought upon Park Policy and Landscape Change in Canada's National Parks: 1885-1911." PhD diss., University of Minnesota, 1972.

Jones, Trevor. *Wilderness or Logging: Case Studies of Two Conflicts in B.C.* Vancouver: Federation of Mountain Clubs, 1983.

Kasperson, Roger E. "Citizen Participation in Environmental Policy Making: The U.S.A. Experience." In *Involvement and Environment: Proceedings of the Canadian Conference on Public Participation,* 2 vols., ed. Barry Sadler, 128-38. Edmonton: Environment Council of Alberta, 1979.

Kemf, Elizabeth, ed. *The Law of the Mother: Protecting Indigenous Peoples in Protected Areas.* San Francisco: Sierra Club Books, 1993.

Killan, Gerald. *Protected Places: A History of Ontario's Provincial Parks System.* Toronto: Dundurn Press, 1993.

Knutsen, Oddbjorn. "Materialist and Postmaterialist Values and Social Structure in the Nordic Countries." *Comparative Politics* 23, 1 (1990): 85-104.

Krasner, Stephen. "Approaches to the State: Alternative Conceptions and Historical Dynamics." *Comparative Politics* 16 (1984): 235-38.

–. "Sovereignty: An Institutional Perspective." *Comparative Political Studies* 21 (1988): 66-94.

Kraulis, J.A., and Kevin McNamee. *The National Parks of Canada.* Toronto: Key Porter, 1994.

Kroeker, H.V. *Sovereign People or Sovereign Governments.* Toronto: Institute for Research on Public Policy, 1981.

Kuch, Dennis, and O.P. Dwivedi, eds. *People and Environment: Proceedings of the Conference on Public Participation in Environmental Assessment at the University of Guelph.* Guelph: University of Guelph, 1977.

Kyba, Patrick. *Alvin: A Biography of the Honourable Alvin Hamilton, P.C.* Regina: Canadian Plains Research Center, 1989.

La Forest, Gerard V. *Natural Resources and Public Property under the Canadian Constitution.* Toronto: University of Toronto Press, 1969.

La Forest, Gerard V., and Muriel Kent Roy. *Report of the Special Inquiry on Kouchibouguac National Park.* Ottawa: Government of Canada and Government of New Brunswick, 1981.

Laframboise, H.L. "Administrative Reform in the Federal Public Service: Signs of a Saturation Psychosis." *Canadian Public Administration* 14 (1971): 303-25.

Lawson, Nicholas. "Where Whitemen Come to Play." *Cultural Survival Quarterly* 9, 1 (1985): 54-56.

Lindblom, Charles E. "The Science of Muddling Through." *Public Administration Review* 19 (1959): 79-88.

Lipsky, Michael. *Street-Level Bureaucracy: Dilemmas of the Individual in the Public Services.* New York: Russell Sage Foundation, 1980.

Lock, Sarah. "Vutnut National Park: A New Kind of National Park." *Borealis: The Magazine of the Canadian Parks and Wilderness Society* 5 (1994): 27-32.

Locke, Harvey. "A Summary of the Brief Presented to the Standing Committee on May 16, 2000." Typescript.

Lothian, W.F. *A Brief History of Canada's National Parks.* Ottawa: Minister of Supply and Services, 1987.

–. *History of Canada's National Parks, Volumes 1-4.* Ottawa: Minister of Supply and Services, 1987.

Lowenthal, David. *Possessed by the Past: The Heritage Crusade and the Spoils of History.* New York: Free Press, 1996.

Lowry, William R. *The Capacity to Wonder: Preserving National Parks.* Washington, DC: Brookings Institution, 1994.

Lucas, Alastair R. "Fundamental Prerequisites for Citizen Participation." In *Involvement and Environment: Proceedings of the Canadian Conference on Public Participation,* 2 vols., ed. Barry Sadler, 43-57. Edmonton: Environment Council of Alberta, 1979.

–. "Legal Foundations for Public Participation in Environmental Decisionmaking." *Natural Resources Journal* 16, 1 (1976): 73-102.

Lynch, Wayne. "Our Unknown National Parks." *Canadian Geographic* (July-August 1992): 18-28.

Macdonald, Douglas. *The Politics of Pollution: Why Canadians Are Failing Their Environment.* Toronto: McClelland and Stewart, 1991.

MacEachern, Alan. *Natural Selections: National Parks in Atlantic Canada, 1935-1970.* Montreal and Kingston: McGill-Queen's University Press, 2001.

MacEwen, Ann, and Malcolm MacEwen. *National Parks: Conservation or Cosmetics?* London: George Allen and Unwin, 1982.

Macklis, Gary E., and David L. Tichnell. *The State of the World's Parks: An International Assessment for Resource Management, Policy, and Research.* Boulder: Westview Press, 1985.

Manzer, Ronald. "Public Policy-Making as Practical Reasoning." *Canadian Journal of Political Science* 27 (1984): 577-94.

–. *Public Schools and Political Ideas: Canadian Educational Policy in Historical Perspective.* Toronto: University of Toronto Press, 1994.

March, James G., and Johan P. Olsen. "The New Institutionalism: Organizational Factors in Political Life." *American Political Science Review* 78 (1984): 737-49.

–. *Rediscovering Institutions: The Organizational Basis of Politics.* London: Collier Macmillan, 1989.

Martin, Chester. "Dominion Lands Policy." *Canadian Frontiers of Settlement,* ed. W.A. Mackintosh and W.L.G. Joerg. Toronto: Macmillan of Canada, 1938.

Martin, Claude. "Introduction." In *The Law of the Mother: Protecting Indigenous Peoples in Protected Areas,* ed. Elizabeth Kemf, xv-xix. San Francisco: Sierra Club Books, 1993.

Marty, Sid. "Homeless on the Range: Grizzlies Struggle for Elbow Room and Survival in Banff National Park." *Canadian Geographic* (January-February 1997): 28-39.

Maurer, K.F. *Public Participation in Environmental Assessment Hearings: An Analysis of Current Practice in Canada and the United States with Proposed Options for the Ontario Environmental Assessment Board.* Toronto: Institute of Environmental Studies, University of Toronto, 1979.

May, Elizabeth. *Paradise Won: The Struggle for South Moresby.* Toronto: McClelland and Stewart, 1990.

McNamee, Kevin. "Expanding and Preserving Canada's National Park System: A Brief on Bill C-27: An Act Respecting the National Parks of Canada." Tyepscript, 16 May 2000.

–. "Pay Per View: The Federal Government Is Turning to User Fees to Help Pay for Canada's National Parks." *Nature Canada* 25 (1996): 34-41.

McNeely, Jeffrey A. "Afterword: People and Protected Areas: Partners in Prosperity." In *The Law of the Mother: Protecting Indigenous Peoples in Protected Areas,* ed. Elizabeth Kemf, 249-57. San Francisco: Sierra Club Books, 1993.

Miller, Melanie. "Origins of Pacific Rim National Park." In *Pacific Rim: An Ecological Approach to a New Canadian National Park,* ed. J.G. Nelson and L.D. Cordes, 5-25. Waterloo: n.p., 1972.

Moe, Terry. "The Positive Theory of Public Bureaucracy." In *Perspectives on Public Choice: A Handbook,* ed. Dennis C. Mueller, 455-80. Cambridge, UK: Cambridge University Press, 1997.

Montjoy, Robert S., and Laurence J. O'Toole. "Toward a Theory of Policy Implementation: An Organizational Perspective." *Public Administration Review* 39, 5 (1979): 465-76.

Nash, Roderick. *Wilderness and the American Mind.* New Haven: Yale University Press, 1967.

Nelson, J.G., R.D. Needham, S.H. Nelson, and R.C. Scace, eds. *The Canadian National Parks: Today and Tomorrow – Conference II: Ten Years Later.* 2 vols. Waterloo: Graphic Services, University of Waterloo, 1979.

Nelson, J.G., and R.C. Scace. *Canadian Parks in Perspective.* Montreal: Harvest House, 1970.

Neufeld, Keith Timothy. "Ranching and the Grasslands National Park: An Historical and Institutional Analysis." Master's thesis, University of Waterloo, 1984.

Newman, Peter C. *The Distemper of Our Times.* Toronto: McClelland and Stewart, 1968.

–. *Renegade in Power: The Diefenbaker Years.* Toronto: McClelland and Stewart, 1963.

Nielsen, Erik. *The House Is Not a Home: An Autobiography.* Toronto: Macmillan of Canada, 1989.

Niskanen, W.A. *Bureaucracy and Representative Organization.* Chicago: Aldine Atherton, 1971.

North, Douglass C. *Institutions, Institutional Change, and Economic Performance.* Cambridge, UK: Cambridge University Press, 1990.

Nowlan, David, and Nadine Nowlan. *The Bad Trip: The Untold Story of the Spadina Expressway.* Toronto: New Press-House of Anansi, 1970.

Olsen, Barry L. "The Role of Public Participation in Parks Canada Planning." Master's thesis, University of Calgary, 1976.

Olsen, Barry L., and Brendan O'Donnell. "First Nations Involvement in National Park Establishment and Management – Interim Measures." Paper presented at the Interim Measures during Treaty Negotiations Conference, Vancouver, 22 April 1994.

Olson, Mancur. *The Logic of Collective Action.* Cambridge, MA: Harvard University Press, 1965.

O'Riordan, Jon. "Public Involvement Program in the Okanagan Basin Study." *Natural Resources Journal* 16, 1 (1976): 177-96.

ORRRC (Outdoor Recreation Resources Review Commission). *Wilderness and Recreation: A Report on Resources, Values, and Problems.* Washington, DC: Wildlands Research Center, University of California, 1962.

Paldam, Marin. "Political Business Cycles." In *Perspectives on Public Choice: A Handbook,* ed. Dennis C. Mueller, 342-70. Cambridge, UK: Cambridge University Press, 1997.

"Park." *Oxford English Dictionary.* Vol. 11. Oxford: Clarendon Press, 1989.

Pierson, Paul. *Dismantling the Welfare State? Reagan, Thatcher, and the Politics of Retrenchment.* Cambridge, UK: Cambridge University Press, 1994.

–. "The New Politics of the Welfare State." *World Politics* 48 (1996): 143-79.

–. "Not Just What, but *When:* Timing and Sequence in Political Processes." *Studies in American Political Development* 14, 1 (2000): 72-92.

–. *Politics in Time: History, Institutions, and Social Analysis.* Princeton: Princeton University Press, 2004.

–. "When Effect Becomes Cause: Policy Feedback and Political Change." *World Politics* 45 (1993): 595-628.

Potyondi, Barry. "Wood Buffalo National Park: An Historical Overview and Source Study." Internal manuscript report, Environment Canada, 1979.

Priddle, George B. "Role of the Public." In *People and Environment: Proceedings of the Conference on Public Participation in Environmental Assessment,* ed. Dennis Kuch and O.P. Dwivedi, 20-40. Guelph: University of Guelph, 1977.

Pross, A. Paul. *Group Politics and Public Policy.* Toronto: Oxford University Press, 1986.

Putnam, Robert D. *Making Democracy Work: Civic Traditions in Modern Italy.* Princeton: Princeton University Press, 1993.

Redford, Kent H., and John G. Robinson. "Hunting by Indigenous Peoples and Conservation of Game Species." *Cultural Survival Quarterly* 9 (1985): 41-44.

Roman, Andrew J., and Mart Pikkov. "Public Interest Litigation in Canada." In *Into the Future: Environmental Law and Policy for the 1990s,* ed. Donna Tingley, 165-84. Edmonton: Environmental Law Centre, 1990.

Rounthwaite, H. Ian. "The National Parks of Canada: An Endangered Species?" *Saskatchewan Law Review* 46, 1 (1981-82): 43-71.

Rueggeberg, Harriet. *Involvement of Aboriginal People in National Park Management in Other Countries.* Report prepared for Environment Canada, Parks. Nanaimo: n.p., 1988.

Runte, Alfred. *National Parks: The American Experience.* Lincoln: University of Nebraska Press, 1979.

Russell, Bertrand. *A History of Western Philosophy.* London: Unwin, 1984.

Sabatier, Paul A. "An Advocacy Coalition Framework of Policy Change and the Role of Policy-Oriented Learning Therein." *Policy Sciences* 21 (1988): 129-68.

Sacks, Paul. "State Structure and the Asymmetrical Society: An Approach to Public Policy in Britain." *Comparative Politics* 12, 3 (1980): 349-76.

Sadler, Barry, ed. *Involvement and Environment: Proceedings of the Canadian Conference on Public Participation.* 2 vols. Edmonton: Environment Council of Alberta, 1979.

–, ed. *Public Participation in Environmental Decision Making: Strategies for Change: Proceedings of a National Workshop.* Edmonton: Environment Council of Alberta, 1979.

Samuel, Raphael. *Theatres of Memory.* Volume I. *Past and Present in Contemporary Culture.* London: Verso, 1994.

Savoie, Donald J. *Governing from the Centre: The Concentration of Power in Canadian Politics.* Toronto: University of Toronto Press, 1999.

–. *Thatcher, Reagan, Mulroney: In Search of a New Bureaucracy.* Pittsburgh: University of Pittsburgh Press, 1994.

Scace, Robert C. "The Visitor Service Centre and Developments at Lake Louise, Banff National Park." *Park News* July 1971: 15-26.

Schama, Simon. *Landscape and Memory.* Toronto: Vintage, 1996.

Scharpf, Fritz. "Decision Rules, Decision Styles, and Policy Choices." *Journal of Theoretical Politics* 1 (1989): 149-76.

Schrecker, Ted. "Of Invisible Beasts and the Public Interest: Environmental Cases and the Judicial System." In *Canadian Environmental Policy: Ecosystems, Politics, and Process,* ed. Robert Boardman, 83-105. Toronto: Oxford University Press, 1992.

–. "Resisting Environmental Regulation: The Cryptic Pattern of Business-Government Regulations." In *Managing Leviathan: Environmental Politics and the Administrative State,* ed. Robert Paehlke and Douglas Torgerson, 165-99. Peterborough: Broadview Press, 1990.

Searle, Richard D. *Phantom Parks: The Struggle to Save Canada's National Parks.* Toronto: Key Porter, 2000.

Sewell, W.R. Derrick, and Timothy O'Riordan. "The Culture of Participation in Environmental Decisionmaking." *Natural Resources Journal* 16, 1 (1976): 1-21.

Sheehaan, Carol. "Reid, William Ronald." In *Canadian Encyclopaedia.* 2nd ed. Edmonton: Hurtig, 1988.

Simeon, James C. "The Neilson Task Force on Program Review and the Reorganization of the Federal Government." *Optimum: The Journal of Public Sector Management* 20-21 (1989-90): 7-19.

Skocpol, Theda. "Bringing the State Back In: Strategies of Analysis in Current Research." In *Bringing the State Back In,* ed. Peter Evans, Dietrich Rueschemeyer, and Theda Skocpol, 3-43. Cambridge, UK: Cambridge University Press, 1985.

Skogstad, Grace. "Interest Groups, Representation, and Conflict Management in the Standing Committees of the House of Commons." *Canadian Journal of Political Science* 28 (1985): 739-72.

Sloan, Raymond W. "The Sunshine Village Issue: 1001 Mistakes and How Parks Canada Mismanaged Public Participation." In *Involvement and Environment: Proceedings of the Canadian Conference on Public Participation,* 2 vols., ed. Barry Sadler, 266-73. Edmonton: Environment Council of Alberta, 1979.

Smith, David E. *The Invisible Crown: The First Principle of Canadian Government.* Toronto: University of Toronto Press, 1995.

–. *The Regional Decline of a National Party: Liberals on the Prairies.* Toronto: University of Toronto Press, 1981.

Sproule-Jones, Mark. *Governments at Work: Canadian Parliamentary Federalism and Its Public Policy Effects.* Toronto: University of Toronto Press, 1993.

Steinmo, Sven, Kathleen Thelen, and Frank Longstreth. *Structuring Politics: Historical Institutionalism in Comparative Analysis.* Cambridge, UK: Cambridge University Press, 1992.

Stevenson, Garth. *Unfulfilled Union: Canadian Federalism and National Unity.* Rev. ed. Toronto: Gage, 1982.

Stiven, Shelagh, and Bruce Downie. *National Parks and New Initiatives in British Columbia.* Victoria: National and Provincial Parks Association of Canada, British Columbia Chapter, 1985.

Task Force on Park Establishment. *Our Parks: Vision for the 21st Century.* Waterloo: Heritage Resources Centre, University of Waterloo, 1987.

Taylor, Charles. "The Explanation of Purposive Behaviour." In *Explanation in the Behavioural Sciences,* ed. Robert Borger and Frank Cioffi, 49-79. Cambridge, UK: Cambridge University Press, 1970.

Tennant, Paul. *Aboriginal Peoples and Politics: The Indian Land Question in British Columbia, 1849-1989.* Vancouver: UBC Press, 1990.

Thelen, Kathleen, and Sven Steinmo. "Historical Institutionalism in Comparative Politics." In *Structuring Politics: Historical Institutionalism in Comparative Analysis,* ed. Sven Steinmo, Kathleen Thelen, and Frank Longstreth, 1-32. Cambridge, UK: Cambridge University Press, 1992.

Thomas, Paul, and John Wilkins. "Special Operating Agencies: A Culture Change in the Manitoba Government." In *Alternative Service Delivery: Sharing Governance in Canada*, ed. Robin Ford and David Zussman, 109-22. Toronto: Institute of Public Administration of Canada, 1997.

Tingley, Donna, ed. *Into the Future: Environmental Law and Policy for the 1990s*. Edmonton: Environmental Law Centre, 1990.

Touche, Rodney. *Brown Cows, Sacred Cows: A True Story of Lake Louise*. Hanna, AB: Gorman Publishers, 1990.

–. "The Village Lake Louise Controversy: A Developer's Perspective." In *Involvement and Environment: Proceedings of the Canadian Conference on Public Participation*, 2 vols., ed. Barry Sadler, 274-80. Edmonton: Environment Council of Alberta, 1979.

Trudeau, Pierre Elliott. *Federalism and the French Canadians*. Toronto: Macmillan, 1968.

Trump, Thomas. "Value Formation and Postmaterialism: Inglehart's Theory of Value Change Reconsidered." *Comparative Political Studies* 24, 3 (1991): 365-90.

Tunbridge, J.E., and G.J. Ashworth. *Dissonant Heritage: The Management of the Past as a Resource in Conflict*. Chichester, NY: John Wiley and Sons, 1996.

Tuohy, Carolyn. "Federalism and Canadian Health Policy." In *Challenges to Federalism: Policy-Making in Canada and the Federal Republic of Germany*, ed. W.M. Chandler and C.W. Zollner, 141-60. Kingston: Institute of Intergovernmental Relations, 1989.

–. "Social Policy: Two Worlds." In *Governing Canada: Institutions and Public Policy*, ed. Michael Atkinson, 275-305. Toronto: Harcourt Brace Jovanovich, 1993.

Val, Erik. "Parks, Aboriginal Peoples, and Sustainable Tourism in Developing Regions: The International Experience and Canada's Northwest Territories." In *Social Science and Natural Resource Recreation Management*, ed. Joanne Vining, 219-43. Boulder: Westview Press, 1990.

VanNijnatten, Debora. "The Power Dynamics of Native Participation and Decision-Making in the Establishment of North Baffin National Park." Master's thesis, Queen's University, 1991.

van Osten, Richard, ed. *World National Parks: Progress and Opportunities*. Trans. John Riddel and E.S. Tew. Brussels: Hayez, 1972.

Waiser, Bill. *Park Prisoners: The Untold Story of Western Canada's National Parks, 1915-1946*. Saskatoon: Fifth House, 1995.

Walker, Jack L. "The Diffusion of Knowledge, Policy Communities, and Agenda Setting: The Relationship of Knowledge and Power." In *New Strategic Perspectives on Social Policy*, ed. John E. Tropman, Milan J. Dluhy, and Roger M. Lind, 75-96. New York: Pergammon Press, 1982.

Weaver, R. Kent, and Bert A. Rockman, eds. *Do Institutions Matter? Government Capabilities in the United States and Abroad*. Washington, DC: Brookings Institution, 1993.

Weaver, Sally M. *Making Indian Policy: The Hidden Agenda, 1968-70*. Toronto: University of Toronto Press, 1981.

–. "The Role of Aboriginals in the Management of Australia's Coburg (Gurig) and Kakadu National Parks." In *Resident Peoples and National Parks: Social Dilemmas and Strategies in International Conservation*, ed. Patrick West and Steven R. Brechin, 311-33. Tucson: University of Arizona Press, 1991.

Weber, Will. "Enduring Peaks and Changing Cultures: The Sherpas and Sagarmatha (Mount Everest) National Park." In *Resident Peoples and National Parks: Social Dilemmas and Strategies in International Conservation*, ed. Patrick West and Steven R. Brechin, 206-14. Tucson: University of Arizona Press, 1991.

Weeks, Nancy C. "National Parks and Native Peoples: A Study of the Experience of Selected Other Jurisdictions with a View to Cooperation in Northern Canada." In *Contributions to Circumpolar Studies*, ed. Hugh Beach, 83-150. Uppsala: Department of Cultural Anthropology, University of Uppsala, 1986.

Weir, Margaret. "Ideas and the Politics of Bounded Innovation." In *Structuring Politics: Historical Institutionalism in Comparative Analysis*, ed. Sven Steinmo, Kathleen Thelen, and Frank Longstreth, 188-216. Cambridge, UK: Cambridge University Press, 1992.

Wengert, Norman. "Citizen Participation: Practice in Search of Theory." *Natural Resources Journal* 16, 1 (1976): 23-40.

West, Patrick, and Steven R. Brechin, eds. *Resident Peoples and National Parks: Social Dilemmas and Strategies in International Conservation.* Tucson: University of Arizona Press, 1991.

Westcott, Geoffrey Charles. "Australia's Distinctive National Parks System." *Environmental Conservation* 18, 4 (1991): 331-40.

White, Cliff J. "The Sunshine Village Development." In *Involvement and Environment: Proceedings of the Canadian Conference on Public Participation,* 2 vols., ed. Barry Sadler, 281-96. Edmonton: Environment Council of Alberta, 1979.

Wilson, Jeremy. "Forest Conservation in British Columbia, 1935-85: Reflections on a Barren Political Debate." *BC Studies* 76 (1987-88): 3-32.

–. "Wilderness Politics in B.C.: The Business Dominated State and the Containment of Environmentalism." In *Policy Communities and Public Policy in Canada: A Structural Approach,* ed. William D. Coleman and Grace Skogstad, 141-69. Mississauga: Copp Clark Pitman, 1990.

Wilson, V. Seymour. "What Legacy? The Nielsen Task Force Program Review." In *How Ottawa Spends 1988-89: The Conservatives Heading into the Stretch,* ed. Katherine A. Graham, 23-47. Ottawa: Carleton University Press, 1988.

Wintrobe, Ronald. "Modern Bureaucratic Theory." In *Perspectives on Public Choice: A Handbook,* ed. Dennis C. Mueller, 429-54. Cambridge, UK: Cambridge University Press, 1997.

World Wildlife Fund. *1995-96 Endangered Spaces Progress Report.* Toronto: World Wildlife Fund, 1996.

Index

Rockman, Bert, 19
Rocky Mountain Parks Act, 29
Rodgers, Stephen, 107
Roy, Muriel Kent, 81, 82
Royal Commission on Government
    Organization, 47, 57, 158, 159. *See
    also* Glassco Commission
Royal Commission on Timber Rights and
    Forest Policy, British Columbia, 101
royal hunting preserves, 3
Royal Proclamation of 1763, 85, 93
Runte, Alfred, 2, 25, 26
Rupert's Land, 32

Sagarmatha National Park, 125
Samuel, Raphael, 9
Saskatchewan, planning ideas from, 56
Savoie, Donald J., 155, 157
Searle, Rick, 167
Seton, Ernest Thompson, 100
Sherpa people, 125
Ship Harbour, Nova Scotia, 98
Sierra Club, 26
Sierra Legal Defence Fund, 116, 118-19,
    174, 206n55
Ski Club of the Canadian Rockies, 76
Skidegate Band Council, 101
skiing, 76-77, 119-20
Skocpol, Theda, 17
Skogstad, Grace, 16
Smith, Chief Elijah, 87
Social Credit Party, British Columbia, 104
social policy
  in Britain and Sweden, 21
  and parks, 5
South Moresby, 98-107 *passim. See also*
    Moresby Island; Gwaii Haanas
    National Park Reserve
South Moresby Resource Planning
    Team, 105
special operating agencies, 156
  features of, 157
  privatization of, 158
Spray River valley, and Banff Park
    boundaries, 34
Sproule-Jones, Mark, 135
standing committees, 205n42
statutory trust, 119
Steer, George, 150
Stevenson, Garth, 60
Strong, Maurice, 104
Sunshine Village Corporation, 120
Supreme Court (Canada), 86
  and Nisga'a land claims decision, 124,
    202n57
Supreme Court (US), 85

Suzuki, David, 103
Swanson Lumber Company, 118
System Plan, of National Parks, 37, 65,
    141, 145, 170
  defined, 53

Task Force on Park Establishment, 108,
    111, 112
  and citizens' heritage fund, 109, 204n34
technostructure, 43, 44
Terra Nova National Park, 35,180
Thatcher, Margaret, 146, 155
Thoreau, David, 26
Thorsen, Joseph, 115
Touche, Rodney, 76, 78, 79
transcendentalist writers, American, 26
Treasury Board, 154
  Secretariat, 148
Trump, Thomas, 197n19
Tunbridge, J.E., 9. *See also* Ashworth, G.J.
Tuohy, Carolyn, 19, 20

UNESCO, 55, 103
uranium mining, 118, 125

Valhalla Wilderness Society, 103
value formation, Ronald Inglehart's
    theory of, 44
Vander Zalm, William, 107
Village Lake Louise, 76-79, 93
visitor service centres, 77
Vutnut Gwitchin First Nation, 127-28
*Vutnut Gwitchin First Nation Final Agree-
    ment,* 129-30
Vutnut National Park, 129, 131

Wall Street Journal, 166
Wasagamining, 193n14
Weaver, Kent, 19
Weaver, Sally, 126
Weeks, Nancy, 125
Weir, Margaret, 15
West Coast Oil Ports Inquiry, 101
Western Canada Wilderness Committee,
    103, 106
*Western Canada Wilderness Committee v.
    B.C.* (1988), 116
white paper on Indian policy (1969), 85-
    86, 202n53
Whitehorse, 87
Wilderness Act (US), 73
Wilderness Advisory Committee, 105
wildlife protection, 206n56
Wilson, Jeremy, 101, 104-5
Winter Recreation Policy, 77
wood bison, 117

Printed and bound in Canada by Friesens

Set in Stone by Artegraphica Design Co. Ltd.

Copy editor: Dallas Harrison

Proofreader: Lesley Erickson